Guadalcanal, Tarawa
and Beyond

Guadalcanal, Tarawa and Beyond

A Mud Marine's Memoir of the Pacific Island War

WILLIAM W. ROGAL

McFarland & Company, Inc., Publishers
Jefferson, North Carolina, and London

Frontispiece: Sergeant William W. Rogal in June 1945.

LIBRARY OF CONGRESS CATALOGUING-IN-PUBLICATION DATA

Rogal, William W., 1922–
    Guadalcanal, Tarawa and beyond : a mud Marine's memoir of
the Pacific island war / by William W. Rogal.
        p.   cm.
    Includes index.

    ISBN 978-0-7864-4671-1
    softcover : 50# alkaline paper ∞

    1. Rogal, William W., 1922–   2. World War, 1939–1945 —
Personal narratives, American.   3. United States. Marine Corps.
Marines, 2nd. Battalion, 1st. Company A.   4. World War, 1939–
1945 — Campaigns — Pacific Area.   5. United States. Marine
Corps — Biography.   6. Marines — United States — Biography.
I. Title.
D769.3722nd.R64   2010
940.54'5973092 — dc22   [B]   2010018587

British Library cataloguing data are available

Cover image ©2010 Shutterstock

Manufactured in the United States of America

McFarland & Company, Inc., Publishers
    Box 611, Jefferson, North Carolina 28640
    www.mcfarlandpub.com

Table of Contents

Preface 1

1. Joining the Marines 3
2. Boot Camp 7
3. The Fifth Marines 19
4. The Second Marines 40
5. Tulagi and Guadalcanal 53
6. Respite in New Zealand 109
7. Tarawa 119
8. Saipan and Tinian 148
9. Camp Pendleton 178
10. China 184
11. Rejoining the World 198

Bibliography 203
Index 205

Preface

It is said that all returning veterans have stories to tell, some of them true. I can agree with that adage for I have heard and read wartime accounts which are really wrong, some deliberately so. I have bent over backward to avoid that result in this work and have sincerely tried to hold hyperbole to the barest minimum.

Why write a memoir? I really don't know for sure. In about 1973 when I was a partner in a law firm, Dow, Lohnes and Albertson, one of the associate lawyers, Patrick H. (Pat) Allen, insisted on several occasions that I should write up my Marine Corps experiences in World War II. I don't recall ever telling any tales to Pat. He knew only that I had fought in the Pacific. In retrospect it seems strange that Pat was so insistent that I write a memoir. Perhaps it was his young age — he must have been a small child when the war was fought.

More recently, going back at least ten years, cousin Roy Miltner, my nephew Mike Nifong and my golfing buddies Jack Boag and Frank Reinhard encouraged me to jot something down. They seemed to have a genuine interest in my war stories and urged me to write them down. Also, early on, Brigadier General Ed Simmons, then the head of the Marine Corps History operation and my good friend, and writer and war correspondent Bob Sherrod assured me that my recollections would be useful to future historians. And, I suppose, there is an egocentric element involved, the desire to change the fact that no one in my family had any knowledge as to how I spent six eventful years on Uncle Sam's payroll. And it is kind of comforting to think that writing this gives my life a measure of permanence.

Which brings me to confess that contributing to my thinking was a sense of resentment that the Second Marine Division's contributions to the victory at Guadalcanal have been given rather short shrift in many of the histories and other writings about the battle. The facts that my regiment was attached to the First Division and made "D-Day" landings on Florida Island before the H-Hour landings on Tulagi and Guadalcanal have been underplayed or ignored by many chroniclers. The fact that my division lost almost 300 killed in action and more than 900 wounded illustrates that we spent some time in combat on that island.

But this work would never have found its way to print without the encouragement and assistance of good friend and noted historian and writer William Bartsch. It was he who insisted I should clean up the draft I had sent him and try for publication. But that was only the start of his assistance. Throughout my efforts to produce a printable manuscript he has tirelessly contributed advice and needed historical facts, photos and maps.

Another great source of encouragement and assistance was my friend retired U.S. Army Col. Harry Contos. He was constantly on call to aid in production. He made dozens of trips to my house to unravel the knots produced by my inability to master my computer's word processor.

And, of course, Pearl Rogal, the woman I married in 1945, deserves kudos for her patience and forbearance during the many hours I spent secluded away in my den. She has cheerfully borne the isolation forced by my absorption and always urged me to continue and not get discouraged.

1

Joining the Marines

It is tempting to write that I opted for military service that summer of 1940 because I knew war was coming and I wanted to do my part, but that would be far from the truth. While I was vaguely aware the war in Europe had commenced with Hitler's invasion of Poland in September of 1939 it did not occur to me that the United States would get involved. In short, patriotism had nothing to do with my decision to enlist in the Marines. In the first place, I was not college material. I lacked the desire and discipline to buckle down and study and I abhorred the thought of doing so for another four years. I had coasted through high school and barely passed enough subjects to achieve graduation. I believe the factor which contributed the most to my miserable high school academic record was, strangely, learning to read at an early age. I am not certain exactly how it came about but I could read fairly well before I entered first grade. I vaguely recall lying on the floor trying to read the comics and asking any nearby adult to help. When they passed out the readers on my first day in school I read the book through while they were still being distributed. During my first five or six years in school I read everything I could lay my hands on. I even went through a single-volume encyclopedia during my third school year. This reading ability enabled me to coast through my first six years of school, getting excellent grades without expending very much effort. In short, I did not learn to study and, when faced with the more difficult high school subjects that demanded rote memory, I goofed off and flunked, from top of the class to near bottom.

Lack of study discipline was not my only shortcoming: I developed a love for the outdoors, especially hiking and fishing. All my leisure time was spent in those pursuits. I even learned to tie my own fishing flies. My reading concentrated on the outdoors. I devoured Jack London and

Herman Melville and novelists like Zane Grey. I had no time for algebra, physics and Latin.

My family was dirt poor for my entire life at home. My father was a railroader. He had a hard life as a youngster for his father, my paternal grandfather, was killed in a mine accident in 1907 when my dad was eight years old. As a very young kid he worked at the mine picking slate and other foreign material from coal as it came out of the breaker. When he was about 18 years old he got a job as a trainman on the Lehigh Valley railroad, a position he held for his entire working life. Unfortunately for the family, he was laid off at the outset of the depression in about 1930 and never regained steady employment with the railroad until the onset of World War II. During the 1930s dad worked as a laborer on the railroad track maintenance crews. His pay for two weeks of hard labor was $19. We didn't eat real well during this period, had lots of beans and cornmeal. Of course, money for luxuries such as dental care was not available, a situation which almost kept me out of the Marine Corps.

In June of 1940, when I graduated from high school, there were no good jobs to be had, for the Depression still raged. But even if reasonably good employment had been available I am certain I would still have opted for military service. The principal motivating factor was romanticism, the urgent desire to escape the confines of a Depression-era small town and travel to the far corners of the world. This factor ruled out the army, for the last thing I wanted was to enlist in a service which might place me at a camp such as Fort Dix, located an hour or two from my town, Lehighton, Pennsylvania. No, sir. I wanted what the Navy recruiting posters promised: "Travel, Adventure and Romance."

If blame is to be assessed it could be levied on the ghost of Herman Melville or, perhaps, on that of his biographer, Lewis Mumford. I had devoured Melville's *Moby Dick*, *Omoo* and *Typee*, and developed a fascination for the islands of the far Pacific. Mumford's excellent biography recounts Melville's adventures in those islands and paints an irresistible picture of romantic adventure. For a penniless kid with travel on his mind there was only one obvious career choice, the Navy, and that is where I headed. However, a chance encounter with another recent high school graduate diverted me to another part of the naval service, the Marines.

1. Joining the Marines

His name was Witzel. We called him "Beardy," and he seemed to prefer being called that to his given name, Luther. Witzel and I were not close friends. We both played on the school football team and, of course, had numerous classes together. But he was not a member of the gang I ran around with and, in fact, I don't think we had ever spent any out-of-school time together. One day in late July Witzel stopped me in the Town Park and said he had heard I had joined the Navy. I told him I had visited the recruiting office in Allentown but had not yet signed nor taken the physical. He said he was going to join the Marines. While I had heard of the Marines, I didn't have the least idea what they were or what they did. Witzel enlightened me. He said, "They ride around on Navy ships and boss the sailors around." He also told me Marines wear a fantastically good-looking blue uniform and reminded me that a member of our Lutheran church was a Marine and had worn the uniform to a church service in the recent past. I did remember seeing the uniform and agreed it was mighty sharp. But the thought that convinced me that I should become a Marine rather than a sailor was the vision of me in a sailor suit being "bossed around" by Witzel attired in a gorgeous blue uniform. After a little more discussion we decided to go to the recruiting office together right after "fair week." The Carbon County Fair was the biggest event of the year in Lehighton, and the Marines would have to wait until that important spectacle had been enjoyed.

Early in August, Witzel, I and two additional prospective recruits drove to Allentown for preliminary processing including a cursory medical examination. Witzel and I passed and, since we were underage, were given parental approval forms for our parents' signatures. The two other fellows didn't make it; one had flat feet and the other had a too large overbite. The Corps was certainly picky in those days. Candidates had to be in perfect health, of proportionate height and weight, and high school graduates. At its peak strength during World War II, the Marines fielded six divisions and had a total strength of 500,000 officers and enlisted men. In the summer of 1940 it was seeking to increase its total strength to 28,000.

Shortly after the papers were signed and submitted we were instructed to report to the Marine recruiting office in Philadelphia on September 5 for final processing and induction. I have forgotten how we made the trip or if the Corps paid for the tickets. On arrival we were given a more thorough physical, which I flunked. The doctor, a Navy lieutenant, told the Marine recruiting sergeant and me he couldn't ignore a very large cavity in one of my lower molars. My heart sank, for I had no money to see a dentist and I could see myself returning home to Lehighton in disgrace. But it was not to be. The Marine sergeant had faced this crisis before and had a remedial procedure at hand. He gave me a scribbled note and directions to go to an office in a nearby building and give the note to the occupant. The office was on the third floor of a seedy building. After repeated fruitless rapping on the frosted glass door I was about to leave when a voice from the interior told me to come in. The office was unbelievably cluttered and filthy. Empty bottles and old newspapers were strewn everywhere. The only furniture was a sort of sideboard and what appeared to be a barber's chair. The occupant was a middle-aged man, unshaven, unkempt and very drunk. Nevertheless, I gave him the note and he told me to take a seat in the chair. In a dirty, much used dish on the sideboard he mixed a bit of cement and packed it into my huge cavity. He told me to not bite on anything until I reached Parris Island and to find a dentist when I got there. I thanked the man and returned to the sergeant, who turned me over to the doctor. He looked at the filling, grinned and told the sergeant I was now fit for enlistment.

Later that day we were assembled with about a dozen other candidates in a room which looked a lot like a classroom. We took the oath and solemnly swore to save, protect and defend the United States against all enemies, foreign and domestic. The officer who administered the oath then told us we were no longer civilians and that we were now subject to military justice and bound to obey any orders given by superiors. In the evening we boarded a train for the overnight run to South Carolina and the tender mercies of the United States Marine Corps. We were joining an organization whose function and mission were unknown to us and we had not the vaguest idea as to what faced us on the morrow. We had heard whispers that recruit depot, or boot camp, as it was called, was tough and we spent the night in our coach seats speculating as to what it would be like. As we soon found out, it was unlike anything else in the whole, wide world.

2

Boot Camp

Tired, sleepy and dirty we disembarked from the train at Yemessee, South Carolina, the nearest rail stop to Parris Island. In short order we were greeted — no, that's not the correct word — we were accosted by a most formidable-appearing figure with a voice to match. The khaki uniform, which fitted his Bunyanesqe frame like a second skin, was adorned with row upon row of campaign and medal ribbons and the five stripes of a gunnery sergeant. A feature which riveted our attention was a prominent scar that ran from his right eye to his chin. We were mortally certain that this was a combat wound and subsequently learned our observation was correct; it was a saber wound received in Nicaragua. Needless to say, we gave the utmost attention to every word spoken by this apparition as he got us to line up in a military formation and explained what standing at attention was. That done, he gave us a very instructive "welcoming" speech. The gist of it was that we were not welcome at all! He repeated several times that nobody had invited us to come down, that we were uninvited scum who would never be Marines but who would, in the interval until we were kicked out in disgrace, cause him and the other training personnel at the base unending work and trouble. While I had not anticipated a warm and fuzzy "Gee, we're glad you're here" speech on arrival, I was floored to hear that they didn't even want me and would, in fact, be happy, or at least unconcerned, if I flunked out.

As intended, the sergeant's lecture set the stage for what was to follow. We were on our own in a cold and unfeeling place. If we were lucky we might survive, but nobody was going to help us. To me, at that time, the worst possible thing that could happen would be to fail and be forced to go home in disgrace. That would be a fate worse than death. That fear of failure dogged my every step in boot camp and stayed with me for a few months after I graduated.

Following the lecture we were loaded onto flat-bottomed trucks with no seats and rather low side rails. It seemed a bit dangerous to ride standing up with only a knee-high railing between you and a fall to the roadside. Clearly, we weren't being coddled. Upon arrival at the base we were assigned to platoons of about 64 men and introduced to our drill instructors, Sergeant Daniel Cummings and Private First Class H.A.F. Von der Heyde Jr. The scarfaced gunnery sergeant who lectured us at Yemessee had forewarned us that our drill instructors would be our absolute masters in boot camp. They would be our "mommies and pop-pies," our confessors and mentors. Their word was final, with no right to appeal and no shoulder to cry on. Sergeant Cummings repeated this warning and added the additional information that there was a medical facility, a "sick bay," on the base but it was run by the Navy, and Marines never, never asked anything of the Navy. If any of us did go there for sick call it would make Sergeant Cummings "very unhappy and jealous." He used that expression a lot when instructing us as to things we should avoid doing. That opening lecture shot down my hopes of having my teeth repaired; the emergency filling I got in Philadelphia had fallen out during the train ride.

Sergeant Cummings appeared to be in his middle to late twenties. He was somewhat under six-feet tall with a well-formed muscular build. He wore khakis of a slightly darker shade than regular issue, which we subsequently learned were of the type issued to Marines on service in China. Private First Class Von der Heyde was a lanky string bean of at least six-feet-three. He had finished boot camp a few months before we arrived but had performed so well while in training they kept him on as an assistant drill instructor. We were lucky in getting these guys as instructors. Neither man had a mean or sadistic streak. They were all business and played no favorites, handing out disciplinary punishments with an even hand. We didn't get an easy ride but we got a fair ride. Haircuts came next. The barbers simply applied the electric shears to the skull and ran it back and forth until we were shorn down to the bare skin. This was less traumatic than it sounds, for in those days young men wore their hair rather short. Mine was no problem at all, for I wore mine about a quarter-inch from my skull in a style the Pennsylvania Dutch called a "schnitzer."

We then were issued uniforms, including underwear and socks. Nothing was tailored and no body measurements taken. The quartermaster sergeant merely looked you up and down and then called out the sizes to his assistant, who handed you the clothing. In my case he fitted me perfectly, with one notable exception. At that time some idiot in Marine Corps procurement had determined that a one-piece blue denim coverall would be the utility garment for recruits. Clearly no thought was given as to how a man in the field, burdened down with a pack and cartridge belt, would answer a call of nature. As one of my friends put it, "Even if you took off all your gear and stripped the thing down to your knees, you would end up shitting in your collar." But that wasn't my immediate problem; the set I was issued would have been a comfortable fit for one of today's gargantuan basketball players. When I donned it the crotch hit me at the knees and the legs were at least 14 inches too long. My drill instructor had a simple solution for this which did not include going back and exchanging it for one that fitted. He told me to pull it up until the crotch was in the right position and blouse the excess over my belt. The legs were still too long so I merely cut them off. Needless to say, I was a sad looking Marine. This garment had another fault. The dye used turned our underwear and our bodies a bright blue; a blue that never came out of the white underwear, "skivvies," and only reluctantly left our bodies. No Marine ever wore this horror in a post-boot camp assignment and I "deep-sixed" mine as soon as I could.

The clothing issue contained one green wool winter service uniform, two pairs of khaki pants, two khaki shirts, three sets of skivvies, a field scarf (tie), two pairs of fair-leather shoes and a "Smokey Bear" campaign hat. We were informed that the cost of this issue came out of and used up almost all of the fixed "clothing allowance" we were allotted for our four-year enlistments. This meant we had to take care of our clothing at our own expense, including shoe resoling and patching of rips and tears. We were also issued a bucket. But this was no ordinary three-gallon galvanized pail. This one came chock full of the toilet articles we would use during our stay at Parris Island. It contained a razor, soap, a bottle of Bay Rum aftershave, a toothbrush and dental cream, shoe polish, a scrub brush, and a sewing kit called a "housewife." To contain and transport our clothing and personal gear we were issued "sea bags," canvas sacks about a meter high and about 18 inches in diameter. Flaps and a hasp on top made it possible to safeguard your treasures with a padlock. We were taught how to fold our uniforms into the bag so that they came out somewhat wrinkled but wearable — no small trick. Finally, we were issued "782" gear, a pack, cartridge belt, mess kit, canteen and cup, and, most importantly, a poncho. After the clothing issue we were required to get rid of our civilian clothing; either mail it home or throw it away. I chose the latter course.

Here are a couple of photos from boot camp days. The one of me standing at "port arms" was taken early in my stay at the facility. Note I was still not squared away — my collar is open and my tie is not properly secured. The other picture of "Beardy" Witzel and me was taken near the end of our tenure when we were sheltered in two-man tents.

A big event was the issuing of our rifles, 30-caliber, model 1903 bolt

Boot camp photo showing the writer with his rifle at port arms, and (at left) in tent with Luther Witzel.

10

action Springfields and accompanying bayonets. They came packed in cosmoline, a sticky Vaseline-like rust preventive. We had to wash all the parts in kerosene or gasoline. In the process we learned the nomenclature of the weapon and how to field strip (disassemble) it. We were told this was a rifle, not a gun, and woe would befall the man who forgot. The difference was firmly fixed in our memories by requiring us to hold the rifle in our right hands, grab our crotches with the left and chant, "This is my rifle; this is my gun; the one is for fighting, the other for fun." Calling your rifle a gun was only second in the panoply of sins a recruit could commit with respect to the weapon. The cardinal sin was forgetting its number. At any time or place a recruit would be asked, "What's your rifle number, private?" The typical punishment if one of our buddies failed this test was to order the entire platoon to hold the rifles over our heads until our arms turned to agonized jelly. I learned my rifle number so well I still remember it — 286238!

The rifle number wasn't the only memorization required. We were given personal serial numbers (mine is 293903) and threatened with unimaginable punishments if we could not recite it to an inquiring superior. A more difficult task was memorizing the ten "General Orders" of a sentry on watch. I don't remember them very well. I recall the first one began, "To walk my post in a military manner...." Another was: "To quit my post only when properly relieved."

I don't recall an actual class in Marine Corps lingo but we soon learned that anything you walked on, floor or ground, was in fact a deck; the ceiling was the overhead, the walls were bulkheads and the privy was the head. In the clothing line, hats were covers, our uniform jackets were blouses, our ties were field scarves and, as I said earlier, our underwear were skivvies. Using these terms became so ingrained that I use many of them to this day.

For a week or so we were billeted in a two-story wooden barracks. The remainder of our stay was spent in wooden-floored two-man tents. Witzel and I bunked together. A pleasant surprise was the quality and abundance of the camp's food. We were not served cafeteria style but were served family style, sitting down at long tables. I was a "Depression kid," raised on beans and cornmeal and accustomed to eating only my allotted portion and always careful to leave an adequate amount for the other kids in the family. By contrast, the meal table set before me in boot camp was a veritable feast. For example, the breakfast table would contain huge aluminum pitchers of cold milk, bowls of hot cereal such as oatmeal, boxes of dry cereal, eggs, bacon and sausage, home fried potatoes, toast and rolls, and some kind of fruit. Despite the physical demands of training I gained weight at Parris Island.

Platoon 103 was a remarkably homogeneous group. With the exception of one very tall American Indian, all were white males between 18 and 30 years old with the very large majority recent high school graduates. Many, perhaps most, were from the South. The majority was from small towns or from farms. There were few, if any, big city slickers. One or two characters stood out from the harmonious mass. A youngster named "Horton" from Lumberton, North Carolina, was absolutely incapable of marching in step. As we marched along, Horton's head would be going up while the other 62 heads were going down. This led to unfortunate results for all of us, as Sergeant Cummings viewed sloppy marching as a reflection on his leadership. We paid the price with many extra hours of close order drill until Private Horton got straightened out.

We lost two platoon members to disciplinary action during training. The first casualty was a real loss as far as we were concerned for he was by far the best recruit among us. He had all the answers with respect to military life and we turned to him for help on all the myriad problems and questions we faced. He gave us additional tutoring on the manual of arms, the nomenclature of our weapons and the proper care of all our equipment. We were devastated when he was suspended from training and eventually discharged. The problem, as he told it, was that he had been dishonorably discharged from the Army and did not disclose that fact to the Marine Corps. In other words, he falsified his admission papers. The Army kicked him out for theft. He told us a vicious female to whom he had been engaged caused it all. When she broke off the engagement she refused to give back the ring. He was caught breaking into her house to retrieve the ring, was court martialed, found guilty and discharged. This was a real tragedy, for I am sure this guy would have been a hellova Marine.

The other recruit who didn't make it turned out to be an alcoholic. One day, when he was excused from drill for alleged illness, he rifled every sea bag in the platoon and drank every bottle of Bay Rum aftershave he found. We returned from drill to find our personal effects scattered and the culprit falling down drunk. The military police removed him and we never heard exactly what happened to him.

By mid–October we could march as a unit without disgracing Sergeant Cummings and had mastered a lot of subjects and disciplines. We had thrown many practice grenades (no live ones), had stabbed straw-filled dummies with our bayonets and mastered the intricacies of military courtesy. One lecture which sticks in my memory like no other was entitled "Field Sanitation." It was delivered in the field with the platoon sitting on the ground in a small arena under some trees. The talk was delivered by a grizzled gunnery sergeant who spoke with an Eastern European accent so thick as to be almost incomprehensible. To digress for a bit, the standing joke at the time was that to make senior NCO rank in the Marine Corps you had to first take a course in broken English. But it wasn't the accent that made such an indelible impression, it was the content of the lecture, which went something like this: "Now I'ma gonna teach you all you need to know about field sanitary. You dig a leetle hole; you sheet in the leetle hole; you cover up the leetle hole. Thatsa field sanitary. OK, class dismissed, smoke if you gottem."

In mid–October we began serious training with our basic weapons, the Springfield rifle and the Model 1911 Colt 45-caliber pistol. The pistol training, which was somewhat perfunctory, included memorizing the weapon's nomenclature, learning how to field strip it and a few minutes aiming and snapping the trigger (dry-firing) of the unloaded piece. On October 15 I shot the "D Course" for record and scored 78 percent, which qualified me as a sharpshooter. There were three levels of qualification: Expert, Sharpshooter and Marksman. Of course, the goal for both rifle and pistol was to make Expert.

Rifle training was a much bigger deal. We were moved to a tent camp adjacent to the rifle range. The first night in that camp still sticks in my mind as one of the worst nights of my life, including some rather hairy evenings in combat. Although it was the 19th of October, it was hot and humid. We were in two-man tents on canvas cots equipped with sheets and a blanket. The horror started after taps. The mosquitoes arrived en masse. They came not singly or by the dozen, but in squadrons.

There was simply no escape; the heat and threat of suffocation prevented pulling the blanket over your head, and pulling up the sheet was to no avail for they bit right through it. I'm not sure how we survived. In all probability a breeze came up and drove the rascals away. At any rate, it was an unforgettable experience.

For the next couple of days we received intensive instruction from coaches on the four firing positions: off-hand, i.e., standing, and sitting, kneeling and prone. We learned how to adjust the rifle's sling so the piece felt almost a part of you in each position. We spent a lot of time dry-firing at targets from each position. Finally, after endless hours of this, we actually fired the full course with live ammunition as a sort of dress rehearsal. As I recall we fired ten rounds off-hand at a ten-inch bullseye at 100 yards, ten rounds in the prone position at a 20-inch bullseye at 500 yards, and 20 rounds rapid fire at a silhouette target at 200 yards. It was great; I scored at the Expert level and couldn't wait to "shoot for record" on the following day. Ah, but glory was not to be mine. Record day dawned cold, windy and with a light drizzle. I shivered through the entire round and couldn't hit a thing. Shame and ignominy was mine; I ended up *unqualified*! It wasn't until five years had passed that I fired the range again at Camp Pendleton and erased this black mark on my escutcheon.

I don't remember any "big deal" graduation ceremony when we completed boot camp. But we had our picture taken. Witzel and I are first and second from the left in the second row down from the top. Sergeant Cummings and Private First Class Von der Heyde are seated in the second row center. Note the campaign hats on all hands. Unlike present times, when only drill instructors wear the hats, they were issued to all recruits in 1940. In my view the campaign hat is undoubtedly the best headgear for outdoor work or recreation. It protects from sun, snow and rain. You can protect your face and neck when going through brush by merely lowering your head and pushing through. It is cool in hot weather when secured properly with the strap, which goes around the front of the crown, down through holes in the sides of the brim and around the back of your skull. This arrangement keeps the hat securely in place but permits it to flop up and down in the back to admit cool air. Unfortunately, it is impossible to pack in a sea bag, and that feature probably caused its demise as standard issue. Too bad.

Platoon 103's Boot Camp graduation photograph, Recruit Depot Parris Island, October 1940.

On November 2 most of us were transferred to something called Provisional Company G. The only exceptions were the three or four guys selected for sea school. After completion of that instruction they would serve on Navy ships. This is the duty Witzel and I thought we were enlisting for, i.e., to "ride around on ships and boss the sailors around." But that duty was only for a select few; the rest of us were told we were going to the "FMF." The initials stood for Fleet Marine Force. We didn't know what that was, but at least it sounded nautical.

For about a month we practiced all the skills we learned in boot camp. We were even given liberty, and an unremembered friend and I made a foray into the nearby metropolis of Beaufort, where we immediately got in trouble. From some source, legal or illegal I don't remember, we bought a bottle of wine, which we took to a secluded alley to consume. We had just opened the bottle when a loud Southern voice scared the s — — out of us with the message, "Don't you know it's against the law to drink on a public street? Give me that bottle and come along; I'm taking you to jail." There, blocking the entrance and only exit to the alley stood every Yankee's nightmare, the quintessential Southern rural cop, complete with bulging belly, puttees and a huge holstered pistol. What went through our minds were arrest, jail, and a Marine brig, a dishonorable discharge and home in disgrace. Maybe those fears were exaggerated but we had been told repeatedly for more than three months, "You get in trouble, and you're out of here!" At any rate, without a word between us we charged the cop, knocked him on his ass and took off running. We figured, correctly, as it turned out, if we could get through

The USS *Henderson*, AP 1. She was commissioned in 1918 and was the Navy's only troop carrier in the Atlantic between the World Wars. She was converted to a hospital ship in 1943 and served out World War II as the USS *Bountiful*, AH 9 (Naval Historical Foundation).

the camp gate before the cop got there we would be absorbed in the general mass of troops and never discovered. We learned later the MPs had been alerted and everyone returning from liberty was questioned at the gate. Needless to say, I didn't go ashore again while at Parris Island.

On December 18 we were trucked to Charleston Navy Yard where we boarded the USS *Henderson*, a troop transport which had served continuously since 1918. To my inexperienced eye the ship was huge. There were three or four decks in the superstructure (the structure above the main deck), which contained the officers' staterooms and were "off limits" to enlisted peons. We were housed deep in the hold in bunks stacked four deep with only about 18 inches from your nose to the bulk of the guy above you. About all that can be said for the accommodation was it was warm and dry. I don't remember if we were told where we were going, although it seems logical we knew, either via scuttlebutt or officially, but we were bound for Guantanamo Bay, Cuba. Then, as now, Guantanamo Bay was a principal U.S. Navy base, although it has no major ship repair or resupplying facilities. Originally a coaling station, its strategic importance waned when coal was supplanted by oil as fuel to generate steam. However, it does have a large protected harbor.

As we sailed past Fort Sumter and into the Atlantic the ship began what is best described as a corkscrew motion. It dipped its bow and raised its stern and, at the bottom of the dip, rolled gently to starboard and then to port. When the bow came up it repeated the routine over and over and over for the next three days. This was my first experience with mal de mer. While I felt pretty bad, a lot of the troops appeared to be in far worse shape, hanging over the side again and again. I reasoned, correctly I believe, there would be less motion in the exact center of the ship and I found a place to sit as near as I could get to that fulcrum of the nautical seesaw I was riding. It seemed to work, although I continued to feel somewhat queasy for a few days.

The *Henderson* probably had a mess hall or dining compartment for the crew but no such luxury was provided for the troops being transported. We lined up on deck with our own field mess gear and were served from huge pots manned by the ship's mess cooks. In nice weather this was no great hardship, but the first night afloat was a real horror. The sea was heavy and a stiff wind pelted us with sleet. Shivering in line

17

on that cold wet night, I experienced an epiphany of sorts. Our chow line snaked past the windows, or portholes, of the officers' dining room. Such splendor, rows of white tableclothed tables attended by stewards in white jackets, and the crowning feature, a sideboard holding the ship's highly polished silver service. Standing there with sleet going down my neck, I truly felt like a homeless vagrant peering at the rich entering a classy restaurant. It struck me then. The difference between the men dining in luxury and comfort and me was a college education! That was all. In America, you don't have to be a peer of the realm to become an officer; all it takes is a bit of education. It was a lesson I never forgot.

On December 23 we sailed into Guantanamo Bay and anchored among a flotilla of warships, including the battleships *Arkansas*, *New York* and *Texas*. I began to feel I was part of a larger effort. We cooled our heels aboard ship and did not disembark until the 27th. I spent Christmas Day on a working party aboard the *Texas* and enjoyed my turkey leg sitting on the deck beneath a five-inch gun. While on the battleship I bought a pair of blue denim Navy pants to replace the absurd coveralls issued in boot camp. I also bought two cartons of Camel cigarettes, 60 cents per carton. Old Golds were 50 cents a carton and "off brands" such as Wings were even cheaper, only 30 cents a carton. The prices were low because state and federal taxes were not assessed on cigarettes sold outside the country. Back home, with state and federal taxes included, Camels sold for about a dollar-and-a-half per carton.

3

The Fifth Marines

Witzel and I were split up when we got ashore. I was assigned to A Company, First Battalion, Fifth Marine Regiment. Witzel went to M Company, Third Battalion of the Fifth. My company was a regular "line" company while Witzel's M Company was a weapons company which manned 81-millimeter mortars and the Browning 30-caliber watercooled "heavy" machine guns. "Heavy" was a correct term for this gun for, with tripod, it weighed about 95 pounds. The term also distinguished it from the "light" air-cooled machine gun assigned to the line infantry companies. Both machine guns used the same belted ammunition.

The regiment was housed in six-man pyramidal tents on a high promontory called, if memory serves, Caravela Point. The tents were undecked and the bunks were canvas cots. With the sides rolled up the tents were quite comfortable day and night. Our sea bags were stacked around the tent's center pole. In addition to six Marines, the tent housed a lively population of gecko lizards. We welcomed these little rascals for they preyed on numerous insect pests. The heads were plank seats over a pit. The pits were flooded with kerosene and ignited once a week. I can still remember the smell of that operation! We had outdoor showers and wooden racks with spigots to do our toilet and wash our clothing. The only permanent large buildings were mess halls, one for each battalion. In due time I would become intimately acquainted with the First Battalion mess hall and its major domo, Mess Sergeant Flannigan.

Captain Phipps, a World War I veteran who wore the Purple Heart, commanded A Company. He wore leather puttees and a Sam Brown belt. I remember thinking at the time, "Ye gods, he's been in the Corps for many years before I was born and he is only a captain!" We had only one other officer, a second lieutenant who served as company executive

19

officer. None of the platoons had an officer platoon leader, a condition not remedied until we returned to the States. In actual practice the company was run by the first sergeant, "Slug" Slusser. Slusser was about 35, six-feet-two-or-three, with a booming voice that could wake the dead. In fact, when the battalion was marching in step, Slusser called cadence for the whole unit. The first thing you learn about first sergeants is to stay the hell away from them. This applied doubly to Slug Slusser. The mere sight of a private stimulated him to think up some onerous task to foist upon the innocent. A buck sergeant, Kennedy, led my platoon. But he and the other high officials of the company were of no concern to me. I had a more immediate boss who stayed in my face every minute of the day, Corporal "Horse" Evans, my squad leader. Evans' physique earned him his nickname. He was a solid mass of muscle with the strength of a bull. Needless to say, I gave him no backtalk. When he said jump, my only response was, "How high?" Evans was always on my case about the acne I still sported. He insisted I didn't scrub my face hard enough and threatened to do it himself. It bothered the hell out of him to see a Marine with acne. It bothered me too, but fortunately I quickly grew out of it. He also got on my case about not cleaning my teeth before breakfast. I argued futilely that I had been taught to brush after eating. But he wouldn't relent until another corporal, Gook Maitland, whose father was a dentist, convinced him I was right.

Shortly after I arrived I was issued a tropical pith helmet as a replacement for my cherished campaign hat. This pith helmet was the most impractical headpiece ever invented. It did shelter you from the tropical sun but was almost impossible to keep on when worn in the field. A bit of wind would send it flying. It would also depart if a rifle touched it while doing the manual of arms. The other headgear issued was a steel helmet; not the pot-shaped one we wore later during the war, but the same type worn by our fathers in World War I. It was awfully uncomfortable, for it had an inner leather-covered steel harness that pressed on your forehead. It also bounced when you ran. While on the subject of stuff we wore, I should bring out that we were allowed to wear whatever we desired while training in the field. We had no set field uniform. The "herringbone" utilities we wore during the war had not yet appeared. I wore the Navy jeans I bought on the battleship and a khaki shirt. Some men wore blue Navy shirts with khaki pants and some wore shirts with the sleeves removed. All in all, we were a salty looking bunch, truly "Raggedy-Ass Marines."

In training we marched around the boondocks a lot and, among other things, learned to get by on one canteen of water for the day, a skill which would come in handy later. We learned to field strip and fire the Browning Automatic Rifle (BAR) and spent some time firing at a sleeve towed by a low-flying plane. The Guantanamo area, "Gitmo" as we learned to call it, was semi-arid with little vegetation other than high grass and cactus. The cactus was a mixed bag: The fruit was delicious but the thorns were lethal. I was picking thorns from my legs long after we returned to the States in April.

In mid–January we embarked on the USS *McCawley*, a former Grace Line passenger ship newly acquired by the Navy and fitted out as a troop ship.

The USS *McCawley*, AP 10, with troops descending cargo nets into LCVP landing craft. During the Rendova operation she was hit by an aerial torpedo and, while being towed away, was accidentally torpedoed and sunk by our own PT boats (Naval Historical Foundation).

The quarters and mess facilities on *McCawley* were far better than those of the old *Henderson*. I made my first amphibious landing from the *McCawley* onto the lovely little tropical island of Culebra. We clambered down cargo nets hung from the ship's side into a large motor launch and departed for the beach. However, there is a problem when you try to land troops from a large motor launch; the only part of the boat actually on the beach is the bow, but it is far too high, at least six feet, to permit men to merely jump off. The remedy was to drape a cargo net off the bow to permit men to climb down, an impossibly slow process. In response to orders, some men started jumping over the sides of the launch and instantly disappeared from sight in more than six feet of water, for the beach sloped abruptly. Some of us had to strip off our gear and jump to the rescue of our sunken comrades. All in all, the landing was as fouled up as a Chinese fire drill. Some other units of the regiment did better, landing from small boats manned by Coast Guard coxswains. These boats were the forerunners of the Higgins boats we used in the war.

Once ashore we formed into a skirmish line and moved off into the grassy hills. The realism of the maneuver was shattered by the presence of small native boys dragging burlap sacks containing soft drinks and a chunk of ice. The kids would crawl behind you as you bellied through the grass whispering, "Coca Cola, cinco centavos." Despite shouted curses and threats from NCOs, few of us could resist the temptation, for "snooping and drooping" through tropical boonies is thirsty work. The maneuver we were participating in was named "Flanex 7." I guess the Marine Corps and Navy learned a lot from the operation, lessons vital to success in the coming war.

From Culebra we sailed to San Juan, Puerto Rico, for shore leave. This was my first visit to a foreign city and, unfortunately, I made the most of it. Accompanied by a friend I'd made aboard ship, Mike Adamoyurka from the coal regions of Pennsylvania, I visited the sights, including the Morro Castle. We patronized an ice cream bar where I encountered the largest cockroach in the world! The three-inch monster emerged from under the bar and began lapping the melted ice cream which had spilled from my sundae. When I recoiled in horror the attendant merely shooed the creature back under the bar and revealed it was a pet! We had been warned about drinking rum in the hot tropical sun but I had to experiment for myself. The result was disastrous. I left Mike and went pub crawling on my own. At a wharf-side bar I must have offended one of the local gals, for she belted me in the face with a bottle. I staggered aboard ship, where Mike and others cleaned me up and got me into a bunk. I had two black eyes and a badly swollen nose. Fortunately, the young heal fast and I was able to resume activities in the Company with no need for disciplinary action. I apparently dodged a bullet, for some of the shore party didn't fare as well. Some had been slashed with razor blades by women.

We went back to Gitmo and disembarked on February 20, where I was detailed for mess duty. When I made this known to the old hands in my tent one of them sabotaged me by telling me to ask for pot washing duty. He made it sound attractive by pointing out "pot wallopers," as they were called, did not have to get up before dawn with the other mess men but could sleep in until almost mid-morning. That part was right, but what he didn't point out was that I would be scraping pots long after dark and after the rest of the troops were enjoying a movie. He also failed to warn me that the field oil stoves used in the galley coated the pots with a black patina, which was almost impossible to remove, and that Mess Sergeant Flannigan insisted that every damned pot must shine like a mirror before he would use it. My time on mess duty was an absolute horror, only relieved by my ability to enrage Flannigan by singing, sotto voiced, "Oh, the Irish flag is a dirty old rag but it's too damned good for the Irish." Flannigan would retaliate by throwing large chunks of coral rock down the hill toward the lean-to where I labored over the pot washing tubs and burners. He never hit me, but he came close. The only bright spot in this duty was the view from the worksite of the beautiful crystal clear water of the bay. I was enthralled by the antics of the giant rays, which cruised near the surface.

My potwalloping duties kept me busy long after sunset. Disgruntled, tired and dirty I would make my way to one of the outdoor showers for a much needed bath. Our showers were placed on raised wooden platforms. The floor was slotted to let water pass through. One dark night, as I was taking my solitary wash, my only bar of soap slipped out of my hand and, of course, found its way through the slotted floor to the mud beneath. I couldn't lose that soap. It was my only bar, and they cost money. So I crawled into the mud below the platform and began to search on hands and knees. While thus employed, I was loudly turning the atmosphere blue with the foulest language I knew. Suddenly I heard a voice coming from the blackness above me. It said, "Would you want your mother to hear what you are saying?" I wasn't sure what I had heard and stammered back, "What did you say?" The answer came back, "Would you want your mother to hear what you were saying?" This angered me, so I shouted back, "Keep my mother out of this!" The answer came back, "Don't you know that there is someone above who always hears you?" This nonplussed me for a bit and I blurted out, "Who are you?" The answer came back, "I am Corporal Bill Culp." I don't remember any more of the conversation, but I am sure I didn't make any smartass remark because I was somewhat ashamed, and besides, I had no intention of arguing with a *corporal*! When I found my soap, crawled out of the muck and remounted the shower platform, he was gone. I had no idea as to his whereabouts or unit but when I related my experience to old-timers in my company I was told, "Oh, sure, that was Bill Culp from C Company. He always talks like that and holds prayer sessions with those he can muster." Bill Culp's name will appear again later in this writing.

We were not given prepackaged rations to eat for lunch when out hiking and maneuvering in the cactus laden hills. Instead, the mess hall prepared sandwiches of varied content, which we picked up after breakfast and took to the field in our packs. Sometimes we had cheese and sometimes peanut butter and jelly. One time, while I was on mess duty, Flannigan sent the troops out with deviled ham sandwiches with disastrous results. Everyone who ate the sandwich came down with food poisoning. We had to send out trucks to bring back the fallen. They were laid out in rows on the Company Street, too weak from vomiting and diarrhea to go to their tents. The battalion surgeon and the corpsmen did what they could but they had no medicine for this malady. Our battalion commander moved among the men and asked an A Company sergeant, Chubby Magnum, what he thought caused the problem. Chubby told him it was the sandwich. "What did it taste like?" the colonel asked. "Red Heart dog food, sir," said Chubby. "Hell, I ate one of the things and it didn't affect me," the officer said. But he was wrong. The poor guy didn't make it back to his tent before he started going at both ends with the rest of the troops. Needless to say, I was glad to be safe in camp on mess duty that day.

Our sojourn in the tropics ended on April 4, 1941, when we boarded the *McCawley* and sailed to the States. We disembarked at Norfolk on April 8 and entrained to Quantico. I was impressed with Quantico. Heretofore I'd been bunking in tents and going to outside heads and shower rooms. Now I was housed in a brick barracks with all inside plumbing. On April 11 I started a 20-day furlough, which I spent in Lehighton. The only noteworthy event was an accidental encounter with my high school heartthrob and her new beau, my best friend in school. She had sent me a "Dear John" letter while I was at Guantanamo announcing that she and Sid had become a twosome. I lost my head and temper and knocked poor old Sid on his can. All Anita said was, "You could have talked to him first." I'm sure my pique was mostly from hurt pride rather than from a broken heart. Sid and Anita married and raised a family, facts I learned in 1990 when we met at the 50th reunion of our high school class.

At Quantico we did a lot of "boondocking" through the woods and hills of Virginia. I do not think the training was very good as preparation for the type of combat we would face in the Pacific. For example, we were not shown how to attack a pillbox or how to flank a machine gun. And I don't recall being drilled in the most basic skill of all, how to set up an MLR, a main line of resistance. Heck, I did not dig a foxhole during any of our maneuvers. On the plus side, running around the Quantico woods did keep us in shape.

Our main diversion was weekend liberty in nearby Washington, D.C. However, my enjoyment of D.C. was tempered by a chronic shortage of funds. At the time I was enjoying a salary of $30 a month, an increase from the $21 I got during my first three months. We were paid in cash every two weeks, standing in line in alphabetical order. But, unfortunately, I never got the full $15, for I always owed bills I had run up for toilet articles, cigarettes, laundry or pogie bait (candy). I seldom received more than seven dollars. We resorted to many artifices to make up for the shortage of cash. Although the rail line ran right through the base and the train fare to the city was only 50 cents, we rarely used it, choosing instead to hitchhike. This meant a hike of several miles to the highway, Route 1, but once there I never failed to get a ride. I seldom stayed in Washington overnight but, when necessary, I slept on a bench in Union Station or merely whiled the night away drinking coffee in Thompson's Restaurant at 14th Street and Pennsylvania Avenue. My regular eating place was the White Tower on 14th Street, where you could get two hamburgers and a glass of milk for 15 cents. However, I rarely ate any food while on liberty; it seemed like a terrible waste of good drinking money.

During my Quantico tenure I hitchhiked to Lehighton several times. One time was especially noteworthy. A man and woman of middle years, obviously husband and wife, occupied the car that stopped for me. When he asked where I was headed, I told him, "Pennsylvania." "Where in Pennsylvania?" he asked. When I told him Lehighton, he asked, "Where in Lehighton?" It turned out they were neighbors of my parents, and I got a ride to the Rogals' front door!

I also had some hairy rides at night from Washington to the base. Once, with two drunks in the front seat, I ended up in a frozen cornfield just south of Alexandria. Another time a driver fell asleep at the wheel and almost put me in the Rappahannock River. Route 1 was a dangerous road in those days. A week seldom passed without a Quantico Marine being killed or hurt on the highway.

The routine of peacetime barracks duty was interrupted in early August by the appearance in the Potomac of six Navy warships, destroyers. From the windows in A Barracks they looked sleek and deadly, but in reality they were outdated and, as it was learned at Guadalcanal, they were no match for a modern Japanese destroyer. The ships were APDs, World War I "four-stacker" destroyers, recently converted to carry and land Marine assault forces. The conversion consisted of removing the forward fireroom and creating a compartment to house about 100 Marines. In the process the ships lost their two forward funnels and their torpedo tubes. They retained some antisubmarine capability with depth charge racks on the stern. For armament the ships carried four four-inch/50-caliber guns, which were only useful for surface targets; they could not be elevated to fire at aircraft. The ships had davits for four Higgins-type

26

landing boats. The APDs were about 312 feet in length with a beam of about 30 feet. Top speed was about 28 knots. The six ships slated to transport my First Battalion, Fifth Marines, were named: *Mckean, Little, Manley, Stringham, Gregory* and *Colhoun*. A Company was assigned to the USS *Little*, APD 4.

We soon learned that our battalion, the First Battalion, Fifth Marines, had been selected to be a special assault battalion, similar to the British commando units. To fit on the ships the companies were reduced in size to about 100 men. In short order the battalion packed its sea bags and went aboard the ships. As we sailed down the river and out to sea we learned we were going to practice beach assault landings on Onslow Beach, North Carolina, the beach adjacent to newly opened Camp Lejeune.

We were accompanied in this venture by an armada of Navy transports carrying the remainder of the Fifth Regiment and elements of the First Army Division. Our role was to land first and secure the beach to

The USS *Little*, APD 4. Three hundred-and-twelve feet of misery for its Marine Corps passengers (Naval Historical Foundation).

enable the main body to land. We were told we were "The spearhead of the Spearhead." Once ashore we executed a forced march through the Carolina pine forests, one of the toughest marches in my Marine Corps experience. Apparently our battalion commander, Lieutenant Colonel Merritt A. "Red Mike" Edson, wanted to see how much punishment his "elite" battalion could take. This march, and a speech he gave us during a rest period in which he predicted we would suffer at least 50 percent casualties if we landed on a defended beach, had an unanticipated result, about 30 men went over the hill.

Upon completion of the exercise we returned to our ships and set sail for liberty in Miami. Life at sea aboard an APD in good weather was primitive but not unpleasant. We slept topside, rolled in blankets, for our compartment was stifling in warm weather and close and smelly at all times. My buddy Don Wolf and I commandeered a space in the port side passageway between the forecastle and the well deck. This narrow aisle was protected from the elements, for it was under the wing of the bridge and behind the hatch leading to the forecastle. Food on the ship was pretty basic but edible. Like the *Henderson*, the *Little* had no mess hall or special compartment for eating. You merely squatted down on the deck in good weather or carried your tray back to your bunk. We spent our time reading and watching the flying fish and dolphins. I loved to lie on my stomach at the very peak of the forecastle and watch the dolphins play in our bow wave. They seemed to enjoy racing the ship and showing off for my benefit. On this trip down the coast we enjoyed the only swimming party I have ever experienced while at sea. The skipper just cut the engines, dropped one of the landing boats for safety and invited all swimmers to dive over the side. Of course I did so with gusto. While in the water an officer on the bridge yelled at me to bring him a strange multicolored balloon-like creature that was floating near me. I didn't like the looks of the thing and refused to touch it. In time someone threw me a vegetable crate lid and I scooped the thing up and passed it up to a crewmember on the ship. After the swimming party I learned the creature had been identified as a Portuguese man-of-war, a type of jellyfish that packs a most painful sting. Sometimes it pays to be a bit cautious.

Our liberty in Miami was fantastic. The citizens were worried that the city was vulnerable to a German attack and were overjoyed to have a regiment of Marines pay them a visit. They would stop their cars and ask strolling Marines whether they needed a lift or would like a home-cooked meal. It was an amazing experience for the old salts who were more accustomed to the good burghers of Norfolk, Boston and Charleston, who locked up their daughters and dogs when the fleet was in. The highlight of my 72-hour liberty was a visit to a private home with a swimming pool. The hosts were a couple of college boys, apparently sons of wealthy parents, and they spared no expense in entertaining us. The beer and food never ran out. Come to think of it, I don't remember even seeing a girl during my time ashore. Did the fathers and mothers of Miami emulate the parents in the other Atlantic coast liberty ports? Be that as it may, all hands had a good time ashore.

From Miami we sailed to Charleston and docked in the Navy yard for work on the ships. The only thing that I remember being done to the ships was the welding of sheet metal over the ships' portholes. The Navy was concerned that some eight ball would leave a compartment light on and reveal the ship's position to an enemy. It made no difference to me, for the Marine compartment had no portholes; those luxuries had brightened the wardroom and the crew's quarters.

This time in port gave me the opportunity to seek dental help, for the yard had a dispensary manned by several dentists, and my mouth was a mess. Unfortunately, the day I got there they were mobbed by Marines and sailors from the six APDs. However, that day the Chief of Naval Dentistry, a full Navy captain, was visiting the facility and, because of the crowd, he decided to don a white coat and lend a hand. And, you guessed it, I was ministered to by the captain. This worthy drilled and filled 13 cavities, all without benefit of anesthesia of any kind. You bet I was in agony, and I would have screamed to high heaven if some ensign or junior grade had worked on me. But I was awestruck by the high rank of this torturer and suffered in silence. It still hurts when I think about it.

I had a bit of trouble in Charleston. On liberty one night I got smashed on moonshine I bought in a joint on Bay Street and awakened the following morning on the edge of what appeared to be a swamp. I staggered out to a street where a vagrant accosted me and asked for money for breakfast. I said, "Hell, man, I'll do better than that, I'll buy you breakfast in any restaurant you choose." This pleased the bum and he led me to a nice place where we both had a big breakfast with all the trimmings. When we finished eating I pulled out my wallet to pay and discovered I had not one red cent. I had visions of being in big trouble with the restaurant's proprietor, fearing he would call the police and have me arrested. But rescue appeared from a most unlikely source; the bum pulled out a roll and paid the tab! He was somewhat disgruntled and I was very, very red-faced.

However, my troubles were not over. I was AOL (absent over leave), for my liberty had expired at 06:00 and it was now mid-morning. I anticipated being apprehended at the Navy Yard gate and stuck in the Navy's brig to await a deck court martial, at which I'd probably get a sentence of at least five days incarceration on "piss and punk" (bread and water). But I lucked out. The sentry at the gate admitted me without comment and I fast-stepped it back to the ship. But I didn't get off scot-free. First Sergeant Slusser and my platoon sergeant, Kennedy, did not officially report my tardy return but meted out fitting punishment. I was directed to report to the Navy chief petty officer in the *Little*'s engine room for a work detail. I spent the next few days in the 100-plus degree heat of the engine room polishing brass fittings. At night, after evening chow, I was given sentry duty over several railroad flat cars loaded with depth charges. The flat cars were located in a swampy area far removed from the base's buildings. It was mosquito heaven, and I had no head net or repellant. I gladly accepted these informal punishments, for nothing went in my record book. A clean record was of great concern to me. I learned a valuable lesson at minimum cost.

After Charleston we sailed back up the coast into the Potomac and disembarked at Quantico, where we resumed training, including some weapons firing on the range. The battalion commanding officer, Lt. Col. Merritt "Red Mike" Edson, was a distinguished rifleman and a past member of the Marine rifle team that competed in the shooting meets held annually at Camp Perry in Ohio. One day on the range, while we were shooting slow fire, sitting position, from the 200-yard firing line, the colonel asked me if I had set the correct dope on my rifle. That is, were the sights properly adjusted for the distance to the target? I answered,

"Yes, sir," and, at his request, handed him the piece. Standing next to me, in the offhand position and without a sling, he put five shots dead center in the bullseye! It was an eye-opening experience. The only way I could equal that would be to shoot from the prone position with the rifle resting on a sandbag.

Barracks life at Quantico was busy but monotonous. We spent a good deal of time working on our equipment. Our aluminum mess gear, canteens and canteen cups had to shine like mirrors. Our shoes had to be spit-shined and our web gear had to be blancoed.* We did little physical conditioning except for daily, pre-breakfast "physical drill under arms." This consisted of various exercises with the rifle, or BAR, grasped with both hands and employed as a barbell. The toughest one was "front sweep slow," in which you swept the rifle slowly from overhead to the deck. After a couple of dozen of those movements your muscles complained and your breath came in short pants. The Marine Corps slang term for these exercise sessions was "organized grab-ass."

A most momentous event occurred in October. The battalion was selected to put on a demonstration of Marine Corps expertise in Washington for Navy Day, October 20. The demonstration was, in effect, a skit in which the Marines would land and attack a village inhabited by South American "insurrectos" who had captured and were holding the U.S. ambassador. We, that is, A Company, had the best parts in the play. We were to be outfitted with straw hats, wear our most ragged clothing and paint on mustaches. We were to be the "insurrectos" which the rest of the battalion would attack. We even had one man dressed in a white suit to be the captured ambassador. On October 20 the six APDs showed up in the river and we went aboard for the trip to D.C. I was impressed when we sailed past Mount Vernon. It is a Navy custom to muster all hands on deck and at attention when a ship passes the mansion, and we were mustered to fulfill our part of this duty. We docked at Washington Navy Yard and boated across the Anacostia River to a large grassy field where our "native village" had been set up. Unfor-

---

*Blanco is a brown, paste-like mud to be smeared on your pack, cartridge belt and other web gear to counteract the bleaching affect of sunlight and color everyone's equipment a uniform shade of brown.

tunately, it began to rain rather heavily. This didn't bother us very much but it caused a problem for the rest of the battalion, for they were dressed in their winter service, green wool uniforms complete with collared shirts and field scarves. They were dressed for a parade, not combat! While attacking us they had to fire a few blanks, run a few yards and hit the deck in a saturated field. By the time they had killed or captured us and rescued the ambassador they were a filthy mess. Perhaps it was cruel, but the " insurrectos" of A Company couldn't suppress a few chuckles.

When we returned to the ship, liberty was announced for all hands that could pass inspection. This caused more merriment in A Company, for our liberty uniforms were dry and wearable. In short, we could go ashore and the poor slobs who messed up their uniforms in the demonstration could not. In the spirit of one-upmanship, I determined to go ashore, although I had exactly one dime in my pocket. But I wouldn't need money, for I headed for a USO dance, which the grapevine had told me was being held at the Bureau of Engraving on South 14th Street. That was a pretty good walk from the Navy Yard, but the rain had stopped and walking was one thing I did very well. Besides, I didn't have to walk both ways; the dime would pay for a return by streetcar.

The decisions to go ashore that night and to go to the USO dance were the most momentous ones I ever made, for at the dance I met the girl I would eventually marry and spend the rest of my life with. I had never learned to dance very well and just sort of circulated around the huge ballroom and helped myself to the soft drinks and other handouts. Toward the end of the evening I danced with an older woman, Vicky Zackman, whom I had met a week or two before at a dance at Quantico. Probably in an effort to get rid of me, she told me to stand by, for she had a girl she wanted me to meet. In a couple of minutes she returned with this absolutely stunning strawberry blonde she introduced as Pearl Price, who, after the introduction, said, "Hi," and scampered back to wherever Vicky had found her. I was smitten but instantly concluded I didn't have a chance with a gal like that. Why mess around with a private when Washington was full of far better catches, including thousands of junior officers? But fate, in the form of Vicky Zackman, played a hand, for towards the end of the evening she asked me to escort her and her friend "past the wolves at the door." I accepted with alacrity and walked them past the gauntlet of leering, horny GIs who congregated around the door. We then walked slowly north to Pennsylvania Avenue, where I could get my streetcar to the Navy Yard. During the walk the girls told me about a Halloween party at their boardinghouse the following week and invited me to come. Their boardinghouse, the Marleta, was located on 16th Street, just above Scott Circle. Needless to say, I went to the party and, as the saying goes, the rest is history.

Over the next few weeks I saw Pearl at every opportunity. We went to the movies at the old Capital Theater on F Street for our first planned date and hit a few nightspots, such as El Patio, the Café Caprice in the Roger Smith Hotel, and Café of All Nations on subsequent evenings. The hit popular songs of the time we adopted as "our songs" were "I Don't Want to Set the World on Fire" and "Two in Love Can Face the World Together."

Left to right: Don Wolf and I dating Pearl Price and her roommate, Tilly Sikish, at the Washington restaurant-nightclub, Mayfair — Café of All Nations.

On November 17 the Marine Corps recognized what a catch I was and promoted me to PFC — wow! While this honor didn't exactly elevate me to the peerage, it wasn't to be sneezed at for it increased my pay 20 percent from $30 to $36 per month. On the following payday, December 5, I was flush with cash so Don Wolf and I rented a car and invited Pearl and Vicky to go for a drive — to visit my parents in Lehighton, Pennsylvania. Amazingly, they accepted and we started out on Saturday afternoon, December 6. Don drove, for I did not have a license, and, in fact, because my family had never had a car, I had never learned to drive. We arrived rather late and got my surprised parents out of bed. On the way up the girls kept saying I should telephone to warn them but I demurred; I didn't want to tell them my folks didn't have a telephone.

Vicky was Catholic, so the next morning we all went to mass at St. Peter & St. Paul Catholic Church and shortly thereafter started the drive back to Washington. In late afternoon after passing through Baltimore, I asked Vicky, who was sitting in the front seat with Don, to get us some music on the radio. She tried several stations but all she could get was excited voices saying something about bombing a place called Pearl Harbor in Hawaii. Thinking this was another Orson Wells *War of the Worlds* spoof, I asked her to try another station. She did and the same message was aired. Still not convinced, I said, "Heck, they are just saying what could happen," to which Vicky responded, "Dammit, Bill, the Japs have bombed Pearl Harbor and we are at war." How right she was! The radio reported few details other than there was a heavy loss of life and repeatedly announced that all military personnel must report immediately to their duty stations. When we got to Washington Don took the car back to the rental agency and I accompanied the girls to the Marleta and sat around talking for a few hours. I thought it would be a long war and the Marine Corps didn't need me that very minute. Moreover, I was afraid that I might not get liberty again once I got back to Quantico. At any rate, I left in time to get back to Quantico before my liberty was up at reveille.

The following day, in the barracks, we listened to President Roosevelt's address to Congress requesting that war be declared against Japan. He was an absolute master of the spoken word. He set the right tone of outrage at the sneak attack ("a date that will live in infamy"), a tone of hatred for the Japanese that galvanized the country and produced an unstinting all-out war effort that didn't slacken until the Japs surrendered on August 14, 1945. The sleeping tiger had been kicked awake!

One day in early January we were informed we were no longer in the Fifth Marines. The battalion had been redesignated the "First Separate Battalion." Shortly thereafter the designation was changed to "First Raider Battalion." Like it or not, we were now "commandos." And, in short order, we were introduced to what that designation involved. In mid–January the six APDs appeared in the river and, within an hour or two, we were aboard and headed downriver. We docked at Norfolk that night and all hands participated in loading a full unit of fire (live ammunition) for the Marines and the ship. My working party loaded the after magazine located in the stern, below the crew's quarters under the after deck house. We finished loading after midnight and immediately sailed. No one told us where we were going or what we were going to do when we got there. I suppose it's true that "loose lips sink ships" but keeping us totally in the dark at that time was ludicrous. For all we knew we were going to attack occupied France. But when we hit the open North Atlantic we had more immediate worries to occupy us: a raging storm!

Riding out an Atlantic nor'easter on an APD is an experience I would not wish on even an experienced mariner. With gigantic waves and a howling blizzard the ship rolled at least 45 degrees and took white water three or more feet deep over the bow on every pitch. Truly, on occasion the entire main deck was submerged with two to three feet of cold green water. On a flush deck destroyer there are no fore and aft passageways below decks, so anyone who needed to move from one part of the ship to another, say from the Marine compartment to the head, located astern in the after deck house, had to traverse the oft-submerged main deck. This would have been impossible if the crew had not rigged a line (rope) from stanchion to stanchion the full length of the ship. We traveled hand-over-hand along that line. Unfortunately, we lost one man, a sailor, overboard that night.

I spent most of the night on lookout watch on the bridge. These ships had an enclosed pilothouse flanked on both sides by wings fully exposed to the weather. Visibility from the pilothouse in that blizzard was absolutely nil, for the windows were coated with a thick layer of ice, as indeed was the entire ship. The lookouts were posted on the exposed bridge wings with instructions to report everything they saw, even floating garbage, to the watch officer in the pilothouse. Of course the real objects of our scrutiny were German submarines. If any were about in that weather I am sure they were resting comfortably well below the heaving surface. The Navy equipped the lookouts with foul weather gear consisting of a heavy coat, gloves with gauntlets, a woolen cap and a facemask. But even so equipped the lookouts on the bridge wings had to be relieved every 15 minutes to avoid injury from exposure. We stood the watch in pairs, with one man outside and the other inside the pilothouse, and exchanged places every 15 minutes. While I was on the bridge we received a message from the flotilla commander to "proceed independently," which meant the ships were to abandon attempts to maintain a formation. We learned our destination the next day, when we sailed into Brooklyn Navy Yard. We were a sad sight, riding very low in the water, for the entire ship was coated with at least six inches of ice, which the crew attacked with axes and fire hoses.

In time we were informed that our purpose in New York was to participate in a practice amphibious landing with the First Army Division. The site of the landing was the Army base, Fort Storey on Cape Henry near the mouth of the Chesapeake Bay. We had come north to escort the transports carrying the Army troops with our six APDs functioning as an antisubmarine screen. By the time we sailed south the weather had abated but the seas remained high and visibility was still limited. Much of the time we couldn't see the rest of the convoy. I was again standing lookout watch on the starboard bridge wing when, for some never explained reason, our skipper cut the engines and we went dead in the water. Suddenly the hatch to the pilothouse flew open and the captain screamed, "Signal 'I am stopped!' Signal 'I am stopped!'" I looked around to see what the fuss was about and saw a sight that chilled me to the bone. One of our sister ships was on a course to hit us broadside. Fortunately, our signalman got on the big 24-inch signal light and flashed our captain's message directly into the other ship's bridge. It changed course and passed astern, missing us by not more than 20 feet. As they say in the Navy, "A collision at sea can ruin your whole day."

Had this one occurred, few of us on the *Little* would have survived a swim in the cold, cruel sea. The rest of the trip was uneventful.

The main thing I remember about the landing and maneuver in the Chesapeake was the cold. We did not have clothing adequate for the temperature and spent two nights freezing our tails off. On the second night we teamed up with some Army guys and built fires from driftwood. I suppose the staff officers learned something from the operation. I doubt the troops got anything out of it. But, I suppose, that is true about most practice operations.

We sailed back to Quantico, where a surprise awaited. We had been transferred; not the whole battalion, only A Company and a platoon, or section, from D Company. We were to travel to the west coast as a nucleus for a Second Raider Battalion, which I found out later had been formed on February 19 as a component of the Second Marine Division. We went by train, in Pullman cars, if you can believe it! It was an enjoyable ride. I had no strong feelings about leaving the First Raiders but I did regret one thing. For some reason I've never learned, Don Wolf stayed behind with the First. We had talked a lot about sticking by each other in combat and now that small comfort was not to be. Upon arrival in Camp Elliot, California, another surprise awaited us. We would not automatically become part of the Second Raider Battalion but would have to undergo a selection procedure personally conducted by the battalion commander, Lieutenant Colonel Evans F. Carlson.

Lt. Col. Carlson was a storied and controversial officer who served in the Army in World War I and received a Marine Corps commission shortly thereafter. In the thirties, while serving three tours in China, he spent a good deal of time living with and observing the tactics of the communist guerrilla units led by Mao Tse-tung. He became enamored with the concept of guerrilla warfare and posited, correctly as it turned out, that Mao's forces would eventually win out. He urged support of those forces as the only viable Army capable of opposing Japanese aggression in Asia. Such comments went over like a lead balloon in Washington. Carlson became somewhat of a pariah and was looked upon as at least a bit pink, if not an actual commie. He resigned his commission to speak out on his China views but regained it when the war broke out. As an expert on guerrilla war his selection as commanding officer of a

Raider Battalion was a natural. While his standing with Marine Corps brass was, at best, marginal, his standing with the president was high. In fact, it was so high that the president's son, Major James Roosevelt, was made executive officer of Carlson's battalion.

While I did not know all the facts about Carlson, the grapevine, "scuttlebutt" as we called it in the Corps, had armed me with enough information to cause me to question whether I really wanted to volunteer my services to his unit. Thus, when the day came for my face-to-face interview, I entered the colonel's office with a rather blasé mindset which may have been detectable. To say the interview was weird understates the event. Carlson was seated in a darkened room with the window at his back, thereby forcing the interviewee to squint in bright light while being questioned by a silhouette. My interrogation went something like this. He began with, "What is your nationality?"

I knew what he meant but mischievously responded, "American, sir."

Testily, he barked, "Dammit, I mean where did your family originate?"

"Prussia and Germany," I responded.

He commented, "That could be a good combination." And followed up with, "Can you march 30 miles in a day?"

I was proud of my marching stamina, puffed out my chest and proudly responded, "I've never fallen out on a hike yet, sir."

I expected a complimentary comment on my response but didn't get it. Instead, he roared, "THAT'S THE WRONG ANSWER! When I ask, 'Can you march 30 miles a day?,' I want you to scream, 'YES, SIR.'"

I quickly got the message; he was looking for zealots! Moreover, I was beginning to dislike the guy. Nevertheless, I determined not to show any weakness and responded, "OK, sir, I can march 30 miles a day."

The next question was the clincher, the one to separate the goats from the sheep. He asked, "If selected for my battalion, are you willing to live for months in the boondocks with only a poncho for shelter, only rations to eat and no liberty while we are in the States?"

My answer killed any chance I had to join his "elite" outfit. I asked, "No liberty, sir?"

3. The Fifth Marines

Within hours I was directed to report to A Company, First Battalion, Second Marines, Second Marine Division.

I was not alone in being a "Carlson rejectee." In fact, he rejected 75 percent of my fellow transferees from the First Raider Battalion. Since I knew most of the guys reasonably well I was perplexed by his choices. Some of the selected were definitely not fire-eaters, and the rejected group included a lot of first-class Marines. The manner of our rejection so angered Lt. Col. Edson that he wrote a letter to General Price, the CO of the Second Marine Division, in which he said:

> In my opinion and the opinion of others who have seen [my battalion] perform in the field and in maneuvers, it was, until I sent this detail to Carlson, the best battalion on the east coast and as good or better than any similar outfit in the 2nd Division.... Whatever Carlson's so-called standards may be, his refusal to accept three out of four of these men only confirmed my opinion that the Marine Corps had lost nothing by his resignation a few years ago and has gained nothing by his return to active duty.*

*Jon T. Hoffman, *Once a Legend: Red Mike Edson of the Marine Raiders* (Novato, CA: Presidio Press, 1994), 158.

4

The Second Marines

Five other men from my former company who failed to pass Carlson's inquisition joined me in A Company, First Battalion, Second Marine Regiment, A-1-2, one of the three infantry regiments which, together with the Sixth and Eighth Regiments and the Tenth Artillery Regiment, made up the Second Marine Division. The rejected five were Cyril Throneburg, Leonard Williams, Joseph Czmackowski, Victor Guilmino and William Carter. All of the companies of the regiment got a similar quota of Carlson's rejects. He was even picky about 81-millimeter mortar men, and my Lehighton buddy, Witzel, ended up in M Company of the Second. The Second Regiment was a green outfit, manned for the most part by young patriots who had enlisted after the Pearl Harbor attack and had just finished boot camp. However, in addition to the rejects from the Raiders, the regiment had a sizeable number of seasoned Marines from the reserve battalions, called up when the war started. My platoon sergeant, Julius Novak, had come in when the Kansas City battalion was activated. Friends I made later, like the Boyd brothers, Bob and Paul, had been in the Indianapolis reserve battalion.

Within a few days I was promoted to corporal and put in command of the Browning Automatic Rifle squad of the Third Platoon. This weapon, always referred to by its initials, BAR, was the infantry's basic automatic rifle. It fired the same cartridges as our Springfield rifles from 20-round refillable clips. It was rather heavy, weighing about 21 pounds with a loaded clip. In addition to the weapon, the BAR man was loaded down with a belt holding eight clips of ammunition. The BAR squad had three BAR teams consisting of a gunner, assistant gunner and a scout, all supervised by the squad leader and his assistant.

The Corps discontinued having a separate BAR squad after Guadalcanal and distributed the BARs among the other squads of the platoon. The other three squad leaders of the platoon were Kenneth Casity, Thurman Price and James Sorensen. Jim Sorensen died in 1981 but left an excellent but unpublished memoir chronicling his experiences on Tulagi and Guadalcanal, which I will refer to as the *Sorensen Memoir* when I describe the events of November 3 to 11, 1942. In addition to the platoon sergeant, a four-striper, platoons had a position known as "platoon guide," typically manned by a buck sergeant. The platoon guide's primary duty is to keep the platoon supplied with ammunition and rations. He also takes over if the platoon sergeant becomes a casualty. In our platoon the position was occupied by Sergeant Ernest Denely Jr.

The company officers, all reserves, were headed by a captain from Texas, Paul W. Fuhrhop. He was a kindly man of a somewhat religious bent. We watched our language in his presence. First Lieutenant Jack M. Miller was the executive officer. He was a somewhat chubby man who enjoyed talking about his family, the wife and small girls he left behind. My platoon leader was a reserve second lieutenant named Russell Johnson. He was a nice guy who was smart enough to know that he didn't know everything.

The men of A Company were an amazingly homogeneous group. Almost without exception they came from blue collar households and farms. While there were some city boys, the great majority came from farms and small towns. We were heavy with Westerners, for the regiment had been formed on the West Coast. There were some Southerners and some Northeasterners, especially among the NCOs. The company was nearly all white, all Christian and all Northern European. The monotony was broken by a couple of American Indians, one Latino and one or two Mediterranean types. A cross section of America we were not. We all spoke the same language — foul. In fact, if the "F word" hadn't been invented we would have been almost tongue-tied. The men had the same immediate interests — women, booze and chow. And, I believe that, to a man, we had one overriding goal — survival with honor. The "with honor" qualification was important to this group for it had been taught and believed that "showing the white feather" in combat was, for a Marine, unthinkable.

Everybody needs a buddy and I soon made fast friends with Bruce

Coote, a sergeant who headed the 60-millimeter mortar section of our weapons platoon. Bruce was an extremely likable guy, in fact too likable to be a sergeant. His section was always in trouble of some kind. But I liked him and we went ashore together on many occasions and to the Camp Elliot "slop chute" (enlisted men's beer hall) when we didn't have liberty. I also went ashore once or twice with the company police sergeant, Wilbur Burgess, but in time discovered we were not simpatico. I had a lot of adventures while ashore in San Diego, including losing a front tooth in a stupid altercation with a Marine who appeared to be molesting a woman. When I charged to the rescue he stripped off his "fair leather" belt, wrapped it around his fist and caught me full in the mouth with the heavy brass buckle. I wreaked revenge but the next day my tooth was too loose to save and was pulled. Playing Sir Galahad isn't always a walk in the park.

From March 23 to April 18, 1942, I attended and satisfactorily completed the Division Rifle Platoon Tactical School. The school was a tent camp located a few miles east of Camp Elliot in a place appropriately named "Green Valley." The students were all junior NCOs drawn from the entire division. We learned a few things I had not previously encountered or mastered, including basic demolitions. While there I spent a few days in sick bay with something diagnosed as "cat fever." The symptoms were similar to those of influenza. My most vivid memory of the school is of the rattlesnakes. Our efforts to crawl through the grass and cactus to attack a simulated Jap pillbox were constantly disrupted when one of us would come face-to-face with a coiled rattler. The maneuvers had to be stopped until the interloper was dealt with. We would hit the deck and start over only to be forced to stop again and again; the valley was lousy with snakes.

One day in May my platoon was selected to explore the possibility of infiltrating an enemy locale by launching a rubber landing boat from a seaplane. We trucked down to San Diego and boarded a Higgins boat which took us out to a PBY Catalina (a flying boat) anchored in the harbor. The plan was to eject the deflated rubber boat from one of the gun blisters on the side of the aircraft, inflate it and have the squad enter the boat from the blister. Seems simple, but it was a debacle of the first order. We couldn't get the boat out of the plane or the men into the boat.

Scratch one novel idea. I didn't relish the thought of flying behind Jap lines in a "Dumbo" anyway!

By June, A Company had progressed to the point where it could handle its assigned tasks as well as my old company in the Fifth Marines. We were as combat ready as we were going to be. At least that is what we thought at the time. Unfortunately, we had no training in jungle fighting, an omission of consequence as it turned out.

On June 9, 1942, we, that is the First Battalion, Second Marines, embarked on a ship which would be our home for the next two months, the USS *President Jackson.* The *Jackson* was one of three American President Line passenger ships converted to carry troops. She was not an old ship, having been launched at Newport News in 1939. The ship was 491 feet in length with a beam of about 70 feet. She could carry about 1,400 troops. The other two ships, the USS *President Adams* and the USS *President Hayes*, together with the USS *Crescent City* and the cargo ship USS *Alhena*, carried the Second and Third Battalions and the Third Battalion, Tenth Marines, our artillery regiment. The four passenger ships operated as a unit throughout the war and became known to sailors and Marines as "The Unholy Four." Their Navy crews formed a looseknit postwar group which still meets annually for a reunion. In Navy parlance these ships were APs, the designation for troop transports equipped with landing craft to land troops on a hostile shore. The *Jackson* was AP 18.

The landing boats on the ships were the early model Higgins boats, not the drop ramp LCVPs (Landing Craft, Vehicle-Personnel) used later in all theaters.

For the next three weeks we made practice landings on nearby beaches. This was old stuff to me but new and novel to most of the men. They had to be taught to grasp only the vertical cords while descending or climbing the cargo nets slung over the side of the ship to provide access to the landing boats and to make doubly sure that all the equipment they carried was tightly secured. A dislodged entrenching tool or rifle falling 20 or 30 feet onto the men already in the landing boat could injure or even kill. And, a slow learner who grasped the horizontal cords of the cargo net received a painful lesson when the man above him stepped on his hand in descending the net. While leaving or boarding a

The USS *Jackson*, APA 18 (Naval Historical Foundation).

ship via a cargo net never becomes routine, we did it enough to master the essentials.

Between practice landings we were docked in the San Diego Naval Station and were given liberty ashore. While it was not a subject of conversation we all realized this would be our last liberty for a long time, perhaps forever. We had a "screw authority," devil-may-care attitude that produced a lot of work for the Shore Patrol. I ran out of money and sent a telegram to Pearl asking for $20 "for one last go-round." Bless her heart, she complied, and $20 was never better spent. I enjoyed myself so much I returned to the ship at 06:00 one morning, although liberty had expired at midnight. Fortunately, the battalion commander took a very lenient view of this infraction and only sentenced me to restriction aboard ship for the remainder of our stay in the States. On the next day, July 1, we sailed for the South Pacific. In addition to the four transports, the flotilla contained an aircraft carrier, three cruisers and six destroyers.

As transports go, the *Jackson* was slightly above par. Its evaporators had sufficient capacity to afford us the opportunity to take a freshwater shower every third or fourth day, a luxury beyond compare. Clothing had to be hand washed in salt water. Some characters tied a line to their clothing and tossed it over the fantail to permit the churning of the ship's wake to do the washing. I didn't think much of this procedure since the ship's heads emptied into the sea and the extreme agitation in the wake almost destroyed the clothing.

Converting a civilian liner to a Navy transport was a pretty simple job; the passenger staterooms could be left as they were to serve as quarters for the officers. The huge cargo holds were fitted out with steel bunks, three or four tiers high, to house the troops. The heads (toilets) were rather stark, consisting of stainless steel troughs with folding seats interspersed along their lengths. Salt water continuously coursed through and out a pipe into the sea. The wash basins and showers ran salt water except for the much-anticipated freshwater periods.

Life on a transport is awfully monotonous. Unlike the old *Henderson*, this ship had no library, and reading material was at a premium. I don't recall reading anything other than military field manuals. We played endless card games, usually poker for very small stakes. Guys who had no money played for matches — what the hell, it was something to do. I played chess endlessly with anyone I could talk into a game. Whenever the weather permitted I slept topside, on the deck, rolled in a blanket. There was competition for space so you had to stake out a spot right after evening chow. The ships were completely blacked out at night and even smoking on deck could get you brig time. Since there was no place to show a movie below decks we saw none during the trip. Of course things were different in officers' country since they had a large dining room, but I am not certain they had movies.

As for dining rooms, we stood in a cafeteria line for chow and ate standing up at chest-high tables. The food was typical Navy chow but only two meals a day. The menu was long on beans, even at breakfast twice a week, when the meal consisted of Navy beans, a chunk of cornbread and an apple. We didn't gain weight but neither did we suffer. Since we had little else to occupy our minds the meals were the highpoints of the day. Even standing in the chow line was accepted without the usual ill-tempered complaints, for it broke the monotony.

Speaking of monotony, it was shattered one day early in the cruise by a "short arm inspection." This is the Marine Corps term for an examination of each man's most private parts by a flashlight wielding doctor or corpsman to determine if any alien life forms have taken up residence. In this instance what they were looking for were crabs, a species of lice partial to human pubic hair. We had other names for them, such as "crotch pheasants" and "shimmy lizards." I faced this examination with aplomb, for I was certain I was clean. Wrong! The doctor found only one of the creatures but this forced me to undergo the humiliating procedure of a complete pubic shave and painting the entire area with a purple concoction to eliminate any embryonic invaders. Of course I wasn't alone; about half the company was infected. Apparently, a crowded troopship is nirvana for these pesky critters.

Shortly after this incident we had another personal hygiene experience. I, and one or two others who bunked near me, became acutely aware of a foul odor strong enough to make your eyes water. After a day or two of this I conducted an inspection of my squad members and their personal effects. The culprit was my youngest private, John Taylor, a kid who may have been 18 but looked to be about 15. The problem was his feet! They weren't diseased but their odor was indescribable. And, of course, the cache of his dirty socks we uncovered could only be handled with a long stick. We quickly got Taylor into the washroom and gave him a GI bath with a scrub brush. He washed his socks under supervision until they were almost threadbare. For the remainder of the cruise he washed his feet and socks every day and reported to me when the task was completed. Obviously Taylor was a kid newly separated from his mommy who needed parental guidance. I will discuss Taylor again when writing about the fighting on Guadalcanal.

While cruising on a large ship like the *Jackson* was not as exhilarating as riding a bucking destroyer transport, I enjoyed the lazy days of sailing. There is always something to watch: the other ships in the convoy, the porpoises which play endlessly with our bow wave, and the flying fish, which apparently assume our ship is a large predator and leap from its path in long, skittering flights. At night the stars at sea are especially brilliant, and as we approached the Southern Hemisphere, a new constellation appeared, the Southern Cross. It is possible that my contentment with the transit was based, at least in part, upon trepidation as to what awaited me at the end of the cruise. At this stage the Marine Corps had not enlightened us as to our destination or role on arrival. Were we really going to make a combat landing or perhaps merely occupy some island and defend it from Japanese attack? Of course, we speculated endlessly but no one came close to guessing we were going to attack the Japs in the Solomon Islands since none of us had ever heard of them or knew they were occupied by the enemy.

On July 10 we crossed the equator and were ceremoniously inducted into the realm of King Neptune, a suitably clad overweight petty officer who, we were assured, boarded the ship with his retinue of mermaids through the anchor hawse pipe. We "pollywogs," those who had never crossed the equator before, were subjected to all sorts of indignities by the "shellbacks," the veterans of prior crossings. Clad only in skivvies we were forced to run a gauntlet of shellbacks wielding leather belts and a bunch of maniacs armed with various colors of food dye. It was a lot of fun and a welcome diversion.

At about this time an unusual and, to me, noteworthy event occurred. My company commander, Captain Furhop, deemed me worthy of promotion to sergeant. But the battalion had concocted an ad hoc promotion procedure which provided that each candidate for promotion must first pass a quiz to be administered by a senior NCO from a different company who did not know the candidate. The knucklehead who concocted this scheme to take promotion authority away from company officers who knew the man and give it to an enlisted man who did not know him should have been drawn and quartered. What purpose was served by this inanity has never been explained to me but I assume they did not trust the company officers to give and grade a quiz.

Anyway, a date was set and I was told the test would cover the functions of the BAR squad and infantry tactics. I was given books to study, U.S. Army Field Manual 7–5 and a dissertation on the employment of the BAR squad in combat. I studied these for a few days and felt I knew the BAR material very well, but the Army's infantry manual was much too long to master in such a short time. On the big day I donned a clean set of khakis and reported to my interrogator, who was seated on one of the upper decks. When I saw him I thought, "Uh-oh, this may not be easy." I recognized him as one of the sergeants from weapons company of the Fifth Marines who was part of my group dispatched to form Carlson's Raiders. I don't know why, but I had a premonition of disaster, and I was right. One of his first questions involved the Army Field Manual. He asked, "What is a closed corridor?" I got by that and he then asked, "What are the functions of the BAR squad in combat?" Of course I was ready for that and laid out everything I had learned from the booklet I had studied. It was not enough, when I concluded he told me I had flunked, that the only words I had to say in response to the question were "Base of fire."

And so, I did not become a sergeant. I have the feeling to this day that my questioner looked at me as too young and unworthy of becoming a sergeant. After all, he probably had ten or more years in the prewar Marine Corps before he made sergeant. I have to look on the incident as kismet, it wasn't meant to be. Moreover, I survived the Guadalcanal fight. As a sergeant I might have been in the wrong place at the wrong time.

About a week later we made our first landfall, the island of Tongatabu, as pretty a place as can be imagined, palm trees, sandy beaches and a reef-protected harbor. At the time it was a British protectorate ruled by a 400-pound black queen who had recently attended the coronation of Edward VIII in London. We were given shore leave and I spent it just walking around enjoying the feeling of solid ground under foot. In fact, there was very little to do ashore other than walking, for the little town had no bars or restaurants and I had not a red cent to buy a coconut or bunch of bananas. During my walk I was approached by two native women who emerged from the brush carrying long machetes. My uneasiness was dispelled when one of them, in a beautiful British accent, said, "Good morning, sir." The incongruity of upper class English coming from these primitive looking natives has stuck in my memory all these years.

A day or two after sailing from Tongatabu our convoy merged with a much larger group of ships, carriers, cruisers, battleships and more transports and cargo vessels. Wherever we were going and whatever we were going to do it was plain we were part of a large operation. On July 28 we made a practice assault landing on the island of Koro in the Fiji Group. The landing was pretty much a disaster, for coral prevented the boats from reaching the tiny beaches and units came ashore piecemeal in knee-deep water and in anything but combat formation. Had any Japs been present to witness the operation they would have died laughing. The island was uninhabited but signs of recent occupation, chickens, pigs and fruit trees, were present. We threshed around in the jungle for awhile and in late afternoon rendezvoused near the shore for an overnight bivouac. What still sticks in my mind about that night was the brilliance of the light from a full moon. It was unbelievably bright, in fact so bright that Jim Sorensen and I passed the time playing pinochle. We went back aboard ship the next day and sailed away in an intense rainsquall, which cut visibility to a matter of yards. The ship's carpenters got busy reinforcing the plywood bottoms of our Higgins boats that had been damaged and even pierced by contact with the coral reefs.*

At long last we were told where we were going; the Solomon Islands was the target and, specifically, the islands of Guadalcanal, Tulagi and Florida. The reason for attacking these targets, we were told, was to prevent completion of an airfield the Japs were building on Guadalcanal. Such an airfield in enemy hands would threaten the sea lanes to Australia and New Zealand. We were also told that this was the first offensive by the United States in World War II. For this campaign we, that is the Second Regiment, would be attached to the First Division. One of that division's regiments, the Seventh, was occupied defending American Samoa. Tough duty! Under the operation plan the First and Fifth Marine Regiments, less the Fifth's Second Battalion, would land on Guadalcanal; the remainder of the Second Regiment, together with the Fifth's Second Battalion, First Raiders and the Parachute Battalion, would attack and subdue the enemy on Tulagi and Florida and two little islands nestled between them, Gavutu and Tanambogo. The honor of being the first unit to attack the enemy in World War II would fall to my First

---

*For a detailed description of the Koro practice landing see William H. Bartsch, "Operation Dovetail: Bungled Guadalcanal Rehearsal," *Journal of Military History*, April 2002.

Battalion Second, for we would hit Florida Island before any of the other outfits made their landings. Company A, my company, would land on the Halavo Peninsula of Florida and attack the shore installations of a seaplane base.

At the time of our attack the Solomon Islands were largely unpopulated and mostly undeveloped. There are several hundred islands, lying about 800 miles east of New Guinea. They are mountainous and, for the most part, heavily wooded. The chain runs northwest to southeast in a double line separated by a navigable channel which the American forces later dubbed "The Slot." Our airmen and sailors came to know it well. Guadalcanal is near the bottom of the southwest line of islands. It is not the largest of the group. That distinction belongs to Bougainville, located about 300 miles to the northwest. Bougainville was the next invasion target after Guadalcanal.

The Solomon Islands' natives are Melanesians who, we were informed, at that time had only recently been persuaded to give up head-hunting. Guadalcanal and the neighboring islands of the southern Solomons were British Protectorates. The civil affairs on each island were administered by a British district officer who reported to a resident commissioner residing on Tulagi. As related later in this work, some of the district officers remained behind when we invaded and performed outstanding service as "Coast Watchers," manning radios and reporting on Japanese naval movements in the entire island chain.

Guadalcanal itself is about 75 miles long and about 30 miles wide. For the most part it is mountainous and heavily wooded. The mountains reach 8,000 feet in elevation. On the tops of the ridges which ran down to the sea on the north side, the jungle gave way to high grass. These ridges became very familiar to me as my sojourn on the island developed. The land on much of the north coast is flat and arable. About in the center of the coast the flat area extends southward towards the mountains for about a mile. This was the site of the airfield the Japs were building, and which we finished. The airfield site was separated from the beach by a very large coconut plantation owned by Lever Brothers. This was a beautiful sight — in fact, Guadalcanal is a very beautiful island. The heat and humidity prevents it from becoming a tourist resort.

Twenty miles north of Guadalcanal lies a small cluster of islands.

4. The Second Marines

The largest, Florida, dominates its smaller neighbors, Tulagi, Gavutu and Tanambogo. Florida is undeveloped, covered with dense jungle. The other three were quite civilized, with commercial and government buildings and docks. The Tulagi harbor is excellent, sheltered as it is by the bulk of Florida. The 20-mile stretch of water which separates these islands from Guadalcanal became known as "Iron Bottom Bay" for the large number of our and Japanese ships sunk there during the war.

August 5 and 6 were spent in last-minute preparations. We were ordered to take no personal items, such as photos, address books, letters from home and girlfriends, ashore. We left all that stuff, together with all uniforms and shoes, in our locked seabags, to be reclaimed after the battle. Unfortunately they were never seen again. Rumor had it they were put on a ship that was subsequently sunk, but I have my doubts since I suffered the same loss after each of my three campaigns. Apparently the Navy and Marine Corps assigned very little value to the personal effects of combat Marines. According to the plan we would spend only two days ashore during this phase and would then reboard the ship and strike other islands, the Santa Cruz group located about 300 miles southeast of the Solomons. Accordingly, we were issued rations for only two days, six cans of "C rations." We left our shelter halves behind and carried only ponchos for protection from the elements, a command decision soon much regretted. Most men carried an entrenching tool, either a small shovel or pick. I selected a pick. I reasoned, correctly as it turned out, the shovel would be next to useless in hard compacted soil. You could throw the dirt out of your "pick dug" hole with your hands or helmet. A few, probably one out of four, carried machetes, which proved to be very useful in the jungle and in constructing shelters and fortifications. Infantrymen carried 100 rounds of 30-caliber ammunition for their Springfields in their cartridge belts and an extra 100 rounds in a bandoleer. The BAR men and their assistants carried about 20 clips between them. Each BAR clip contains 20 rounds. Rounding out everyone's armament were two fragmentation grenades and, for riflemen, a bayonet. Our rifles, BARs and heavy water-cooled machine guns, were of World War I vintage. However, they worked well and could stand a lot of abuse. The Japs' rifles were of similar vintage, but their machine guns, especially the light Nambu, were modern and probably superior to our light machine guns. The Japs also had one unique weapon, a spring-operated grenade thrower that could launch a grenade a good deal farther than hand-throwing distance. The curved base plate of this tube-shaped weapon gave rise to the erroneous speculation it was designed to be fired from the knee of a crouching man. In actual fact the weapon was placed on the ground for firing. Our erroneous speculation gave rise to calling the weapon a "knee mortar," an appellation we continued to use long after we learned the truth about it. The effectiveness of Jap grenades was limited by the high explosive charge, which produced very fine fragments, too fine to cause disabling wounds.

During this preparation time many of the riflemen filed their bayonets to razor edge keenness. I wouldn't let my squad do that. I reasoned, correctly as it turned out, that filing away the bluing to get an edge would make it impossible to keep the weapon from rusting. Besides, the thing was sufficiently sharp as issued. It is a penetrating tool, not a slicer. On "D-Day" eve we were treated to an inspirational message over the ship's public address system from the admiral in overall command of the operation. The vignettes I vaguely remember from the message are: "Tomorrow is the day you have all been anxiously waiting for.... You have the finest weapons in the world," and "This is the first offensive of the war!" Only the third of the three statements was completely accurate.

I slept reasonably well that night and have no recollection that I was highly concerned about going in harm's way on the morrow. Mine was more a feeling of resignation — whatever will be, will be. Sure, I had a knot in my stomach but it was no greater or more intense than the knot associated with stage fright. For me the fear of personal bodily harm was far outweighed by the fear of disgracing oneself, i.e. "showing the white feather." The feeling that you must evince resoluteness is enhanced by command, even command of a squad, for the leader knows all his subordinates will look to him and follow his lead whenever an unfamiliar or threatening event occurs. Thus, in a perverse sort of way, it is easier for an NCO to conquer fear because more is expected of him. A private's reputation among his peers can survive an instance of panic, but such a showing by an NCO or officer could never be lived down.

5

Tulagi and
Guadalcanal

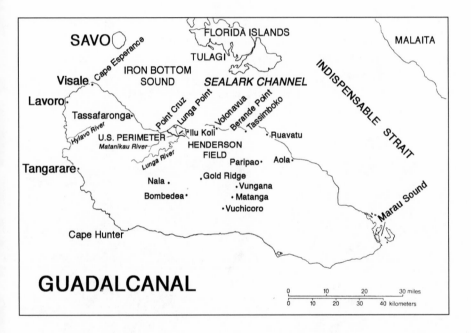

I went to breakfast on "D-Day" morning expecting a better than usual pre-combat meal but, alas, it was not to be. August 7 was a Friday and the breakfast consisted of the standard Navy breakfast for Friday: Navy beans, a square of cornbread and an apple. They didn't coddle Marines just because they were going into combat.

At dawn the target islands became visible. We were stationary a mile or two off the south coast of Tulagi. The light cruiser USS *San Juan* was shelling the beach where the Raider Battalion and the Fifth Marine's Second Battalion were scheduled to land. The *San Juan*–type cruisers were the most beautiful fighting ships of the Navy. Their five-inch guns were chiefly useful as antiaircraft weapons. However, she had a lot of them, with three dual turrets forward and two dual turrets aft the superstructure.

Around 06:30 we clambered down the cargo nets and embarked in the landing boats for the trip to our target beach. In a long line of boats we skirted the shore of Tulagi, well out from shore but under the trajectory of the *San Juan's* guns. The cracking thunder forced the realization that this was the real thing, there's a war going on and we are in it. We motored around the end of Tulagi and past the tiny island of Gavutu. A heavy gun emplacement was clearly visible on the peak of the hill that made up most of Gavutu, but not for long. As we passed the island, a dive bomber eliminated the emplacement with a huge bomb. We cheered and were heartened by this show of accuracy and devastating power.

The light cruiser USS *San Juan* (Naval Historical Foundation).

5. Tulagi and Guadalcanal

Maybe we were invincible, as our leaders had been telling us. Our landing was sort of an anticlimax. We stormed ashore unopposed, not onto a beach but into a mangrove thicket. Our target, the seaplane base, was several miles away and we moved toward it as quickly as the jungle permitted. When we got there the base turned out to be merely a collection of grass shacks the Japs had confiscated from the natives. They had skedaddled just in time, leaving warm prepared food on the tables. We set up a perimeter defense around the village and prepared for the night attack that was sure to come. Shortly after dark one of our machine guns fired a burst and all hell broke loose. Our entire line opened fire, filling the night with a cacophony of noise and mowing down every piece of vegetation within 50 yards. Man, I thought, this is combat; we're showing those dirty rascals! Wrong! What we were showing was the tendency of green troops to waste ammunition firing at nothing. Eventually cooler heads realized that there was nothing out there and put an end to the panic firing. It wasn't a total loss, we realized how stupid we were and never repeated such nonsense. It's a rite of passage almost every green outfit experiences.

The next morning, chastened and red-faced, we reboarded the landing boats and, after a short trip, disembarked on Tulagi at the same spot the Raiders and Fifth Marines had landed on "D-Day." While we could hear firing in the distance it was quiet in our immediate area. In fact there was nothing to indicate that any fighting had taken place in the vicinity. We learned the Japs had not defended this area but had concentrated their defense on the north side of the island, where all the warehouses, residences and government buildings were located. A high, wooded ridge runs the length of Tulagi and, after some delay, we started to climb the ridge and join the action on the north side. As we started up the hill we came under fire from one or two riflemen concealed in the jungle near the crest of the ridge. I took shelter beneath an overhanging rock face and said to myself, "So this is what being under fire feels like." Can't say I liked it very much. After a short wait we got word the troops on the other side didn't need our help and we settled down to wait for orders. We were located in the middle of a native graveyard. Interestingly, each grave was outlined by a 10-to-12-inch high cement wall. The graves made perfect above-ground foxholes, which we quickly appropriated.

In late afternoon Captain Fuhrhop called me to the company command post (CP) and told me I was detailed as bodyguard for the assistant division commander, Brigadier General William B. Rupertus, who had just landed and wanted to go over the ridge to oversee the fighting on the other side. First, he said, they had to issue me an automatic weapon, a Reising gun. Why a Reising gun, I wondered. Its unreliability was well known, but I recognized it was the only light automatic weapon available. At any rate my tenure as a bodyguard for the general was to be short-lived. Apparently his staff had not forewarned him that he was getting a protector, for he blew up when I reported, screaming he didn't want "any goddamned bodyguard" and, turning to me, roared, "Stay the hell out of my sight!" I hung around his CP for a while until they dismissed me when he decided not to attempt the trip to the north side.

I got back to the company about dusk, rolled up in my poncho and settled down in my "grave" for the night. Unfortunately, it started to rain and the walls around my "grave" proved very effective in preventing any runoff and I soon found myself marinating in a cold puddle. Not to worry, we were rousted out shortly after midnight to unload supplies, rations and ammunition from landing boats grounded by shallow water about 30 yards offshore. We formed a line from the shore to the boats and passed the boxes from man to man. It was cold and miserable work but child's play compared to what was going on at sea just a few miles away. Our Navy was suffering the most humiliating defeat of its history. We could clearly hear the thunder of guns and see the sky light up from explosions but knew only what the crews of the landing boats told us, that there was a naval battle going on. We were not told the results of the battle and I didn't learn until after the war that the Japs had sunk four of our cruisers and killed more than 1,000 sailors and Marines of their crews. The Japs suffered only a handful of casualties and minor damage to their ships. This was the first of several losing battles for our Navy in the Solomons. These losses had their effect ashore in reduced supplies for the Marines. The transports and cargo ships had left the area with most of our food and other supplies still onboard. For more than a month, we almost starved.

Later that night a single Jap wandered into our bivouac. Someone in the battalion CP disposed of him with a single 45-caliber round right between the eyes. In the morning we all gawked at the body. It was the first enemy we had seen. And he was the last we would see for many weeks, for the battalion had received orders to garrison and defend Tulagi from any sort of counterattack either from the sea or from nearby Florida Island. We in A Company were assigned a heavily wooded area near the west end of the island, where only a narrow waterway separated Tulagi from Florida. The shoreline in our area was covered by mangroves, which extended about 30 yards out from shore. The land behind the shore rose rather steeply and we prepared our defensive positions on this slope. One did not have to be a military genius to immediately conclude that a landing in force through the mangroves was impracticable and the only thing we had to watch out for was the possibility that some of the Japs isolated on Florida might try to infiltrate our position.

After we dug in I got permission to go to the area on the north side, where all the action took place, to locate a dentist. A large filling had dropped out of a molar and I didn't relish the thought of a long campaign with a toothache. Also, I wanted to visit the Raider Battalion to see if any old friends had been killed or hurt in the heavy action they experienced. My trip was a complete success; a corpsman packed my cavity with some sort of gunk and I located the Raiders and found my old buddy, Don Wolf. He was unwounded but seemed greatly subdued and not the talkative Don I remembered. I doubt that I asked, and he did not volunteer any comments on the previous days' action. My guess is he was in the throes of post-combat shock, a short duration syndrome when your mind is so full of the horrors you experienced you want to be left alone with your thoughts. I did learn from him that one of my Raider Battalion acquaintances, Bill Culp, the unseen corporal at Guantanamo who shamed me for my foul language, was being transferred to my battalion as assistant to our chaplain, Navy Lieutenant W. Wyeth Willard. According to the story, Culp wanted to hold a church service after the battle but was denied permission by Lt. Col. Edson, the Raider CO. There ensued some sort of a dustup and Culp was banished to the Second Marines. Culp did yeoman's service to the chaplain during the Solomons campaign but was commissioned and assigned as a platoon leader when we got to New Zealand. Unfortunately, like so many others, he died on Tarawa.

Life on our defensive line was abysmally boring, terribly uncomfortable and unhealthy. But the single overriding emotion during the weeks we existed in that jungle retreat was *hunger*! Not nearly enough food had been gotten ashore before our Navy was run out of the area and what got ashore was severely rationed. We were allotted one C Ration meal per day and sometimes not even that. To supplement that starvation diet we sent scavenging patrols to the other side of the island, where Japanese-stocked warehouses had been demolished on "D-Day." The ruins contained broken sacks of barley, which we pounced on and carried back to our positions. When you are seriously hungry most anything edible tastes good and I remember fondly the barley mush I made. Typically the conversation among young Marines deals with sexual exploits, alcoholic binges or physical feats. Not on Tulagi; almost all we talked about was food. We regaled each other with detailed descriptions of favorite meals as prepared by our mothers and/or grandmothers. Restaurant meals were rarely discussed because few of us had frequented quality restaurants. We really didn't know what combat was like and occasionally speculated about it and how we would perform. One of my fellow corporals in the third platoon, Jim Sorensen, startled us by stating he wanted to get a Purple Heart. He knew you only get that medal by being wounded but insisted he wanted one because his father had gotten one in the first World War.*

We tried to make our jungle home as comfortable as possible, which wasn't easy, for the only building materials at hand were our ponchos and scrounged communication wire. But some effort was necessary, for sleeping on the wet jungle turf week after week was unthinkable and unbearable. I improvised a sort of hammock by weaving six-foot, pencil-thin reeds with wire. None of the vegetation in the vicinity had large leaves suitable for roofing, so I just had to roll up in my poncho when it rained. For almost my entire stay in the Solomons the poncho was my only shelter. We finally were issued shelter halves, pup tents, on Guadalcanal, about a month before we sailed to New Zealand.

Ostensibly for military purposes, but most likely just to give us some-

---

*Jim Sorensen got his wish for, as I report below, he was badly wounded on November 10.

thing to do, Captain Fuhrhop ordered construction of a fence along our entire front. But this was not an ordinary fence, no, siree. This was a cheval-de-frise of sharpened stakes (six-foot saplings) rammed into the ground at a 45-degree angle, with the sharpened ends pointing outward toward the mangroves. Scouring the island for suitable saplings, cutting, sharpening and placing them occupied us for a couple of weeks. I questioned the efficacy of the construction but reasoned it might serve to slow down a charging enemy, if one could envision any humans capable of charging from a mangrove thicket. What the heck, we weren't doing anything anyway to occupy our time. I assume keeping the men occupied played heavily on Captain Fuhrhop's mind for he soon ordered the construction of a second line of defense, a stockade! This highly doubtful project, erected just inside our cheval-de-frise, was constructed of four-to-six-inch logs, about eight feet long and sharpened on one end. They were sunk into the swamp, sharpened ends up, and lashed together with wire or vines to form a solid wall. Sure, this monstrosity would have delayed any attackers, but to my mind it would also have helped any intruders, for we couldn't see through the stockade. An entire company of Japs could sneak up behind that wall without being seen. Not to worry, our leaders opined, we would set up listening or observation posts in the mangroves from dusk to dawn each night. Manning this lookout was the most uncomfortable, miserable duty ever foisted on our men. They had to wade to the outer fringe of the mangroves, try to climb out of the water and perch like a bird for the duration of their watch. Of course, nothing was ever seen, for the few Japs who had fled to Florida were in no condition to attack or even swim the 100-yard channel between the islands.

These make-work schemes and scavenging for food and sitting around talking about food occupied us for more than two months. In the meantime, the First Division guys were repulsing Japanese attacks over on Guadalcanal, 20 miles away, but they might have been in Africa for all we knew. We got no news of the fighting, not even scuttlebutt. Guys at the other end of Tulagi got a little excitement, for Jap destroyers and submarines would shell them or shell and sink the small ships in or near Tulagi harbor. These little ships, the Navy called them YPs, constituted the only onsite Naval presence. YPs were about the size of West Coast tuna fishing boats. They did yeoman service ferrying people and supplies between Tulagi and Guadalcanal. It was hazardous service for their crews, for the Japanese Navy owned the seas around the islands during these early months. They and the Marine pilots flying out of Henderson Field on Guadalcanal were our only protectors.

While I didn't know it at the time, the night of September 5 saw the tragic end of my old friend the USS *Little* and of the USS *Gregory*, another of the APDs that carried us around the Atlantic before the war. The ships had transported First Raider Battalion Marines to Savo Island in the early morning hours. After landing, the Marines they encountered a Japanese cruiser and three destroyers, which were about to bombard Guadalcanal. A PBY searching for the enemy mistakenly illuminated our ships with flares and the Japs immediately opened fire. *Gregory* sank almost immediately, at about 01:30, and *Little* went under about two hours later. While both ships were dead in the water, the Jap destroyers steamed between them firing at pointblank range. Twenty-two of *Little*'s crew and 11 from *Gregory* died that night. About 70 men were wounded on the two ships. This information is from a study called *A Family Saga, Flush Deck Destroyers 1917–1955* by John L. Dicky and Richard B. Frank, *Guadalcanal*, especially pages 211–212.

One day in late September, Paul Boyd, a six-foot, three-inch string bean from the second platoon, told me we were going to have a "smoker" with all kinds of games and contests. He told me — didn't ask, told me — that I was scheduled for a three-round fight with his brother Bob. I didn't know Bob from Adam but tried to weasel out by complaining, "Isn't he a lot bigger than me?" Paul said we were the same size but that wasn't quite accurate, Bob had me by a couple of inches. At any rate somebody had scared up boxing gloves and the bout took place. I survived until midway through the second round when a punch I never saw got me square on the button and projected me backward through the air in a sitting position. I wasn't completely out but couldn't stand without help, and the fight was over. Only later did I learn Bob had been a professional fighter in his hometown of Indianapolis and that tough guys from all around the city would try to make a reputation by calling out Bob from the bistro where he tended bar. They always left the site — usually were helped from the site — sadder and much wiser. The guy was good!

5. Tulagi and Guadalcanal

My encounter with Bob on Tulagi was the start of a close friendship which continued until Bob's death in 1984.

About this time I came down with my first malaria attack. I would lie on my makeshift bunk drenched with sweat and shiver with chills until my teeth rattled. The chills were interspersed with fever, which was accompanied by headaches and, during sleep, bad dreams. We did not know what it was and I waited it out. It went away by itself in a few days. In time we all had it. Malaria was a minor and temporary inconvenience compared with the chronic dysentery we lived with. This condition affected everyone but, with a few exceptions, did not result in hospitalization. My buddy Bruce Coote and my platoon sergeant, Julius Novak, were especially hard hit and were absent from the company much of the time. It was so bad and so prevalent that a solid bowel movement was a cause for rejoicing.

In October rumors began that we would soon be shipped to Guadalcanal to take part in the heavy fighting still going on. The First Division Marines and our Third Battalion, Second Marines, had formed a perimeter defense around the airfield, now called Henderson Field, and were fully engaged repelling repeated enemy attacks. Soon the rumors became fact and we began preparations for action on the "Canal." But we were not going to relieve one of the battalions on the front lines. Rather, our assignment was to attack and reduce a Jap unit of uncertain size at Aola, a native village located about 30 miles east of the Henderson Field perimeter. Shortly after dusk on October 10, we departed Tulagi packed into two YP boats and eight Higgins boats. Four Higgins boats were towed behind each YP, but instead of securing each boat to the YP by a separate towline, the boats were tied one to the other in a column. Thus the lead boat, the only one tied directly to the YP, had to bear the strain of the three loaded boats tied to its stern. This unseamanlike procedure caused heartbreaking tragedy.

My platoon was embarked on the YP itself; a placement I first felt was fortunate but soon regretted. The problem was we were not alone on the bay that night. After an hour or two of chugging along at a speed of no more than four or five knots the sky to our rear lit up with flashes of light and the booming of heavy guns reached our ears. We didn't learn what was going on but sharing that confined waterway with enemy warships was discomforting. In fact, it scared the hell out of me. My discomfort was not helped by the highly visible sparks that spewed from my YP's stack. To escape this danger the YPs picked up speed, with disastrous results. The lead boat being pulled by the other YP couldn't take the strain and its entire bow was pulled off, dumping its occupants, the first platoon of B Company, into the sea. Fourteen men, including a well-liked platoon leader, 2nd Lt. Floyd Parks, drowned.

At dawn we disembarked at Aola and were greeted by a white male civilian and four or five armed natives. This was Martin Clemens, an Australian "coast watcher" who had stayed on Guadalcanal during the Jap occupation. He was one of several "Aussie" coast watchers deployed on islands throughout the Solomons to observe enemy activity and radio results to their headquarters in Australia. Their existence depended on the cooperation of the natives, with whom they lived. Clemens' helpers were members of a "constabulary" formed by the British in prewar years

Captain Martin Clemens and his constabulary. Corporal Daniel Pule, my companion on the patrol from Aola, stands at left.

to keep order in the colony. Their assistance throughout the campaign was of great value to the Marines. To me, Clemens was a romantic and heroic figure. His ability to live in the jungle of an enemy occupied island and spy upon the occupiers was heroism of the highest order.

The exploits of Clemens and his native crew are described in his excellent book, *Alone on Guadalcanal: A Coastwatcher's Story*. Naval Insitute Press, 1998.

After the confab with Clemens we were divided into two groups. C Company would attack a nearby small Jap camp while A and B Companies would hit a larger position some distance away to the west. Led by one of Clemens' Melanesian scouts, we moved off into the jungle in a southerly direction. The plan was to circle the target by making a loop through the jungle, returning to the beach west of the Jap position and attack moving from west to east with our left flank on the beach. The trek through the jungle was exhausting and harrowing. The trail led through a wooded swamp, with the trees emerging from murky water of undetermined depth. The trail consisted of floating or grounded logs laid end to end with waist-high stakes spaced every ten feet or so on either side to serve as a rudimentary railing. Needless to say, none of us made it through the mile or more to solid ground without slipping into the muck at least once. My concern during the passage was that we were absolutely helpless to resist an attack.

In time we emerged to solid land and commenced climbing hills and fording streams. I was impressed by the clarity and coolness of the swiftly running mountain streams. I had expected turgid rivers choked with vegetation. We were able to drink from these streams and fill our canteens. That night we bivouacked in a native village composed of large, obviously communal huts with floors raised off the jungle floor. They were constructed of woven reeds and roofed with palm fronds. We were not permitted to even see the women and children of the village. During our stay they were secreted in the huts, where they could be heard but not seen. I hope it was just a native custom and not because they feared their women needed protection from sex-starved Marines. Our group was far too large to shelter in the structures even if they had been vacant. We merely rolled up in our ponchos and slept on the hard packed ground between the huts.

At dawn we moved down out of the hills to the coast and formed a skirmish line facing east. We were probably five or six miles from our landing place at Aola. We did our best to maintain a line abreast but the impossibility of that procedure soon became apparent. A wide sandy trail or path, called "Government Trail," ran here and along the entire north shore of Guadalcanal. The parts of our line on or near the trail had easy passage but the guys in the jungle and brush on either side could not keep up. In short order we abandoned the skirmish line formation and moved east on the trail in column expecting to hit a large concentration of Japs at any minute. But all was peaceful until we had almost completed the circle back to Aola. Then, someone in the point spied the enemy, not en masse, as expected, but only a single soldier standing on the beach looking out to sea. Sergeant Wilbur Burgess killed him with a single offhand shot. The body was quickly stripped of everything of value for use, such as his beautiful wristwatch and binoculars, or for souvenirs, such as insignia and his pistol. What this fellow was doing all alone at this spot soon became apparent. Within minutes we discovered a large pedestal-mounted cannon which had been placed, under camouflage, on the Government Trail. Nearby we found a heavy machine gun and a large stack of ammunition for both weapons. Our lone victim apparently was the caretaker of the weapons. We destroyed the machine gun by field stripping it and scattering the parts far and wide. The ammunition was dumped into the ocean. Rendering the cannon unserviceable was a tougher problem. We solved it by dropping an incendiary grenade down the muzzle. This seemed to work, for thereafter we were unable to open the breech.

Our eastward trek had barely been resumed when Platoon Sergeant Ernest Denley began firing his Thompson submachine gun (Tommy gun) at the brush on the right of the trail. He had heard movement in the brush but, unfortunately, what he heard were Marines, my platoon leader Lt. Russell Johnson and his runner, Pvt. Joseph Sparks. Johnson was badly wounded but Little Joe Sparks, as we called him, achieved the dubious honor of being the first man of A Company to die for his country.

Within a short time we met up with the rest of the battalion. C Company had encountered and eliminated an encampment of about 30

Japs with only one casualty, its company commander, Captain Richard Stafford, shot dead by a sniper. We rested awhile and waited, without enthusiasm, for the boats to return us to the boredom of our jungle retreat on Tulagi. But an opportunity to remain on the Canal was offered to those who would volunteer to participate in a combat-reconnaissance patrol along the coast from Aola to the defensive perimeter around Henderson Field, a distance of about 30 miles. Although I had been in the Corps long enough to have learned one of the cardinal rules of service — "Never volunteer for anything!" — I opted to give it a try. Anything, I reasoned, would be better than crawling back into that stultifying, mindless inertia watching the mangroves grow.

None of the men in my squad volunteered so I went along as just another trooper. But it was decided that the firepower of Denly's Tommy gun might be needed and that Corporal Rogal would man it. This weapon was not basic armament for Marine infantry and I had never received any instruction on it. However, I was intrigued and welcomed the opportunity to see what it could do. I soon regretted my acceptance of the honor bestowed on me for the weapon was awkward to carry; it would not hang by its sling vertically from your shoulder like the 03 and BAR would. Its balance was such that unless you held it firmly in place it would swing into a horizontal position and bang your ribs. I had to give up slinging it from my shoulder and carried it in my hands at port arms or one-handed at my side. I quickly replaced the 50-round drum for one of the half dozen 20-round clips to facilitate carrying the thing. Another disadvantage was soon made apparent; the carrier of this awesome weapon was permanently assigned to the point of the patrol, where quick reaction rapid fire might be needed.

About 90 of us under command of a 2nd lieutenant from battalion Headquarters Company, Thomas M Leineweber, set out westward on the Government Trail. I was accompanied in the point by two of the native constabulary, a corporal named Daniel Pule and a private whose name I never learned. They spoke only pidgin but I soon mastered enough of the language to feel comfortable with my companions. Moreover, they bolstered the C rations I carried with the fruits that constituted their only food. They taught me to scrape the soft insides of green coconuts with a chip sliced from the outer shell and I learned to enjoy green bananas roasted in a brush fire. The tried to teach me to climb coconut trees with a loincloth looped around my feet but I lacked the musculature to manage it, although I weighed no more than 140 pounds at the time. I allowed the natives to go ahead by a few yards for I believed they had an almost animal awareness of their surroundings and would be far better at smelling out an ambush than I. Besides, we moved much faster with them on point. This was their country and they led with confidence. I suspect they could smell Japs, an ability some of us picked up later in our tenure on the island. At any rate, I enjoyed soldiering with the natives and greatly appreciated their services.

The patrol was almost uneventful insofar as contact with Jap soldiers was concerned. In fact we saw none until the third and last day, when we neared the Henderson Field perimeter defense line. During the three-day patrol we destroyed tons of Jap supplies, including landing boats and ammunition. Items which could be destroyed by immersion, we carried into the ocean. Most of the boats, strange looking collapsible things, we piled up and burned. At one point in our trek we came upon the remains of a Christian mission. There was evidence of hasty evacuation and looting. Photographs of clerically clad women (nuns) and men were scattered on the ground. We heard the nuns had been raped and killed by the Japs but I subsequently learned most had escaped to the south side of the island. The mission's buildings were in good shape. The ocean inlet at the mission was home to two large, six-to-eight-feet, crocodiles. I wondered if they had been there when the missionaries were in residence.

On the third day of our venture, October 13, we were fording a sizable stream when three Japs were spotted on the opposite bank. With several others, I moved to the beach on the right in an attempt to flank the enemy soldiers. However, I was distracted from that endeavor by an airplane, one of our Grumman F4Fs, splashing into the sea about a quarter mile offshore. It was a controlled dead stick ditching but the plane almost instantly upended and sank. The pilot escaped, for we could see his head bobbing in the choppy waves. Without pausing to think, I whipped out of my shoes and clothes and waded into the surf. Sergeant Wilbur Burgess, who was east of me by about 50 yards, also entered the light surf but stopped and yelled something about a riptide. There may have been some unusual current for him, for he was located right in the middle of the river's flow into the sea. I couldn't detect anything unusual where I was and began the long swim to the pilot. When I reached his vicinity I could see he was bleeding from a head cut. He was barely afloat and seemed dazed. Remembering that drowning victims not infrequently panic and pull would-be rescuers under, I warned him, "I'm coming up behind you. Don't turn around and try to grab me!" He said, "Okay." I repeated the warning when I got to him and he responded, "I won't grab you." With that formality out of the way I seized his collar and started towing him to shore. At one point in our journey he became discouraged and said, "Save yourself and let me go." I assured him we were making progress, although, I have to admit, I was getting awfully tired. Fortunately, I didn't have to tow him the last hundred yards or so, for a group of guys, including the Boyd brothers and Burgess, had floated a driftwood log and paddled out to relieve me of my burden.

I was awarded the Navy and Marine Corps Medal for this afternoon swim. This is a low-level medal awarded for acts not involving combat. I wasn't the only recipient of this medal for going for a swim in the Solomons. President John F. Kennedy received one for swimming to rescue three of his crew on August 1, 1943, after his PT 109 was rammed and sunk by a Jap destroyer. Other than Purple Hearts, it is the only personal medal I got for wartime service. I have always been apathetic about it, for Marines get paid to kill people, not to save them. And I fail to see anything heroic in a strong swimmer going to the rescue of a floundering fellow human.

If I learned the name of the rescued pilot at the time I have long forgotten it. In 1973 a friend, Robert Sherrod, author of the book *History of Marine Corps Aviation in World War II,*[*] tried to find the name of the pilot without success. But just recently the historian and author William H. Bartsch found the name which we believe is the name of the rescued pilot. He was Marine Lieutenant Joseph L. Narr, an ace credited with downing eight Jap planes. Sherrod's book mentions him only once (p. 108), crediting him with shooting down two zeros and a bomber on October 25, 1942, 12 days after his rescue. Unfortunately he

*Washington: Combat Forces Press, 1952.

THE SECRETARY OF THE NAVY

WASHINGTON

The President of the United States takes pleasure in presenting the NAVY AND MARINE CORPS MEDAL to

CORPORAL WILLIAM W. ROGAL, U.S.M.C.,

for service as set forth in the following

CITATION:

"For heroic conduct while serving with the First Battalion, Second Marines, Reinforced, during a patrol on Guadalcanal, Solomon Islands, on October 13, 1942. As part of the point of a large patrol, proceeding from Aola to the airport, Corporal Rogal, immediately after fording a deep stream and attacking a small group of Japanese, saw an American plane crash into the sea near Koli Point. Despite his exhausted condition and the imminent danger of enemy attack, he unhesitatingly started swimming in the direction of the wrecked plane and, by his cool and daring courage, contributed in a large part to the saving of the pilot's life. His conduct was in keeping with the highest traditions of the United States Naval Service."

For the President,

Secretary of the Navy.

My Navy and Marine Corps Medal citation.

did not survive the war. He was shot down and killed on November 11, 1942.*

When we got the pilot ashore we radioed for a boat to return him to the airfield. He was still in shock but we did learn from him that he had been in a dogfight and believed a Jap bullet had gotten his oil line. A Higgins boat arrived in a short time. Possibly because he believed I was exhausted from the swim, Lt. Leinweber directed me to accompany the pilot to the perimeter and report to the Island Commander, General Vandegrift, on the location of the patrol and what it had accomplished. During the ride I pumped the coxswain for the latest scuttlebutt on conditions and the overall situation on the Canal. He told me things were not looking up. The Japs had landed troops and supplies west of the perimeter, had stepped up the frequency and severity of air raids and had commenced shelling the perimeter with long-range artillery. A jeep met us at Lunga Point and took the pilot to a tent hospital and dropped me at the First Division's CP, General Vandegrift's HQ. I told a hanger-on I had been ordered to report the results and status of the patrol to the general. In short order I was taken to the general, who listened intently as I told him we had encountered no significant opposition on the patrol, but had destroyed a lot of Jap equipment. I had the impression he had other things on his mind for he asked no questions. He dismissed me by telling one of his staff to see that I got chow and a place to bunk. I don't remember what I ate but I met a couple of guys at the mess tent who invited me to share their dugout for the night. They also filled me in on the latest scuttlebutt, including that the Japs had landed and begun using artillery with sufficient range to reach the airstrip. These 105-millimeter rifles, which were soon dubbed "Pistol Pete," outdistanced any guns the Marines then had and were immune to our counter-battery fire. Japanese artillery played hob with A Company about three weeks later, as I will subsequently relate.

A gigantic coconut plantation took up much of the land between Henderson Field and the sea. The tall palm trees were planted in orderly rows and, for the most part, evidenced little damage from the earlier

*John Lundstram, *The First Team and the Guadalcanal Campaign: Naval Fighter Combat from August to November 1942* (Annapolis: Naval Institute Press, 1994), 299, 472.

fighting and bombing. The dugout maintained by the two Marines who invited me to spend the night was located under the palms, about 50 yards from the beach. It was not a fighting hole, just a bomb and naval gun fire shelter. It was about five feet deep, six feet long and about four feet wide. A rather flimsy sandbag roof kept off the rain and the shell fragments, which plummeted down from our own 90mm antiaircraft fire. As things developed, it was the greatest hole I ever occupied.

The first lethal visitor that night was "Washing Machine Charlie," a Jap bomber that had a distinct "putt putt" sound. My hosts told me he was a nightly visitor who circled for endless minutes over the perimeter dropping a single 100-pound bomb every 15 minutes or so. His purpose was less to do damage than to affect morale by keeping everyone awake. This night there was more than one bomber, for there was at least one aloft at all times until about midnight, when we had a brief respite. I rolled up in my poncho and went to sleep but was soon awakened by flares or star shells exploding overhead turning the night into day. My hosts, who had seen this before and recognized it as the prelude to a shelling by Jap warships, dove into the dugout and I wasted no time in joining them.

We didn't have long to wait. Suddenly bright orange flashes lit up the sky to seaward followed almost immediately by the roar of projectiles passing overhead. This was not the scream or whine of small shells but the swishing roar of 14-inch monster shells from two Jap battleships. This was flat trajectory fire with the shells arriving almost simultaneously with the sound of the muzzle blasts. Fortunately for me the Japs were uncannily accurate. A single short round would have ended my Marine Corps career, but there were none. The shells passed harmlessly overhead and exploded on the airfield with devastating results. Fuel and ammunition dumps, airplanes and support facilities burned in a monster conflagration that lit the skies. And the bombardment didn't stop! It seemed to go on for hours. As I learned recently, the battleships *Kongo* and *Haruna* began firing at 01:34 and continued for one hour and 20 minutes. About 973 14-inch shells struck the target, burning the entire supply of aviation gas, holing the airfield's runways, destroying most of our aircraft and killing 41 men.*

*Richard B. Frank, *Guadalcanal* (New York: Random House, 1990), 316–19.

5. Tulagi and Guadalcanal

The following day I found the rest of the patrol. They had double-timed it from the place I had left them and made it to the perimeter just in time for the fireworks. Like me, they were shook up but unscathed. We bivouacked in the coconut plantation for about four days awaiting transportation back to Tulagi. And an interesting time it was. Multi-plane air raids kept us alert and diving into hastily dug foxholes. The planes, twin engine Mitsubishi bombers we called "Bettys," would come over at about 20,000 feet and dump their loads on the airfield area. Our antiaircraft fire didn't seem to bother them. At night they looked rather pretty when illuminated by our searchlights but it would have been great to see one of them get hit by our ineffective 90-millimeter fire. The Jap navy returned each night and shelled us but this was smaller stuff, eight-inchers from cruisers. Late one afternoon, I think it was October 16, I was sitting on the beach watching a working party manhandling fuel drums from a converted four-stacker, the McFarland, AVD 14, to a steel barge. Suddenly a Jap dive bomber at treetop level dropped a bomb squarely on the fantail of the ship. The barge and its contents erupted in roaring flame but the ship withstood the blast marvelously. It managed to get underway and limped to Tulagi for repairs. The only thing left of the work party on the barge was their steel helmets. The dive bomber was one of a flight of about nine "Vals" that carried out the attack. For a while the air was filled with roaring airplanes as a lone Grumman F4F came to the rescue. In seconds the pilot splashed three of the bombers. I learned much later that the pilot, a Major Harold Bauer, got the Medal of Honor for his afternoon's work.*

The shelling and multiple air raids we endured during this three or four-day period were part of the Jap's last all-out effort to retake the island. The day after the battleship shelling saw six large Jap transports unloading troops and weapons at Tassafaronga, just a few miles west of the perimeter. While our crippled Air Force managed to force three of the ships to beach themselves, the group managed to unload at least 5,000 soldiers and many tons of supplies. For our part we were wondering, "Where in the hell is our Navy?" The terrible truth was we didn't have much naval strength in the area and what we had was greatly inferior in armament and ability.

*Thomas G. Miller, Jr., *The Cactus Air Force* (New York: Harper & Row, 1969), 132–33.

At this stage in the war the Japanese admirals and ship captains outclassed the officers who manned our few ships. This would change as our guys learned their trade, but the Navy's early ineptitude nearly lost Guadalcanal. Our Navy was long on courage but short on knowhow. And it cost us, for more than 5,000 sailors and seagoing Marines died in naval clashes around the island. Less than 1,800 Marines and soldiers were killed in the land fighting.

About October 21, a YP boat ferried us back to Tulagi. While I appreciated the quiet and relaxed climate of our rear area bivouac I sort of resented being removed from the action and excitement on the Canal. I felt I was sitting on the bench while my buddies were playing the game. I didn't like that in high school football and I didn't relish it now. Moreover, I had a crazy inner feeling that the great expenditure of money and resources needed to equip and train me would not be justified until I had personally killed at least one Jap. Once I accomplished that the United States and Japan would be even. Then, if I and enough other Yanks got one or two more of the enemy, we would be on the road to victory. I can't say I felt grateful to the United States for making me a Marine, but I did feel an obligation to fulfill the expectations of the system that put me here. It wasn't a Marine thing, I would have felt the same in any uniform.

I didn't have long to stew over being relegated to the backwaters, for a week later, about October 30, we went back to Guadalcanal. This time the entire battalion made the trip. And this time there was no uncertainty as to our mission. We would be taking part in an offensive to take the western part of the island, the part controlled by the Japanese army. This was it, the real thing, and I doubt that many of us were certain we were up to it. As a troop leader I felt obligated to exhibit unconcern and a savoir-faire I certainly didn't feel. In a very real sense it is somewhat easier for a leader to quell his inner fears, for the fear of disgracing yourself by showing the white feather before the men who depend upon you overwhelms your personal fear. Fear of disgrace is more potent than fear of death or injury.

On October 31 I left our bivouac area to find the First Raider battalion and my friend Don Wolf. I found the Raiders but my inquiry for Don produced the worst possible news; he had been killed the preceding week in hand-to-hand combat repelling a Japanese night attack. For the first time I began to hate our enemy. Don was posthumously awarded the Silver Star and, in April 1945, a new destroyer escort, DE 713, was named after him.

On November 1 we moved out westward on the well-traveled Government Trail, which skirted the beach along the entire north coast of the island, the same trail we had traversed on the patrol from Aola. We had to step aside frequently to allow vehicles of many kinds to pass. Ominously, some were jeep ambulances carrying wounded to the rear. We crossed the Matanikau River on floating footbridges hurriedly thrown up by First Division engineers. We were following my old regiment, the Fifth Marines. In fact, our mission was to pass through the Fifth and take up the assault. But heavy Jap resistance changed those plans. We bivouacked that night about 500 yards west of the river and about 100 yards behind the Fifth. We received some scattered mortar and artillery fire that night but had no casualties.

At 0800 we deployed as skirmishers and moved up close behind the Fifth, who were now heavily engaged. Machine gun and rifle fire directed

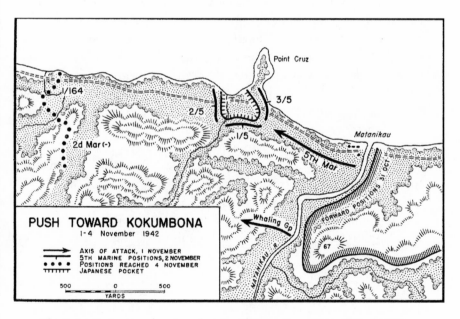

The Point Cruz area, showing where our lines were on November 4, 1942.

73

at them kept us flat on our stomachs. At this time, one of the saddest events of my time in the Marines occurred. My platoon leader, who had been showing signs of nervousness, whispered to me, "I'm sick — tell Denley (the platoon sergeant) I'm going to the rear." I was thunderstruck! This guy was chickening out while under fire, a thing Marines never do. I tried to talk him out of it. I said, "You can't do that, lieutenant." But he only mumbled, "I'm really sick," and scuttled to the rear. I crawled over and told Denley what happened and suggested he relay the news to Captain Fuhrhop. The word was passed that the company executive officer, Captain Jack Miller, (recently promoted from first lieutenant) would take over temporarily as platoon leader. This was a good choice; I liked Miller.

After several hours of hugging the dirt to avoid the Jap fire aimed at the Fifth Marines, we were pulled back and directed to move inland and encircle the pocket of Japs the Fifth was trying to eliminate. We completed this maneuver about dusk and dug in with our right flank on the beach facing west. During the night we killed about six Japs trying to escape the pocket. One of these incidents was somewhat amusing. I heard Paul Boyd in a stage whisper call to his brother, "Bob, is anyone supposed to be on your left?" The immediate answer was, "No. Shoot the son of a bitch!" Almost instantaneously the loud "POW" of an 03 rifle closed the door on a Japanese life. Shortly after dawn I almost became the victim of a Jap who had apparently penetrated our line and lay hidden about ten yards behind me in the tall kuana grass that covered the crest of the ridge we occupied. This stalwart, armed only with a pistol, emerged from the grass to a kneeling position and banged poorly aimed shots at me and the men stirring around in the company CP. Before I could respond, First Sergeant Raymond Sadler disposed of the threat with one carefully aimed shot from his 45. In retrospect, I concluded the Jap was shooting too wildly to have had lethal intent. I believe he was committing suicide, i.e., just inviting us to kill him. There was no surrender in those guys.

The next day, November 3, was not a good day for the battalion. After a short artillery preparation we attacked westward in a skirmish line about 400 yards in breadth, with the right flank on the beach and the left on the coastal ridges. A Company was on the extreme left flank and my platoon was on the left flank of the company. Captain Miller put my squad on the extreme left and cautioned me to look out for another Marine unit, the "Whalen Group," which was supposed to be somewhere inland of our position. I never did see them. The jungle was thick, too thick to maintain an orderly skirmish line, and we soon decided to have the squads in column. For some reason I don't recall I stayed in the van of my squad as we moved slowly westward along the side of a ridge. We could hear an occasional shot from the units on our right but no sounds of incoming fire. It wasn't exactly a Sunday stroll through the park but it was almost eerily quiet. Perhaps, I thought, the Japs have moved out and this is going to be a cakewalk.

My wishful thinking was suddenly interrupted by a movement of the underbrush about ten yards to my front followed by the emergence of a Jap soldier, helmet-less and armed with only a small shovel. Wide-eyed, muscles frozen, we stared at each other for several heartbeats. I don't remember who first broke the trance but he whirled, dove back into the bush and disappeared. Why didn't I chalk up my first trophy? I still blush to admit it — I couldn't get the safety off on my rifle. By the time I got it off my target was not in sight. The round I fired at the spot of his disappearance penetrated only leaves.

One would think that this commotion would have alerted every Jap within several hundred yards. Surely the man I faced and shot at would spread the word that the Yanks are coming. But, strangely, that was not the case. We moved out again, more cautiously and a bit slower. After advancing for not much more than a hundred yards, I moved through a screen of brush and stared in disbelief at a mind-boggling sight not more than 20 yards away, a group of three Japs, squatting close together, their packs and rifles on the ground beside them. Compared to my ragtag appearance these troops wore neat and clean uniforms. They appeared to be fresh troops and not the tattered remnants of the units which had attacked the perimeter in the preceding months. For a few seconds we stared at each other wide-eyed. The soldier nearest to me was very young, probably no more than 17. I can still see the look of absolute terror in his eyes. My mind was working at top speed and I determined the only viable solution was to shoot the first one who moves and try to get them all. And that's what I did. When number one stood up I shot him in the chest. He dropped and lay motionless. Number two spun away and started to run but only took one or two steps before my second round drove him into the dirt. While his comrades were dying the kid stayed frozen, his eyes glued to my face. He was on hands and knees, his right side toward me. Slowly he started to rise, his rifle in his left hand. I shot him in the chest and he died quickly and, I think, painlessly. The look in his eyes has stayed with me all these years.

So far it had all gone my way, three to zip, but the game wasn't over. A bullet cracked by my left ear and then another hit the shale directly beside me. I was crouched completely in the open on my left hip with my right leg stretched out down the slope. The shots were coming from a green wall of vegetation about ten yards beyond the bodies of the three dead soldiers. Soon another shot cracked by my ear, and this time I saw the shooter. He was standing behind the trunk of a very large tree. It was dark under this jungle canopy and all I could see was a half-hidden black silhouette when he emerged to bang a quick shot at me. He would hide completely behind the trunk when he worked his bolt. I traded shots with him but only succeeded in knocking bark off his tree. Then, horror of horrors, my bolt hit the follower, telling me my weapon was empty! If there was a record for getting a cartridge clip from an ammunition belt and reloading five rounds into an 03 I'm sure I broke it. By this time I realized that I was going to die unless I killed the man behind the tree and I determined that the next time Tojo stuck his head and rifle into sight I was going to slowly squeeze off a shot, as I had been taught in Boot Camp. He didn't keep me waiting. His rifle and arm slowly appeared and I drew a bead on the edge of the trunk slightly above them, where his head would emerge. When it came into view, my shot went true. The impact of the bullet drove the body sideways, sort of cartwheeling down the slope to the right.

What a relief! That shooter had me cold, completely in the open at a range of 30 or 35 yards and he misses with three or four shots. I'm sure he was green, but so were we. The difference — Marine Corps training — those endless hours spent practicing with the rifle on and off the range until you learned to load and aim by reflex with little mental effort needed.

After this minute or two of action some of the men from Jim

Sorensen's squad moved up on both sides of me and we continued the advance. At this juncture the rest of the company on the low ground to our right had not encountered resistance. In fact, the CP sent up a rather accusatory message asking what was holding me up and what all the firing was about. This peed me off and I yelled back, with a certain amount of exaggeration, "We've run into the whole dammed Jap army and have killed a bunch of them!" About this time we started taking casualties. A Marine named Verne Ramey was hit in both thighs and had to be dragged back. Private Raymond Hesslink died with a bullet between the eyes. And things started to heat up for the rest of the company on our right. They started taking mortar fire and a heavy machine gun pounded them mercilessly. Corporal Price was killed, along with several others. We were taking so much fire a fast advance was out of the question. At the time I toyed with the idea of taking a couple of men and trying to flank the machine gun which was causing so much havoc to the men on my right. In fact, I should have done it but was concerned that I would have been hit by the friendly fire of the troops I was trying to save. It may have been a foolhardy attempt, for there were a lot of Japs between the machine gun and me. All the same, I wish I had tried it.

About this time I heard a voice somewhere to my left screaming, "I give up! I give up!" The brush screened the source of this hollering from me and I asked the men on my left what was going on. George Gardner yelled, "It's a fucking Jap." Without hesitation I ordered, "Shoot the son of a bitch." George complied, although it took him two rounds to do the job. I'm not proud of my action in that situation. We may have been able to take the man prisoner and save his life. But we had been taught the Japs were very tricky and would try to kill you with their last breath. Moreover, we were in the middle of an attack with no time or men to handle a prisoner. Nevertheless, my direction to George still bothers me.

We received orders to hold our position. In a short while the firing on our right died down and we stopped taking fire. The company gunnery sergeant, Everette Dunkle, crawled up behind me and said the attack had been called off. We formed a rough defensive line but did not dig in. I took a position prone behind the rotting trunk of a fallen tree and

Gunny Dunkle squatted behind me. This seemed like a good time for a smoke, if I could bum one from the gunny. I looked back at him and asked for a cigarette. He was handing it to me when his eyes suddenly widened as he stared at something over my head. I spun around and there, not 30 feet away, stood the biggest Jap I had ever seen. This bearded guy had to be at least six feet tall. He was carrying his rifle at port arms and was looking from side to side. He had obviously been sent out as a scout to determine our position. But my god, I thought, he must be blind, for the gunny and I were in plain sight only 30 feet to his front. He was so close I didn't have to aim; I merely pointed the rifle and hit the trigger. The round hit him in the chest and knocked him off his feet to the left. He bounded back up and I shot him again in the chest. He got to his feet and started to run away. I could see two large blood spots on the back of his shirt. I triggered a third round, which knocked him down for good.

During the action, Jim Sorensen's squad was on my right at a lower level. Jim, who died of leukemia in 1982, wrote a brilliant memoir of his time in combat while it was still fresh in his mind, and shortly before his death made a return visit to Guadalcanal. Here is his description of the action on November 3:

> Our lines were getting pretty well extended so Rogal and his B.A.R. Squad were assigned to reconnoiter from the flank at each rise. At one rise they moved out and found trouble. Their B.A.R. chattered away [Wrong, that was no B.A.R., just my rifle.] and Rogal hollered down to me that they had just dispatched three Japs on the big ridge to my left.... The center of the line and the flank of [on] the beach were moving with no opposition. Seems our end was destined to smell gunpowder. We crossed another hollow and encountered no troubles. Then we came to a rather extensive hollow. The rim in front of us being the big ridge to our left curved toward the shore. Rogal's squad was up on the ridge when all hell broke loose up there. His B.A.R.s cut loose and the Jap rifles answered. My squad was nearest to him and there was considerable distance between us so we began to angle up the slope and moving forward at the same time. My idea was to hit the Jap's pocket from the flank while Rogal's guns were engaging them on the front. I lay behind a log on the slope trying to locate the Jap's position. I couldn't see them so most of the detecting was forced to be done by sound. The other two platoons were stalled while we were mopping up. Guess we delayed them so someone hollered up, "What's holding you up? A couple of snipers?" Rogal

roared down, "Snipers hell. The whole dammed Japanese army. We've already got five of them and there's more up here." I relayed the message with a few remarks of my own. At about this time a lull in the fighting occurred.... This stop gave Cassidy [He means Cassity, Kenneth D.] time to move his squad up and fall in on my left and fill in the gap between Rogal and me while Price and his squad moved into the hole between my bunch and the second platoon. None of the corporals had been given any orders on what to do in a case like this but it seems like the right positions were taken up nearly automatically. I spotted a big tree on a slight bump of the slope so I raced for it, but the last man in the Cassidy [Cassity] squad, Heslirh [He means Hesslink, Raymond H.] got there ahead of me.... Things wasted no time in happening. Heslirh stood up behind this big tree and poked his head around the left of the tree. Almost immediately a Jap rifle sounded. Heslirh just seemed to shutter [sic], then stiffen like a ramrod and almost in slow motion he fell over backwards with his arms spread out straight from his shoulders. His helmet fell off as he dropped and his head swiveled in my direction, and I looked into a pair of eyes that seemed frozen in their sockets. Right between his eyes was a nasty little red hole. This was the first marine I'd actually seen killed, and I always remembered it.

This was the third platoon's baptism of fire and we caught hell; the man next to Heslirh [sic] was killed and in a few more minutes and when a corpsman with the platoon crept up to see if he could help him, the sniper got him too. I felt the breath of eternity around me, the three nearest men on my left all killed in what seemed a few minutes but was probably more — I'm sure I said a fervent prayer....

Price's squad, on my right flank, caught it next and part of Boyd's squad. First off, Miller, one of Boyd's B.A.R. men, tried to cross the gully mouth and caught a bullet through the chest and died while the fracas was going on. Cox, one of Boyd's riflemen, poked up from a log at the gully mouth, and tried to get the sniper somewhere up the gully — the sniper caught him first though and he dropped with a dum-dum slug through his right collar bone and shoulder. The captain ordered Price to take his squad across the gully mouth and establish an anchor for the line on the other side. Price, instead of taking his men across individually in quick jumps, moved squarely into the gully and shouted to his men to follow — they probably would have, only he proved an excellent target and the Jap felled him with a shot through the stomach. He too died while the scrap went on....

After things quieted down I had time to think about what I had done. I had killed five human beings and I conducted a self-examination to see what my inner feelings were about these acts. I thought about it for awhile and concluded that, as a Christian, at the very least, I should feel remorse or shame and sorrow for the slain. I tried, but I couldn't muster up those feelings. But, on the other hand, I couldn't feel elated or victorious. I am sure there was a certain amount of smugness and satisfaction at having fulfilled my self-imposed duty to justify my existence by killing at least one Jap, but it wasn't a feeling of joy. The best way I can describe my mental state is that it was one of numb acceptance — this is a war and this is the way it's going to be. Of course I did feel thankful for survival and probably mouthed an appropriate prayer.

My minor victories on November 3 were overshadowed by the severe casualties suffered by the battalion that day. A Company had 18 casualties, seven killed and 11 wounded. In addition to Cpl. Thurman Price, our dead were Raymond Sanders, Doyle Miller, Dalton Whittington, Blaine Hyde, Dooney Armstrong and Harold Baker. As a whole, the battalion suffered 74 casualties, 20 or more killed in action. As I said above, it was a bad day. And, but for the ineptitude of two of our pilots, it would have been worse. Just before dusk we moved back a bit and started to dig in across the crest of a grass-capped ridge. I noticed two low-flying SBDs circling our position and obviously looking us over. Surely they mean no harm, I reasoned. Wrong! Suddenly the lead plane banked and, machine guns spitting, dove right at us and dropped a bomb. It was a miracle none of us was killed or wounded. The bomb soared over our heads and detonated in the valley to our rear. Our leaders tried to contact Henderson Field to have them call off their hawks but couldn't make contact in time to prevent a second attack, but it too caused no casualties. While the planes were diving we were waving our arms and flapping dirty skivvy shirts to show the pilots we weren't Japs. Finally they got the word and flew back, banking from side to side as if to say, "Sorry about that."

We spent a quiet night, except for killing one Jap who invaded the battalion aid station. The next day we took up positions straddling the eastern end of a ridge. B Company, which had been in support the previous day, moved up on our left. It was good to have someone over there, I had been nervous about my exposed flank. One of our water-cooled machine guns was set up between us on the crest of the ridge, where it had a good field of fire westward along the ridge line. Like most Guadalcanal ridges, the heavy jungle which covered its sides gave way to a crown of tall grass at the peak. The grassy crown of this one was only about 30 yards wide but it ran westward for at least 100 yards. I positioned one of my BAR men next to the machine gun position, two riflemen to his right, then my position followed by the rest of the squad to my right in the trees. It was a flimsy line with the men protected by only shallow foxholes. But, thank goodness, B Company had protected the heavy machine gun with sandbags.

The following night I was on watch an hour or so after midnight when my ears picked up a rhythmic swishing sound. It was difficult to locate for a second or two but it grew gradually louder until the source appeared to my direct front. There, coming down the ridgeline, swishing their way through the tall grass and moving directly toward us, was a mass of Jap soldiers. They were not in a military attack formation but were bunched up. Clearly, they did not know they were blundering into a Marine defensive line. I lay there dumbstruck for a second or two wondering if that knucklehead behind the heavy machine gun was awake. He either was asleep or was an awfully cool character, for he let them get within 20 yards before he pulled the trigger. The first bursts from the machine gun killed or wounded most, if not all, of the forward elements of the Jap advance and the remainder of the group melted away in the darkness. But not for long. Within a few minutes we could hear the rattling of gear and guttural commands from an area about 40 yards to our front. I assumed they were forming up for one of their spectacular "Banzai" attacks. Fortunately, this enemy group was more circumspect. They did not mount an all-out charge but set up three light machine guns and began firing from a fixed position. At this juncture we riflemen got into the action, banging away with our rifles and throwing grenades. Company members in the woods behind us kept us supplied with grenades by forming a line and passing them hand to hand. The fight was weird in one respect. The Jap machine guns did not lay down a continuous volley, with at least one gun firing while the others reloaded, but rather all three fired simultaneously in long bursts until their magazines were empty. When they stopped firing we could hear rather loud clickety clacking as their gunners seated loaded magazines in the guns. Then all would be silent for a few seconds until the firing recommenced on the shouted command of a Jap officer. This was duck soup for us. We stayed prone in our foxholes while the Jap guns were firing but could emerge with impunity during the periods of silence. We would bang off an entire five-round clip with the 03 and could even stand up to get the needed distance for grenade throwing.

During this fracas I noticed the man in the foxhole to my immediate left was not firing his weapon nor participating in the grenade throwing. This was the same kid, Taylor, who had the stinky feet on the transport. I thought he had been shot and whispered a couple of times, "Taylor, are you hurt?" Finally he answered in a tremulous voice, "I'm scared!" This time he had cold feet. I ordered him to get up and start firing, but he seemed almost catatonic, muttering, "I can't, I can't." I put an end to that by the simple expedient of making him more afraid of me than he was of the Japs. By reaching out with my left arm fully extended I could stay in my hole and poke him in the side with the bayonet affixed to my rifle. I told him if he didn't start firing I was going to push the bayonet through him. To this day I am not certain whether I would have carried out the threat, but I wasn't put to the test, for Taylor emerged from his stupor and started firing.

After 30 minutes or so word was passed up to me that our artillery was going to fire some ranging rounds and I was to watch for them and pass back directions to place the fire on the enemy. The first rounds hit in the trees about 200 yards too far and too far right. I yelled back, "Bring it down a little and give it a little left windage." This was apparently a bit too inexact, for some uncouth character yelled, "Give it to us in yards, asshole!" I yelled back, "Left 25 and down 50." Almost magically, the next rounds hit exactly where I had directed them. But they were too far out, well behind the Jap gunners, so I directed they be lowered another 50 yards. They were now "battery firing," that is at least four guns (75mm pack howitzers) were firing simultaneously. I kept bringing them down in 25-yard drops until they were hitting on the Jap guns. At one point somebody in my squad yelled, "Don't bring it down no more, Rogal!" But I was determined to get the barrages on the target and persisted in dropping the range until they were hitting less than 50 yards in front of us. That was too much for the Japs and the machine gun fire ended and all was quiet.

I learned later that my sightings were relayed to our company CO,

Captain Fuhrhop, who had a phone line through to a battery of the 11th Marines, the First Division's artillery regiment. We were lucky. These were seasoned gunners who had been in continuous action since August 7. I still feel indebted to those guys. Dropping that volume of fire on a black night with pinpoint accuracy, and without a single short round, was expertise of the highest order.

The following morning we were relieved by a newly arrived Army outfit, the 164th Infantry. They had been in reserve behind us for the past few days. The platoon sergeant who brought his men up to take over our positions was, to put it mildly, a bit apprehensive. He told me he thought we should stay there with them for a day or two because the Japs were afraid of the Marines and not of the Army. I laughed at that and told him, "Those clowns can't tell a Marine from a soldier." I tried to bolster his morale but doubt I succeeded. At the time I wondered how this guy's platoon would react to his obvious fear. I left him with the admonition that the dead Japs laying around would soon start stinking something awful if he didn't crank up a working party to bury them.

I found out that morning that both A and B companies had not suffered casualties during the night battle. Apparently the Japs didn't realize we were on lower ground and all of their fire went over our heads. We don't know how many they lost for we did not send out a patrol to examine the entire area. B Company sent a squad led by Emery J. "Stud" Noble to gather up the Jap machine guns and any material which might be useful to intelligence. They had to finish off a couple of enemy wounded. I am sure Captain Fuhrhop's estimate of 400 Jap casualties is too high. Stud Noble counted only 18 bodies piled around the abandoned machine guns but it is reasonable to estimate that at least twice that many were hit and managed to make their way back to their lines. Regimental CO Col. John Arthur's report states: "Approximately 100 Japs were killed during this action." That's possible, but no one will ever know for sure.

First Battalion's Record of Events Journal entry for November 5 makes this statement with respect to the artillery that night: "By using Lieut. Gunter as a spotter on the frontline Lt. Col. Robert E. Hill [our Battalion CO] was able to summon very effective artillery fire." As the old saying goes, "Success has many fathers." The Lt. Gunter mentioned was 2nd

Lt. Howard G. Gunter of B Company who, no doubt, was also calling back the shots.

A funny thing happened when we went into bivouac that evening. Taylor came to see me. I could see instantly he was not antagonistic. Quiet the opposite, he was bubbling over with good spirits and walking on air. He wanted to thank me for the bayonet jab of the preceding evening. He explained the fact that he was able to overcome his fear, and taking part in the firefight had freed him from the fear of cowardice he had been burdened with since he joined the Marines. He was now free of doubt and confident he could handle anything that came his way. He kept thanking me and telling me what a great thing I had done until it became embarrassing. I tried to tell him it wasn't his welfare in my thoughts that night, I was motivated by concern for my own safety. Nevertheless, I precipitated his epiphany and he was ecstatically grateful.

For the next few days we remained in a static position about 500 yards to the rear of the front line, now manned by the Army. We received some scattered mortar and artillery fire but suffered no casualties. On November 9 we moved about 500 yards south, inland, and took up positions to resume the westward assault. The next day, November 10, is the Marine Corps' birthday, but no one mentioned it. The day began on a sour note. The Eighth Marines, newly arrived on the island, situated somewhere in our rear, dropped a barrage of 81mm mortar rounds on us. Several men in our battalion CP, including the Battalion CO Col. Hill, were wounded and evacuated. We lost a couple of guys from our weapons platoon. The battalion executive officer, Major Wood B. Kyle, took command, although he was wounded in his legs.

The day was the hottest I can remember on the Canal. We formed a skirmish line on the crest of a ridge and lay there waiting for our artillery preparation and the word to push off. I can remember those minutes distinctly because of a singular attitudinal change I experienced. Perhaps influenced by the sight of all the guys bloodied up by the Eighth Marines' mortars or just general malaise, I was thinking of all the relatives and friends I had back home and all the good times I had then and might never experience again. I kept thinking along those lines to the point where tears started forming in my eyes. I was one miserable puppy! Suddenly, like Paul on the Damascus Road, a light came on in my brain and

84

A Marine 81mm mortar squad (photograph by Abraham Felber).

I said to myself, "Do you know what you are doing, asshole? You are feeling sorry for yourself. Stop it now and never, ever do it again!" It was a most noteworthy epiphany and I was free of self-pity for the rest of my time in combat, or anywhere as a matter of fact.

In due time the word came to move out and we advanced into a heavily wooded valley. The descent into the gorge was uneventful as was most of the climb up the opposite slope. However, when we reached the crest of the hill and started to move into the tall grass which covered the crest all hell broke loose. As we entered the grass a hail of machine gun and rifle fire cut into us. Sgt. Burgess, who was then platoon sergeant of the weapons platoon, did one of the stupidest things I have ever seen. Apparently convinced we were taking friendly fire, Burgess stood erect on the crest and yelled to figures we could vaguely see about a hundred yards away on our left front, "Are you Marines?" The answer was a burst of machine gun fire. He took a round through the stock of his rifle and another through his blouse but was unhurt. The Japs then went to work with mortars, dropping round after round on us. I don't think they wasted a single round either long or short. Sergeant Denley and I curled up in a far too shallow shell hole. During the barrage Denley screamed, "I'm hit! I'm hit!" and started to rise. I threw an arm over him to hold him down and asked him where he was hit. "In the ass!" he screamed. I looked at his stern quarter and, sure enough, there was a shell fragment sticking out of his rear. But it was a tiny crescent shaped fragment, which had hardly broken the skin. He calmed down when I pulled it out and showed it to him.

Meanwhile, A Company was taking a beating. Richard Gill, William Schreiner, James Majercak and Amos Gray lay dead. At least ten others were wounded, some very badly. Included were Sgt. Otis Thompson, Cpl. Jim Sorensen, and Privates James (Dub) Taylor, Otis Davis, Henry Hale, Oliver Smith, Eugene Campbell, Frank Freeman, and Elmer Goetz. The Battalion Muster Roll reveals two Corpsmen were killed that day, Alfred Schuler and James Gage, but I have no recollection as to which, if either, was with us. My squad was decimated, with all three BAR men down. Fortunately the Japs didn't know what chaos they had caused for they didn't follow up the barrage with a Banzai assault, which would have meant curtains for at least the badly wounded. Moreover they ceased firing all their weapons and we took advantage by getting the hell out of there. Even retreating wasn't easy for we didn't have enough stretchers for the wounded nor enough able bodied men to get them and our weapons back to the safety of our lines. There was no help for it — we had to leave our dead. I took on the job of getting all three of my BARs back but had to leave my rifle which I field stripped, scattering the parts around the jungle and then wrapped the receiver and stock around a tree. I slung the BARs on my back and manned one end of a stretcher. Descending the hill wasn't too bad but going up the opposite slope was a real bear of a task. The man I was helping to carry kept sliding off the stretcher for we could not keep it level on the steep grade. He had several bullet holes in his upper torso and at first I couldn't figure out where to grab him to pull him back on the stretcher. He solved it for me by telling me: "Grab under my chin, stupid." — Still feisty despite his wounds. When we finally emerged out of the jungle and regained the flat hilltop we had kicked off from that morning we saw our former foxholes and positions were occupied by the newly arrived Eighth Marines. They were too spooked by the sight of this bloodied, ragtag crew to leave their holes and offer us any help with the wounded. In fact, a crew of them just looked at me with blank faces when I asked them to help. We ended up carrying our loads all the way to an aid station in the rear of their lines.

Usually, contemporary written accounts of combat action are accurate and reliable but the Battalion's Record of Events Journal for November 10th is the exception that proves the rule. It states: "At 1400 we received word that a Bn of the 8th Mar would pass through us. Our lines held until the 8th passed through." What a crock! The facts are as I have set them out — we had our asses whipped and withdrew back to the line we kicked off from. I suspect the facts had to be slightly laundered for it would have been considered impolitic to disclose even a little retreat in a formal report. Come to think of it, the strategic withdrawal of 10 November 1942 was the only one I witnessed in my combat career.

Jim Sorensen was wounded that day but I was occupied a little ways to his right and didn't actually see what happened to him. Here is Jim Sorensen's version of the day's events as it appears in his memoir:

Over the valley rim we flowed and down into a jungle hell again. This sector was the most dimmable piece of jungle I ever hope to see — We had to hack our way through with bayonets and machetes at each stop. Thorny vines clutched at our dungarees and tore them like barbs on a wire fence, we were bleeding from countless scratches and deep cuts; we couldn't even plunge headlong through the tangle of vines — they merely swayed with your weight and flung you back again. Hack, cut, chop was the system — light was about what one would receive through dark brown glasses and the heat was stifling, even breathing was difficult. Sweat oozed in driblets — our clothes were soaked through from sweat and the heat increased as we edged forward in a cursing, fuming line through the jungle. The heat got to the point where I expected the men to go berserk — it drove everything from your mind but your loathing for this never ending jungle.... We finally struck the far slope and began whittling a way up to the ridge — daylight and fresh air were up in that direction, so we literally mangled a path upwards. Up here too the Japs lay in wait for us.... Boyd, just ahead of me, reached the jungle edge — from here to the ridge top was a distance of about forty feet, covered with grass about two feet deep. He moved his squad up on the very crest and I moved up right behind him, with both of our squads lying on the ground over a front of about thirty feet and extending back within about ten feet of the jungle. One Squad of "C" company moved up on my left and just as our own company must have been breaking out of the jungle — the Jap ambush opened up on us.

From where we lay Boyd's bunch nor myself could see them, but they opened up on us with machine guns and sprayed right down through us. They sure had our number, two of Boyd's squad were hit with the first burst — one was killed and another fellow — Shanahan, was hit bad and lay there moaning with now and then a pitiful warbling scream.

We yelled for a corpsman — no corpsman could get up to the ridge to us through that fire, but the men cursed and yelled for a corpsman nevertheless. I guessed the Japs to be on our left — probably on a rise on the ridge so they could observe us from above.... I yelled to Cassity who I knew would be on my right, to give us the word did the captain want us to stay here or withdraw. Well the company was in the jungle-so we didn't get the word, and we stuck to our spot on the ridge. Orders were to stay on the flank and we were. I even thought we could anchor a line from our position but we were just an anchor without any line. Suffice it to say — the two squads caught hell....

We couldn't raise up to take a look so we stood pat and waited for developments. Well the Nip boys gave 'em to us, a couple grenades spilled in on us and two more boys got hurt — from somewhere Burgess had crawled up with us and when one of the fellows in front started whimpering from his wound, Burgess crawled right into the potential line of fire and began patching up the two boys. Another couple grenades went off and the kid who was kicking up dirt near my shoulder, gave a scream — Burgess wanted to know who got it. I told him to sit tight and I'd handle this one, so I eased up alongside the boy — McDonald and asked him where he was hit. He gave me a frightened whimper and told me he'd been hit near his hip. I tore his pants leg open — he had a gash about an inch long with very little blood — not more than a skin cut but for three inches on any side of it his leg was already black and blue. Must have been a solid piece, nearly spent that struck him. I kidded him about it but that didn't help, so to help his feelings I rolled over, took off my first aid kit and proceeded to tie on one of my gauze bandages — the other I stuck in my pocket.... Some of the fellows who could were begging me to give the order to withdraw — they wouldn't budge unless they were told to but even that was handled by the hidden Nips. At last they threw the works at us — machine guns and mortar-must have been half dozen grenades from those "knee" mortars that struck squarely in the cluster of men. One shell hit practically on Grey on the jungle's edge and killed him instantly, young Hale, to my right was hit in the spine with fragments. Mosier below me was hit in the chest and kidneys, young Jais was deaf from the shock blast and McDonald caught a load of the stuff in his shoulder and left arm. One damn shell blew up three feet to my left, punctured my pack and me too — my hearing went off, my head felt as though it was floating on air and I had the impression that I'd been flung from a truck. I couldn't see right away — imagined and wondered for a moment if I were dead and this was the first step toward eternity. My hearing came back first and I heard blubbering screams and moans all about me, men whimpering, "I've been hit." And one of my own squad calling Sorensen, Sorensen, I'm hit. My head cleared a little and I heard someone swearing a blue streak and for some reason thought it was Burgess — it wasn't though, it was me and I was outdoing myself. I shut that off and then took a look down my left side at myself— I couldn't feel any pain, but all down my leg below my pack I could see blood oozing through my dungarees, my side and left arm felt awful numb but they didn't hurt. I knew I wasn't dead by a long shot.

Jim and the other wounded were carried off that ridge and turned over to the medics. He was evacuated by air in a few days with other casualties. I wish we could have gotten together after the war for a good confab.

We took some more mortar fire that night but no one was hit. About noon on the 11th we were ordered to move north to the Government Trail and stand by for further orders. We didn't know it at the time but this movement was the first step in the withdrawal of all forces west of the Matanikau to strengthen the perimeter defense of the beachhead. Our intelligence had revealed a large Jap taskforce was headed our way and the only smart thing to do was consolidate forces and await developments. When we reached the Government Trail we discovered the Eighth Marines had gotten there first. There were a lot of men scattered around taking it easy. We joined the throng but most of our people selected a five or six-feet deep dry gully for a resting place. Experienced combat troops will always try to find a defilade area to squat in. I dropped my pack in the gully and joined the company headquarters group who were sitting around a six-foot square Jap foxhole with their legs in the excavation. The hole had been dug at the base of an immense tree, at least three feet in diameter and probably 90 feet high. The group included Captain Fuhrhop, Captain Miller, First Sergeant Sadler and Gunnery Sergeant Dunkle. We were a rather subdued bunch recalling the tragic events of the previous day and wondering why we were now back where we started from a week earlier. Were we really giving up all the ground we had gained at such a huge price? And where were we going next? Our questions were answered at about 16:00 when we got orders to move farther east and set up a defensive line 500 yards west of the Matanikau.

I jumped into the gully and passed the word to get ready to move out. I found my pack and was putting it on when an unbelievable concussion almost knocked me to my knees. I was facing a kid named Alton Corey, who crumbled to the ground. Dazed, I looked down at Corey's prostrate form. He was lying on his back but I don't remember whether his eyes were open. That was of little consequence, for an immense, unsurvivable wound in the top of his right shoulder was emitting red blood and pink bubbles. A huge shell fragment had entered his shoulder and traveled downward into his chest. Private Corey died instantly. I looked to my right where I had been sitting with the headquarters group G and all I could see was a huge pile of green branches. Captain Fuhrhop's voice resounded from the pile. He screamed, "I believe in the Lord Jesus Christ!" I think he said it only once and then lapsed into unconsciousness. I guess those were his last words.

There was no sign of Captain Miller and Sergeants Sadler and Dunkle. I climbed out of the gully but was unable to do anything but stand still in shock. Looking around, I saw the Eighth had suffered casualties. I could see a man I later learned was a battalion surgeon with a huge hole in his side and apparently dead. My platoon sergeant, Julius Novak, came running past me holding his bloody, fingerless right hand aloft. Julius had returned to the company from sick leave just minutes before the explosion. In a few minutes a truck roared past me with Lieutenant Joe A. Mann sitting in the right seat. He was holding his right foot, which was missing its toes. Hey, I thought, there goes our last officer.

In short order I learned what had happened. I heard the shriek of an incoming projectile and hit the deck. It exploded about 50 yards away, too far for me to determine if it had caused any casualties. But it did enlighten me as to the source of the explosion which wreaked such havoc on A Company. A large Jap artillery shell had hit about 30 feet up on the trunk of the tree beneath which our headquarters group had been sitting. Exploding at that height it had the affect of an airburst. I guessed it had to come from "Pistol Pete," the gunner who manned the artillery pieces the Japs had landed in mid–October. He continued to shell us and inflict casualties as we moved eastward on the Government Trail. The Record of Events Journal put it succinctly: "At 1630 Japs shelled government trail resulting in large number of casualties." Wounded that day in the continuing shelling seriously enough to require evacuation were Privates Paul Petty, George Gardner, Orville Stevens, Charles Clifton, Edward Ludlum, Walter Green, Charles Howe, Claud Mosier, John Kernan, and Russell McCullough. The other companies in the battalion also lost a lot of men, killed and wounded. All in all, it was a bad day.

Until recently I was not absolutely certain as to the caliber of the artillery shell which hit the tree over my head nor of the shells which followed us in the eastward march back towards the Matanikau River. I guessed they were either 105 mm from the long-range rifle the Japs had used to bedevil the Henderson field area or, as I was inclined to believe, larger caliber howitzer shells. Now, thanks to William (Bill) Bartsch, I have the answer. Here is what Bill dug up:

> It appears that the firing came from one of the three 150 mm howitzers of the 2nd Company, 21st Independent Artillery Battalion, emplaced on the coast at the White River, three miles west of the mouth of the Matanikau

River. The gun position was wired to the Company's observation post at (Japanese) hill 903 to the south and evidently the battery had been informed by the post of the new location on November 11th of the 2nd Marines' 1st Battalion. In a letter to Akio Tani of April 18, 1990, the 2nd Company's CO, Captain Jinzou Tanaka, indicated that his guns were prepared to shoot "at zero range" as the enemy approached at the beginning of November [letter to William Bartsch, August 21, 1991].

A Company was now leaderless, but not for long. We still had two staff NCOs, Platoon Sergeants Wilbur Burgess and Howard Carpenter. Howard was senior and should have taken over but he declined the honor and, for a short while, we had Burgess as acting CO. We holed up that night on a well-blasted ridge a few hundred yards west of the Matanikau. We were a pretty sad and somewhat demoralized bunch. There were now less than 40 of us. Our morale was greatly boosted later that night by the arrival of hot chow, a glorious feast, baked beans. This had never happened before. We had always subsisted on C rations. I don't know who brought us the food but it sure was welcome.

On the following day we moved back across the Matanakau and dug in for the night. At about this time we received a new company commander, Captain William T. Bray. He had been a first lieutenant when we landed and was serving as our BN 4, Battalion Quartermaster, the officer responsible for supplies and equipment. This was to be his first command of troops. Not to worry, the senior NCOs, especially Wilbur Burgess, would show him what to do. Burgess was promoted to first sergeant.

At about 01:30 in the morning, November 13, we were awakened by the thunder of heavy guns from the sea. We learned later our Navy had intercepted a Jap fleet of two battleships, several cruisers and numerous destroyers on their way to shell and neutralize Henderson Field. The ensuing battle was costly for both sides. We lost two cruisers and four destroyers and the Japs lost a battleship and two destroyers. Over 1,400 U.S. sailors, including two U.S. admirals, Callaghan and Scott, died in the action. While not a clear-cut victory for us, the battle saved Henderson Field from another pasting.*

*Marines and soldiers who served in the ground fighting on the "Canal" tend to overlook or forget the tremendous casualties suffered by the sailors and Marines who served on the ships damaged or sunk in the seas around the island. In fact: "For every United

5. Tulagi and Guadalcanal

Later that morning we received orders to move eastward, all the way across the defensive perimeter, and set up a defensive line in the coconut grove east of the Tenaru River. It took all day to get there and the fox-holes we dug for protection were at best rudimentary, a shortcoming we soon regretted. Its losses the preceding night did not deter the Jap Navy from a second attempt to bombard Henderson Field and, unfortunately, we were in the line of fire. Shortly after midnight flares exploded overhead brightly illuminating our position and the nearby fighter strip which had been bulldozed out of a field a little southeast of the main runway. In very short order it became apparent the illumination was the prelude to a naval shelling. Two heavy cruisers with eight-inch guns and a bevy of destroyers arrived at 01:30 to finish the job aborted the night before. The shells arrived with a roar. Naval shells fired from close range have a very flat trajectory. They arrive at high speed with no advance warning of their approach. And they come in bunches, with six or seven ships all firing broadsides. The shells exploded all around us but most carried over our heads and exploded near the fighter strip. My A Company was dug in on the north end of the battalion's line and, for a change, lucked out with no casualties. The other companies of the battalion didn't fare so well, with three killed and 14 wounded. Late that afternoon A Company was sent to the fighter strip known as "Fighter One" to guard the planes not destroyed by the naval shelling. While we were setting up, a group of F4Fs landed. Two of the bunch crashed on the rough strip but the pilots were unhurt and, perhaps, the overturned planes were salvageable. A pilot from one of the planes which landed safely asked me what outfit I was with. When I told him the Second Marines he was astonished, saying, "Jesus Christ, are you guys still here? This is my second tour at this hellhole."

Being off the western front lines and in a reasonably secure area was not an unmixed blessing for we were bivouacked too close to the island's prime targets, the air strips. Naval shelling was infrequent but bombing by aircraft was a daily and nightly hazard. The attacks were carried out by flights of 20 or more two-engine Mitsubishi bombers we called "Bet-

States soldier or marine ashore who died, almost three sailors and marines in ship companies perished, 4,911." Richard B. Frank, *Guadalcanal*, 613–614.

tys." They bombed from high altitude, around 25,000 feet, and were pretty accurate in that they usually hit Henderson Field. The runway at the field was unpaved dirt covered with perforated steel plates called "Marston matting." The Seabees and Marine engineers became expert at filling bomb craters and getting the runway back in action in time to accept our fighters, which had been scrambled to intercept the bombers. If you weren't directly under the flight path of the bombers it was actually fun to watch our fighters dive into the Jap formation and cut it to pieces. From our safe position on the ground it resembled a pack of wolves attacking a flock of sheep. A bomber would be hit and forced to drop out of the formation where it would be finished off by our fighters.

At least initially, we did not send up fighters against night raids. The field was protected by 90-millimeter antiaircraft guns but the few times I saw them in use against a nighttime raid they appeared ineffective. The Bettys looked beautiful shining white up there when illuminated by our searchlights but the shells from our guns never seemed to explode among them. In fact they exploded all over the sky but not near the Jap formation. And the bad thing about antiaircraft fire is the fragments from the exploding shells come to earth in a lethal shower that scared the hell out of us earthlings. I can still hear them whirring and clunking into tree trunks and the ground. The rain of death didn't bother the permanent cadre around the airfield for they had bunkers and sandbag-roofed foxholes to hide in.

Large-scale air raids at night were somewhat unusual but the enemy did not completely abandon us. Each night a lone aircraft, which soon acquired the names "Washing Machine Charlie" and "Louie the Louse," circled the area for hours on end. Every now and then, at uncertain intervals and from various locations, the pilot would release a small bomb, probably about 100 pounds. Clearly, his purpose was not to destroy or cause injury but only to harass and cause sleeplessness. In that effort he was partially successful but for only a limited time. At first he kept me awake. I would lie awake in my foxhole reassuring myself with calculations as to the extremely long odds in my favor. After a few nights of that I became inured and slept through his nightly perambulations. We kept hearing rumors that a Major Smith, commander of one of the fighter squadrons,* was going to take a fighter aloft some night and knock the sucker down, but to my knowledge it never happened.

At about this time, mid–November, we received replacements to bring us back up to strength, or at least near strength. They arrived at night, in the rain, apprehensive and woebegone. I couldn't help feeling sorry for them but didn't reveal it. I can't remember how many were assigned to me but it was probably about six or eight. I remember two names, Olson and Johnson. When I looked quizzically at hearing these names, one of them said, "Honest, sir, that's our names." One of the group asked the dumbest question of World War II: "What happened to the guys we are replacing?" I mumbled something to the effect that we had a lot of guys shipped out as sick. I then put them to digging their foxholes, explaining that it was decidedly unhealthy to sleep above ground.

Replacement Olson was a fresh-cheeked farm boy from Minnesota with a most peculiar trait. During his first few nights on the island he would say a prayer before going to sleep. The odd thing about it was the prayer was said aloud! Everyone in earshot could hear it. And here is what he prayed: "Lord, help me to learn to swim, and if I am to die in this war let me die like a Marine." After a few nights of this I persuaded Olson that silent prayer was the norm on a battlefield. But I still marvel that this kid's greatest fear was not of getting killed or wounded but of dying unbravely! With recruits like that we were a cinch to win the war.

After about another week in that area just south of Henderson Field we moved back to the western front and sat up a defensive line a few yards east of the Matanikau River with A Company on the right with its flank on the beach. This was a reserve position; there were other Marine and Army units between us and the Japs. We spent the rest of the month patrolling and getting acquainted with our replacements. During this time my company killed but one Jap, an unlucky character who swam ashore one night. The poor guy probably intended to surrender.

Patrolling on the "Canal" was a nerve-racking experience. The jungle afforded the Japs perfect cover and made it impossible for the patrol

*Major John L. Smith was a much-decorated ace who shot down 19 Japanese aircraft.

to move silently enough to achieve surprise. As a result the first thing that alerted you to the presence of the enemy was the wounding or killing of one or more of your men in the point of the patrol. Then you had a helova time getting the wounded or dead out from under the muzzles of the gunners who shot them. For example, two of my friends, the Boyd brothers, Bob and Paul, were members of a patrol that ran into a Jap ambush manned with Nambu light machine guns. Instantly, four of the men were hit and down. When the corpsman went to their aid he was mortally wounded. Two of the downed Marines were dead. The other two, including Bob Boyd, were seriously wounded and evacuated from the island. Bob was particularly lucky; the bullet which found him entered at the point of his chin, traveled downward through his neck and exited from his back. The patrol's efforts to recover the three bodies were repulsed. I was doubly chagrined at this happening for it was my platoon's corpsman that died that day. He had been "borrowed" by the Boyds to fill in for their corpsman, who was ill.

However, the Japs didn't win them all. On December 16, a B Company patrol surprised a large enemy group bathing in the river and lolling about with absolutely no security posted. I wonder where they thought they were. By actual count, 20 of the group paid for their carelessness with their lives. In all likelihood these were newly-landed troops with no concept of proper battlefield conduct. On the following day, an A Company patrol killed seven enemy in the same area.

As a rule neither side took prisoners on Guadalcanal. But there is an exception to every rule and I was instrumental in effecting one exception. We were patrolling south along the east bank of the Matanakau when a lone Jap emerged from the brush about 30 feet to our front. He was unarmed and stood motionless. The BAR man next to me drew a bead on him but I knocked the muzzle up and told the others not to fire. I don't think I was moved by compassion but rather by the thought our intelligence people would be pleased with this rare find. I motioned the Jap to come forward and patted him down when he arrived. This wasn't good enough for my replacement platoon leader, Lieutenant Wickersham, who came up from his position at the rear of the patrol. He became very excited and demanded I reach into the guy's filthy pants pocket to remove an object which bulged there. I argued with him but relented and pulled out a small piece of rotting coconut. I then detailed two men to take the prisoner back. But Lt. Wickersham would have none of that—we, the entire patrol, would take him back. I remonstrated, pointing out that the R2 captain who sent us on these patrols was a hard-assed son of a bitch who would undoubtedly send us right back out. Of course I lost that argument and we slipped and slid the couple of miles back to our lines. As I had tried to warn our peerless leader, the captain was not at all pleased that one of his patrols had returned without orders and he proceeded to explain to Lieutenant Wickersham in purple prose that he had better get his patrol back to its assigned area pronto or face unspeakable disciplinary consequences. My enjoyment at this lively scene was tempered by the fact we had to retrace our steps back into Jap territory. I was stuck with this officer as my platoon leader for the remainder of the campaign. He was an adequate platoon leader but I couldn't get along with him—just incompatible, I guess. He became the company executive officer when we got to New Zealand.

By mid–December my malaria was pretty bad. I could function but had a constant headache. I had lost a lot of weight and had occasional chills, especially when my foxhole filled with water during a nighttime rain. The corpsman who took my temperature now and then told me if I had a temperature over 102 for three consecutive days I would have to go to the rear for quinine treatment. The medics were concerned that the disease could be fatal if it infected the brain, so-called "cerebral malaria." At any rate, I crossed that threshold and was sent to the rear. I hitched a ride on a passing truck and arrived in the rear area near Henderson Field after dark. The driver had no idea where the Navy sick bay was but suddenly said, "There's a hospital," and dropped me off near a group of large tents where I joined a line of figures moving toward a person seated at a table. When I got to the table the seated one looked at the casualty tag my corpsman had hung on my blouse and exclaimed in surprise, "You're a Marine!" In my addled state I didn't know what he was talking about until he said I was at an Army hospital. He at first said they had no facility for treating malaria but after consultation with another doctor assigned me to one of the big hospital tents.

I was assigned a cot and gratefully settled down for the night. But it was not to be. The occupant of the next cot wanted to talk. He told me he was a captain, company commander, hospitalized for an aching back. He said he had been carrying a water can when a mortar round blew him off a ridge. At the time I wondered what a captain was doing carrying a water can. That's privates' work. But I said nothing and tried to get to sleep. I had just dozed off when sirens sounded and voices shouted, "CONDITION RED," the signal for an air raid. We were led out of the tent to a sort of open trench where we squatted for several hours until the all clear was sounded. I don't think any Jap planes came over that night, not even "Washing Machine Charlie."

I was awakened the next morning by loud voices. One of the Army doctors was reading the riot act to the captain in the next cot. The doctor called him a duty shirking, cowardly bastard who was a disgrace to the Army. The captain weakly protested saying his back really hurt and he couldn't go back to his unit. This loud argument went on for several minutes until the doctor gave up and stalked away in disgust. After he left, the captain sought sympathy from me. I wanted to tell him to get his ass out of bed and back to the front but refrained, thinking he would have been of no use to his company with or without a bad back.

In mid-morning I was accosted by an elderly (probably mid-thirties) senior NCO, a first sergeant or sergeant major who was clearly out of his mind. He grabbed my blouse with both hands, thrust his whiskered face close to mine and shouted, "You've been here a long time. You know what it's like — they're in the trees, they're everywhere! It's suicide out there!" As quickly as possible I extricated myself from his grasp and looked up the doctor in charge of the hospital, convinced him that I was completely well and wanted to go back to my unit. After some argument he gave me a chit to recover my rifle from their property sergeant and I was on my way. In retrospect it was apparent that, lacking a malaria ward, I had been assigned to their nut ward, the place they put malingerers, like the captain, and real nut cases, like the sergeant.

Back with the company I popped atabrine pills with enthusiasm and eventually felt better. I had two malaria attacks when we were in New Zealand and nothing thereafter. Our living conditions during our entire time on the Canal ranged between bad and miserable. Our only shelter was the poncho we all carried — no tents, no shelter halves. We always slept in our foxholes and covered up with the poncho if it rained. During a heavy nighttime rain the only warm part of my body was the part submerged in the water at the bottom of the foxhole. My body heat warmed the water. As the campaign wore on, we were able occasionally to set up company messes. Our steady diet of C rations was augmented by rudimentary meals whipped up by our mess sergeant. Canned vegetables, canned fruit, dehydrated potatoes and canned meat, usually Spam. At one point the Spam was replaced by canned tongue from New Zealand. Both of these canned meats were too rich for my stomach. I couldn't keep them down and I frequently gave my portion to a less fastidious comrade.

When in a static position we dug slit trenches to handle bodily wastes. Our diet and chronic diarrhea produced watery bowl movements. Toilet tissue, we called it "shit paper," was always in short supply. Occasionally we got only one roll for the platoon. The platoon leader we had for the last month of the campaign took custody of our platoon's roll and reluctantly doled it out, sheet by sheet, to those in need. That stuff was like gold to us and we watched like hawks to make sure it was equitably distributed. How did we keep clean? Well, actually we didn't. In late November, A Company was assigned the right flank of the battalion, which put us on the beach a few hundred yards east of the Matanakau River. Here we were able to wash ourselves and our clothing in the ocean. Someone even produced a bar of saltwater soap. It didn't work very well but it was better than nothing. My clothing at this stage was pretty rudimentary. My underwear and socks had long since melted away, leaving me with only trousers and blouse. The buttons had rusted out of my blouse necessitating my keeping it closed with little lengths of communication wire. "Raggedy-ass Marines" we surely were! Most of the time we were positioned inland, in the jungle or on the grassy hill tops. There we had no facilities to keep clean. Water had to be carried to us in five-gallon cans, and it was strictly for drinking. It is amazing how one can get acclimated to being filthy for days on end. However, not bathing had one significant advantage, it seemed to discourage mosquitoes. This was made obvious when I occasionally put a little water in my helmet and washed my hands. In short order my clean hands were targeted by rapacious mosquitoes. They ignored my unwashed arms, face and neck, which led me to believe that human skin, if left unwashed, produces a natural repellant. This belief is supported by the fact that the unwashed, near-naked Melanesian natives were not bothered by mosquitoes, while a well-bathed Marine was attacked by swarms.

On December 14 we moved back west across the Matanikau River and took up a position on a ridge about a mile from the beach. This was not a fighting position but was on the reverse slope looking eastward toward Henderson Field. From here we resumed almost daily patrolling to the south. At dawn one morning I noticed an aircraft headed in my direction from the south and at very low altitude. The airplane looked kind of funny. There seemed to be too much dihedral in the wings for an American plane and sure enough when the craft came down the valley abreast of my hilltop position it was a Jap bomber. The bomber turned right and swooped over Henderson Field, dropping bombs on a line of parked aircraft. It then turned north and attacked a ship, a New Zealand destroyer or corvette, cruising about three or four miles off-shore. But this audacious venture was not to go unpunished. While this was going on one of our P-38s was coming from the west toward me, wheels down for a landing on the airfield. He was apparently alerted of the enemy's presence by radio for his wheels came up and he banked left over the ocean. He approached the bomber from the left rear, fired one burst and turned it into a ball of fire. The Air Corps fighter then resumed his landing approach as if the whole thing had been routine. I thought to myself, "Man — that's the way to fight a war, not in the mud of these stinking foxholes!" The incident I just described was witnessed and remembered by others. In his excellent book, *Faithful Warriors,** good friend Dean Ladd reports the event as follows:

> At daybreak on one of the last mornings, a Japanese bomber with its engines quietly idling glided in over Henderson Field and dropped a harassing bomb. Then it climbed to leave. A P-38, returning from dawn patrol, intercepted it and blasted it out of the sky in one pass. Everybody around Henderson Field that morning was awakened by that event and shouted a spontaneous "Hurray." It reminded me of cheering after a goal in a football game.

*Annapolis: Naval Institute Press, 2009.

5. Tulagi and Guadalcanal

This left a very vivid memory for Marine Harry Adkins. He was on a high ridge position watching the enemy bomber glide toward him at the same altitude. The left wing tip cleared him by only ten feet and he surprisingly even had eye contact with the pilot and exchanged salutes.

I wonder if Harry Adkins was standing on the ridge which provided my vantage point?

Christmas Day was miserable. We moved south and west to a new defensive line. It rained like hell all day and, since this was a new front, we made the move in a skirmish line, slipping and sliding up and down some near-vertical ridges. We were wedged between Army units, the "Peep Troops"* on the right and the Army 182nd Regiment on the left. But in this position my platoon again dug in on the military crest of the reverse slope facing east overlooking the Matanakau valley. Unfortunately I didn't dig a proper foxhole but merely dug into the slope far enough to make a level place to lie down. It was a two-man hole, i.e., wide enough for two men to lie down side by side. My companion in the hole was one of the new replacements, a diminutive kid named Romkowsky.

We continued almost daily patrols from this position. I remember one of them I led because of a very embarrassing boo-boo I committed. We had just completed searching an abandoned Jap bivouac when I, the seasoned combat NCO, had an accidental rifle discharge, a goof only raw recruits commit. For obvious reasons weapons are never fired on patrol without lethal intent. The discharge of my piece scared the crap out of the patrol, which scattered and hit the deck. My excuse was good but probably unpersuasive; I had decided to extract and discard the round in the rifle's chamber and carry the weapon with five rounds in the magazine and an empty chamber. I pulled the bolt back and thought the round had been extracted and fallen into the brush in which I was standing. But I was wrong, the extractor had slipped off the head of the cartridge and it was still in the chamber. When I worked the bolt forward and pulled the trigger to uncock the piece the round went off.

*The official name of this battalion-size unit was Mobile Combat Reconnaissance Squadron. When formed in New Caledonia it was equipped with jeeps to operate as a mobile strike force but the terrain on Guadalcanal was not amenable to this concept and they fought on foot. And fought well, I must add. Jeeps were called "peeps" when they first appeared in the Army in New Caledonia and hence the name "Peep Troops."

The night of January 5 was among the worst I have spent on this earth. At about dusk that evening a new private reported to me. I have forgotten his name and the reason he was transferred to us from his original outfit. He asked me where to dig in and I told him this was not a fighting position and it didn't matter where he dug his foxhole. He chose a spot about ten feet to the right of my spot. At about eight o'clock the first round arrived. It exploded 20 or 30 yards from my hole. I knew it was a mortar from the brief sssst sound that preceded the detonation. Mortars don't give you a warning whine or shriek as artillery does. When you hear an incoming mortar round it's already there. You only have time to flinch and perhaps pucker your sphincter. That first round was followed by dozens of others exploding all around our position. Shell fragments saturated the air and made a mess out of the poncho I had erected on sticks over my hole. Romkosky began screaming and blubbering. I could hear shouts from other men on the hillside. I don't know how long it lasted but it seemed to span lifetimes. I can't explain why but that mortar barrage was the most terrifying episode of my combat career. Going ashore under fire at Tarawa and a heavy artillery barrage on Saipan were scary, but not quite as bad. I hate mortars to this day.

It seemed apparent to me at the time that this was friendly fire. We had not experienced heavy mortar fire from the Japs, although they had 81-millimeters. I had only experienced their so-called "knee mortars" projectiles, which can't compare in size or lethality to the stuff we were getting that night. Where was it coming from and why did it continue for so long a time? It was coming from an 81-millimeter mortar battery of the 182nd Army Regiment situated behind us on the east bank of the Matanakau. We couldn't get it stopped because the first rounds severed our only telephone line to the rear. A runner carried the word back to battalion CP and it was relayed to the Army from there. When it was over I took a fast check of the platoon and found one wounded badly in the legs and two missing, including the new man who reported in the early evening. The missing were found the next morning. But the discovery was as gruesome as it gets. Both men had suffered direct hits that had literally shredded their bodies into fragments scattered all over the hillside. We gathered up the pieces with entrenching shovels and buried them in their former foxholes. The reason for such complete destruction was the nature of the ammunition the Army was using. The shells were equipped with one-tenth-of-a-second-delay fuses which may have actually penetrated and exploded beneath the bodies of the victims. The fact that these fuses were used saved A Company from greater losses, for when shells penetrate and explode beneath the ground the shell fragments are directed upwards rather than horizontally as with normal mortar ammunition. The delay fuses were used to penetrate and explode inside bunkers and when the target area was heavily wooded, for regular fuses would cause the projectiles to explode harmlessly in the treetops.

From our position on this hilltop we had a panoramic view of the sea (later called "Iron Bottom Bay" in memory of the many U.S. and Jap ships sunk there), with Savo Island in the foreground and Tulagi and Florida Island in the distance. The view to Jap territory in the west was enhanced every evening by the most spectacular sunsets imaginable. We theorized that the dust kicked up by the explosions of our artillery shells and aerial bombs caused the painted sunsets. At night the Southern Cross constellation dominated our sky and gave us something to think about while standing the endless nighttime watches. When active enemy contact was feared, every other man was on watch. When things were quiet, we might have only one man in each squad awake. The watch lasted two endless hours, but no one was caught sleeping on watch on this island. The indispensable equipment for the sentries was a watch to tell when it was time to awaken your relief and get some blessed shuteye. But watches were few and those available were not equipped with luminous dials. This lack was not a problem on moonlit nights but caused a lot of eyestrain when stars were the only source of light. Illumination or "star" shells lofted intermittently by our artillery helped a lot. My disgraced platoon leader had the only watch in our platoon and, when he finally persuaded the medical people to evacuate him, I insisted he leave his watch with the platoon. Months later, in New Zealand, he showed up at our camp and asked me to return the watch because it was a gift from his parents. I returned it to him without hesitation, just to get him out of my sight as quickly as possible.

On January 10 the Army artillery dropped several short rounds in our area, wounding two men in B Company and one guy in my company. I wished they would stop doing that; it is hard on your nerves.

We were interacting a little bit with the Army. They would occasionally send a few soldiers to accompany us on patrol. Their principal purpose was to become familiar with the territory they would eventually attack and occupy.

Shortly thereafter, on January 13, we kicked off on our final attack, or "push," as we called offensives. The attack started at 0500 and we, that is the battalion, had reached the assigned objective or phase line by 0730. We had 19 casualties with only one Killed in Action (KIA), a lieutenant in C Company. The enemy dead totaled about 50 according to the guys in the front of the assault. My platoon was in support, about a hundred or so yards behind the lead elements. This position gave me the opportunity to watch our 60mm mortar team in action. The guys firing the piece, Bigelow and Howard Boling, were a pleasure to watch. They had prepared their ammunition in advance, removing the shells from their packages and setting the increments for the anticipated range. The gunner, Bigelow, fed the tube with two hands. I don't know how many shells he had in the air before the first one landed but I am guessing at least six or more. It must have been very uncomfortable for the Japs in the impact area.

This was the only time we experimented with using shotguns in the assault. We had been issued a couple of Winchester or Remington pumps a few days before the action. It didn't turn out real well. The buckshot cartridges supplied were of the usual civilian type paper construction which swelled up in the jungle humidity and blocked the action of the guns. One of our new replacements, Channing Miller, came back from the front in tears. He told me three Japs ran out of a bunker less than ten yards from him and got away because his shotgun wouldn't fire. He should have been happy they were running away and not right at him. We never tried shotguns again, although I learned cartridges with a full copper casing were later made available.

This offensive followed on the heels of a three-day army attack in the hills to our south. The Army effort was immortalized by a book, later a movie, *The Thin Red Line*, written by James Jones, an enlisted man in the 27th Infantry. The Army had the toughest job. The Second Battalion of the 27th Infantry had two officers and 29 enlisted killed, but killed an estimated 170 Japs. The battalion's executive officer, Captain Charles W. Davis, was awarded the Medal of Honor for his exploits in the fight.

5. Tulagi and Guadalcanal

At about noon we were relieved by the newly-arrived Sixth Marines and retired to a perimeter defense position near the Lunga River. Of course this put us back in the sights of the high-level Jap bombers. They hit close one time and B Company had a few casualties. Despite our rearward position we still had to conduct patrols to the hills and jungle south of Henderson Field. We were also put to work manhandling supplies for the Army near Lunga Lagoon.

There has always been a bit of resentment among Second Marine Division veterans that our participation in the Guadalcanal campaign has been overlooked by historians and other writers. The first oversight of our role was in the Final Report on the campaign as prepared by First Division personnel. On page 80 in the original draft it is stated that in our Second Division fighting in November, west of the Matanakau, we "...resorted to frontal attacks rather than to methods of encirclement resulted in an extremely slow advance." In a 1945 letter responding to this criticism, Col. John Arthur, Second Division CO, stated, "The statement ... is not, in my opinion, justified ... all assigned objectives were

My platoon's survivors shortly before leaving Guadalcanal. All but seven are replacements. The arrow points to the author.

reached on schedule and according to plan, and the military situation, terrain, enemy dispositions and distance to the final objective did not call for or warrant any encirclement or enveloping movements...."

Col. Wood Kyle, in his memo reviewing the Report, objected to statements which appeared in "Annex N (Intelligence)" of the Final Report charging that the November drive "never achieved the objective of pushing the Japs back beyond the Poha River. So firmly entrenched were the enemy that the Marines were held for 12 days, suffering notable losses." Col Kyle's memo states, "The above statement is not correct," and refers the reader to Col. Arthur's report, which states his directions from Gen. Vandegrift on November 3 were "to establish a small beachhead in the area about a thousand yards west of Point Cruz and to contain the enemy until reinforcements could be furnished."

Before leaving this Guadalcanal discussion I must repeat here the text of a letter I wrote to the editor of *Leatherneck*, the Marines magazine, which was published in the March 1993 edition:

Dear Sir:

Congratulations! The November issue is a real blockbuster. The well written Guadalcanal articles stirred long dormant memories of events and battles, episodes of triumph and, yes, intervals of terror and despair. Of particular interest was Eric Hammel's piece on the November offensive west of the Matanikau River.

Mr. Hammel has done his usual good job in researching and reporting the operation, but I can't let stand the impression one gets from his narrative that the only role played by my unit, 1st Bn. 2d Marines, was to occupy the "newly conquered ground" after the conquering troops (5th Marines) had been withdrawn. It wasn't like that at all, but I can understand Hammel's error, for the usual reference sources, such as the Guadalcanal monograph and First Division history make no mention of 2d Marines participation in the fighting around Point Cruz. I feel strongly about these omissions because our fight on Nov. 3 was as fierce and bloody as the fighting to reduce the Point Cruz pocket on that day.

The original plan as set out in Operation Order 13–42 was for the 1st and 2d Bns. 5th Marines to attack west along the Government Trail with the 1st and 2d Bns. of the 2d Marines following immediately behind. At 0800 Nov. 2, my battalion moved out with orders to pass through the 5th Marines and continue the offensive.

The strong enemy resistance at the Point Cruz pocket made that course impracticable and at 1300 we were ordered to circle the pocket and take up a position on Phase Line 0–2 west of Point Cruz. We accomplished this by 1800 and set up a line facing west with the 5th Marines' line about 30 yards to our rear, facing east toward the surrounded Japs. We killed five or six enemy that night at a cost of two wounded.

At 0630, Nov. 3, we attacked west with our right flank on the beach and our left extending inland for some 400 yards. We met no resistance until about noon when we hit the Japanese main line of resistance and all *hell* broke loose! Heavy and light machine guns firing from perfectly camouflaged emplacements cut into us with terrible effect. Heavy mortar fire, pre-sighted along the trail, pounded into the middle of our line. Within minutes, we had taken 74 casualties with a high proportion killed. (My outfit, A Company, had 7 killed, 11 wounded.)

We built a defense line short of our deepest penetration and remained there until relieved by a battalion of the 164th Infantry on the morning of November 5. Our stay on the line was not uneventful. At 0200 we were attacked by a force of about 200 enemy.

They hit [where] A and B Companies joined, and fortunately, where B Co had set up one of its heavy water-cooled machine guns. With the help of beautifully accurate fire from the 11th Marines howitzers, we survived and disposed of a large number of the enemy, capturing several machine guns, many rifles, swords and several officer dispatch cases.

We again attacked on November 10. This time we were on the extreme left flank, about 500 yards inland from our earlier positions. To say this was a bad day understates the situation which developed. We again ran into well-concealed machine guns and mortars and had to withdraw. We lost our battalion commander, Lt. Col. Hill, and my company lost 20 men with four killed. That was not a great way to observe the Marine Corps birthday.

We withdrew on the 11th, and during the withdrawal, "Pistol Pete" with his long-range howitzer, dropped round after round along our route back to the Matanikau. One "jackpot" round struck about 30 feet high on a huge tree under which A Co was taking a break. That explosion killed the company commander, his exec and a private. It wounded our last remaining lieutenant, first sergeant, gunny and a platoon sergeant. A company was then led by a platoon sergeant.

So, contrary to everything most people have read about Guadalcanal, there were troops there other than the First Division and the Raiders. Indeed, the 2d Marines made the first landing on Aug. 7, and were still on the attack in January 1943, long after our First Marine Division friends had departed.

Finally, in this writing I have tried to describe and memorialize the role one company of the Second Marine Division played in the Guadalcanal Campaign. I recognize our accomplishments pale in comparison with those of the First Division units that bore the brunt of the fight and saved the island from recapture by the enemy. But I hope that future historians will at least acknowledge that the Second Division was there and contributed the lives of 272 Marines and suffered 915 wounded in action.

On January 31 we boarded LCVPs and boated out to and boarded the ship that had brought us to the island, the USS *President Jackson.* We were delighted to get back on board, get cleaned up in a heavenly shower bath and swap tales with the many Navy friends we had made on the long voyage from the United States. I was personally uneasy until we had put a day's sailing distance from "Iron Bottom Sound." It would have been high irony to have survived six months of land warfare and be killed by a Jap bomber or submarine while at sea. Happily, nothing untoward happened and we disembarked on February 7 in the beautiful harbor of Wellington, New Zealand.

6

Respite in New Zealand

If the Marine Corps had known what an ideal "liberty port" New Zealand was we would probably not have been sent there for fear we would become soft and lose our fighting edge. For ideal it was, not only because of the brisk climate to aid in recovery from malaria and other tropical diseases, and not because of the beautiful hills and streams for outdoor recreation, but primarily because of the welcoming, open and sincerely friendly New Zealand people. Almost without exception they opened their hearts and homes to us. What greatly added to our good fortune was the almost total absence of young New Zealand males. They were away fighting as part of the British Army in North Africa. This left all the young ladies, "Sheilas," to use the New Zealand appellation, bored and lonely. What more could a lonely and lusty young Marine ask for. Truly, most of us thought we had died and gone to heaven.

In retrospect, our living conditions left much to be desired. However, after six months in a foxhole, a cot and a roof over our heads felt downright luxurious. We were bivouacked in pyramidal six-man tents. Each tent had a small potbellied coal stove whose heat became mighty welcome as the season progressed. We had outdoor privies which had to be burned out periodically. Cold water showers and cold water wooden wash racks kept our bodies and clothing reasonably clean.

The camp was located at a place called McKay's Crossing. We were connected to Wellington by about 30 miles of narrow-gauge railroad. The nearest town, really a small village, was Paekakariki, which we shortened to "Piecock." After a bit we learned to emulate the natives by calling McKay's Crossing "Mackie's Crossing. We picked up a lot of the native expressions. Instead of pals or friends we had "cobbers." If something was okay or all right we said it was "fair dinkum." If it was really outstanding it was "too right," or if a superlative was needed it was "too bloody right." But after awhile I learned not to say "bloody" in polite company.

Apparently the Marine Corp's first objective was to fatten us up, for the mess halls put out huge servings of food, most of it pretty good, and urged us to load up. I accepted the invitation, for my weight had dropped to 138 pounds, 30 pounds or so under my normal weight. We were even permitted to fill our mess gear with ice cream and fruit, an invitation I frequently accepted. In very little time I hit the scale at 169 pounds or, in New Zealand terms, "13 stone." The Corp's other objective was to get everyone back to good health, and I was swept up in this campaign. For several weeks the doctors and corpsmen attached to our battalion had tried in vain to heal jungle sores I had on my right foot and left elbow. Nothing they tried worked and I was dispatched to the naval hospital at Silver Stream, a large, rambling facility equipped to handle all kinds of wounds and diseases. My treatment was radiation of some type. But the problem was that they could give me only one shot at a time and the shots had to be spaced a week apart. This kept me out of action until the treatment ended. Unfortunately I could not wear a shoe and thus could not go ashore. I was bored, angry and apprehensive as to my position back at the company. I had been promoted to sergeant and appointed Acting Platoon Sergeant of the First Platoon. I didn't have a platoon leader but new second lieutenants were expected any time. I had high hopes of getting a competent replacement for the disgrace I was blessed with on the Canal.

I had one adventure while in the hospital. One of my frequently-filled molars had finally given up the ghost and only the double root remained. The hospital had a dental clinic that competently and painlessly removed the now toothless roots. With the extraction completed the doctor packed the cavity with a white powder that tasted a bit sweet. Shortly after I returned to my ward my back began to itch intensely. I stood it for awhile but eventually asked a nurse to look at it. She took a look and told me I had a rash of some sort. About this time we both noticed my chest and stomach were turning red. She became alarmed and said she had to get a doctor to look at this strange phenomenon. He arrived shortly, took one look and said, "We have to get this guy out of here and into isolation." They wheeled my bed the length of the ward and into a small separate room. Soon other doctors arrived and noted that the rash now covered me from head to foot. Eventually one of them asked what I had eaten that day. When my answer offered no clue as to the cause, he asked what I had done during the day. I told him about the dental work and he asked what medication I had received. I said I didn't know but that the cavity had been packed with something that tasted like sugar. A look of relief came over him and he said, "Hell, take him back to the ward. All he has is an allergic reaction to sulfanilamide." Needless to say, I too was relieved to know I didn't have bubonic plague or some other noxious disease. The rash and itching went away in a few hours. The radiation therapy healed my "jungle rot" before I went completely bonkers in confinement.

The first thing I discovered when I got back to the company was my 03 rifle had been replaced with an M1 Garand. What a blow! That old World War I–type bolt-action rifle had saved my life and dealt severely with the enemy. It would always work under all conditions and I did not trust this semiautomatic replacement even though it was capable of firing eight rapid shots. Would the son-of-a-gun work in a landing if you had to drag it through wet sand or in a swamp if covered with mud? I never put it to a real test but millions of soldiers and Marines did and found it eminently satisfactory.

During our stay in New Zealand we were given only one lengthy liberty. I do not remember if it was for one week, two weeks or ten days. Bruce Coote, Ed Clark and I reasoned we would have a better time if we got away from the horde of reveling Marines who descended on nearby Wellington. Someone had read or heard that the coastal town of Napier was the place where New Zealanders vacationed so we boarded the train and set out. The 150-mile journey took most of a day for the train contained freight and stock cars as well as passenger cars. It stopped at every village and feed lot. We discovered that the country was one big sheep ranch and train moved sheep from one farm to another. It takes a bit of time to drive sheep from a pen into a railroad car but the ranchers and their dogs were fun to watch. I don't remember where we stayed the first night in Napier but I suspect it was the YMCA hostel or something of that kind.

The next day we explored the town and found to our delight we seemed to be the only Marines to have found the place. It was quite beautiful with wide beaches and a paved walkway along the shore called, rather appropriately I thought, the Marine Parade. We had finished a delightful fish and chips lunch and were strolling along the parade when three young ladies stopped their car next to us and asked if we would like to go to a party. We were almost too stunned to reply. We had not spoken to or even seen a girl for eight months and here were three lookers asking if we wanted to party! Never in our wildest dreams did we imagine getting female companionship, except the type that frequents bars and speakeasies. We stammered our acceptance and squeezed into the car. When we arrived at the private home of one of the girls we were served tea and cookies. This was a comedown for we had anticipated somewhat less staid refreshments. When we voiced this feeling things improved, for some beer and a bottle of gin appeared. After a few drinks we danced to music from the radio or from records, I don't remember which.

The girls were about our age, early twenties, and, to put it nicely, of proportionate height and weight. One was married to a soldier serving somewhere in Africa, and two, Vi and Poppy, were single. While all were comely, Poppy was clearly the prettiest and liveliest and I zeroed in on her as my date for the evening. She apparently liked my company and we exchanged life histories. Her name was Beth Poppelwell. A radio station employed her as hostess of a children's show. Her mother worked at the local hospital as a nurse and her father was a "commercial traveler," that is, a traveling salesman. She had a brother named Bill who had been crippled in an earthquake and was away in college, exempt from army service. Bill was going to school in Wellington.

Beth and I became good friends in short order and she invited me to her home to meet her mother. We hit it off pretty well for she was a no-nonsense type of woman. It was through Mrs. Poppelwell I was able to inform my parents I was in New Zealand. Our censors would not permit us to reveal our whereabouts, although Tokyo Rose told the world many times the Second Marines were in New Zealand. She even described one of our practice maneuvers, which had turned into a fiasco. To get the word to my parents Mrs. Poppelwell wrote them a letter couched in terms to lead any censors to believe they were friends of long standing. She wrote that "Bill" had visited her but did not write anything to reveal that "Bill" was a United States Marine. It worked and my folks got the word that I was well and content.

Early in our stay in New Zealand the time arrived for officers, usually company commanders, to appraise and grade the men under their commands. The men were assigned numerical grades on a scale from zero to four in five categories: Military Efficiency, Neatness and Military Bearing, Intelligence, Obedience, and Sobriety. The marks or grades were entered in the Marines Record Book, which goes with each man throughout his Marine Corps career. This gives new commanding officers a view of the past performance of a Marine as opined by past COs. In my view the most significant of the categories was Military Efficiency.

As stated above Captain William T. Bray became our new Company Commander when Captain Fuhrhop was killed on November 11, 1942. Bray had never commanded troops and, of course, had never marked or graded them and, as I learned, had not the least idea as to how that duty was to be accomplished. When I heard our record books had been marked I asked to see mine and, to my horror, discovered that my grade for Military Efficiency had been lowered from 3.6 to 2.4. When I confronted the captain he explained that I was only a corporal during the grading period and that 2.8 was the highest grade he gave to corporals. I remonstrated, asking how it would look to future COs to get a Marine whose Military Efficiency was downgraded after six months in combat? He said this was his system and I was stuck with it. Being somewhat of a sea lawyer I wasn't going to let that be the last word and I borrowed an officer's manual from one of the lieutenants and showed the section to Bray which instructed the grading officer that the ideal Marine would rate a 4.0 no matter what his rank was and lesser marks would be given to Marines which fell below that ideal. Thus privates and corporals could and frequently were given higher grades than sergeants and staff NCOs. But the captain was unmoved and refused to upgrade the mark. My annoyance at this obstinacy in the face of proof that he was wrong was heightened by the fear that this guy would do the wrong thing in combat and get some people killed.

However, my chagrin over the lowered mark was short-lived. After our first lengthy liberty the ruling powers decreed there would be no more weekend or longer leaves during the intensified training we were undergoing. But the senior NCOs in A Company had an arrangement with First Sergeant Burgess that allowed us to go ashore without being marked absent. If higher authority discovered your absence it was understood that he would report you were AWOL.

One week I accepted an invitation to spend a few days in Napier with the Poppelwell family. One afternoon, when Beth was at work, I went to the local movie theater. While the movie was being screened a typewritten note was flashed on the screen asking Sergeant Rogal to call Mrs. Poppelwell. I immediately got in touch with her and she said Burgess had called and told her to tell me that I was going to be decorated the following morning at a regimental formation. Needless to say there was no way in the world that I could stay out of the brig if I missed that formation. With the Poppelwells' help I got permission to ride the cab of a freight train leaving Napier that evening. Before I boarded, Poppy gave me a rare, and in those times almost priceless, gift, a fifth of scotch whiskey. I got aboard and had a good time talking to the engineer and fireman but the train stopped at every farm along the way and I became increasingly worried I would be late. When we finally got to McKay's Crossing the engineer stopped the train at the camp gate and I hit the ground running. Friends from the company met me and got my shoes shined and gave my pants a quick press. I washed off the cinders, shaved and got into the uniform in time to fall in with the company and march to the parade ground for the formation. The ceremony was quite impressive, with the band and the entire regiment marching by the reviewing stand where I and the other two medal recipients were standing. Our battalion commander, Major Kyle, and a Sergeant Cooper from C Company got Silver Stars and I got the Navy and Marine Corps Medal for my swim to rescue the downed pilot on October 13, 1942. After the formation I was interviewed by a correspondent, Ben Price, who posted a good story with the Associated Press. My hometown paper gave the story a banner headline across the full width of the front page. Never in history has so much been made of so little. But the whole thing was worthwhile, for when I got back to the company area, Captain Bray showed me my record book with the rating for Military Efficiency restored to its former level. Maybe there was hope for this character after all.

At about this time I was given command of the First Platoon. It was great for awhile to run the platoon without a lieutenant but all good things must end sometime and, within a few weeks, I was blessed with a new platoon leader, a newly commissioned "Mustang" second lieutenant, Armstead E. Ross. Lt. Ross had been a drill instructor and wrongly concluded that the proper way to run a platoon was the way it was done in boot camp. The first time he addressed the platoon he told them, "I'm a Marine 24 hours a day and by God that's what each of you will be!" Our green replacements were cowed by this pronouncement but the combat-experienced men rolled their eyes, knowing full well that this clown had no idea as to what being a Marine in combat was all about. In my first conversation with Lt. Ross he told me he had "selected" me to be his platoon sergeant even though he had been told that I was a "Bolshevik." He said he liked Bolsheviks.

It didn't take long for Lt. Ross to get off on the wrong foot with most of the battalion. Shortly after he took over the platoon, the battalion was trucked to a beach to practice rubber boat operations. The problem was that the South Pacific breakers on this beach were too high to permit the boats to be launched. However, we tried without much success. Despite having four men hanging on to each side of the boats it was impossible to get them through the surf. The men soon became soaked so Mr. Ross permitted one of our squads to strip down to their skivvies for a try. That didn't help, and as these winter waves broke over our men's involuntary screams filled the air. This perfectly natural reaction to a cold water dousing greatly perturbed Lt. Ross. With the entire battalion, including the colonel and his staff, looking on, he had me fall in the platoon and bring them to attention. Then, in his best DI manner and voice, he castigated them as a disgrace to the Marine Corps and hit them where it hurt the most by restricting them to camp, i.e. no liberty or weekend passes until further notice. While this was going on the battalion headquarters staff was facing us from a scant 50 feet away. I am sure Lt. Ross thought he was impressing them with this demonstration of leadership.

That night in the NCO club battalion Sergeant Major Charles Funk told me Colonel Kyle was less than impressed with the lieutenant's leadership demonstration and had so commented to his staff. The sergeant major asked me if I would appreciate it if Lt. Ross were taught a lesson and brought down a peg or two. I told him I thought the lesson was overdue and asked how he could bring this about. "It will be easy," he said. The lieutenant would be assigned the duty of court martial recorder. He would be required to submit a report to the colonel on each court martial, a task no green second lieutenant could properly perform without the sergeant major's assistance, which in this case would be denied. It worked like a charm. The reports were all screwed up and Lt. Ross was dressed down and restricted by an irate battalion commander. The moral? Junior officers should keep a low profile when they join an experienced outfit.

We spent the months of September and October in intensive training in the New Zealand hills. We fired a so-called combat range where targets of opportunity appeared suddenly as you advanced through the brush. We went on night compass problems in which you were given three or four azimuths which, if properly followed, would bring you back to the starting point. On many of our hikes through the countryside we were accompanied by stray dogs which had taken up residence in the Marine camps where they had become pets. These dogs soon became a problem when they accompanied us afield for they harassed and mutilated sheep. Orders were issued directing companies to shoot any dog they witnessed attacking sheep. Each company appointed at least one man to carry live ammunition during field excursions and on our next hike into the hills I was assigned the job of executioner. We had marched only a mile or so from camp when the reason for the order became all too obvious. The mongrels that had followed us attacked a flock of sheep. They ran alongside a sheep and bit at its underside until it was disemboweled. It was an awful sight to see the poor animals running with their intestines trailing on the ground. But I had an accident which prevented me from taking a shot at their tormentors When I clambered over a fence to get a good shot at the miscreants I twisted my right knee out of joint. The knee had been injured in high school football and re-injured when I was at Quantico. Each occurrence was accompanied by excruciating pain and an inability to straighten out the leg. Needless to say I was unable to shoot the dogs and had to be carried off the field and driven back to sick bay.

After a day or two of examinations and treatment the doctors told me they could not correct the matter with their facilities and I would be sent back to the States for surgery. That sounded fine to me but alas it was not to be. My company CO, Captain Bray, told the doctors I could not be spared, and within a few days I was back limping around the company area. In a couple of weeks I could walk without pain and, in Navy medical parlance, was "fit for duty." Bray's insistence on keeping me was because he had selected my platoon as the "assault platoon" for the next operation. When I asked, "Why me?" I was told the platoon was picked because neither Ross nor I was married and at least either the platoon sergeant or the platoon leader of each other platoon was a married man. Big deal! I do not know to this day if they were pulling my leg. At any rate the platoon was soon engaged in maneuvers as a unit separate from the company. The scenario as explained to us was that during the next operation the battalion would be charged with attacking on a very narrow, two platoon front. A platoon from B Company would be on the left and my platoon on the right. Attached to each platoon would be a plethora of support forces, including tanks, heavy 50-caliber machine guns and demolition men. We trained with this mission in mind. We met the leaders of the support forces, including the tank platoon leader. I concluded we would have the heaviest platoon in Marine Corps history. We were given no information as to the identity of the target but guessed it was either a small island or a peninsula of some sort.

During this period the battalion embarked on the transport USS *American Legion* for assault landing practice. I remember nothing of this activity but remember with fondness a blackjack game on the ship. I had only a few bucks in my pocket but sat in the game for something to do. A Sergeant Stanley from A Company was dealing. I started playing only a dollar or two each round but soon discovered I was "hot" and increased my bets to ten or $20 a crack. I simply couldn't lose. In a short time I had won $300 or $400. At this point Stanley threw the deck to me and told me to deal but he had no money before him on the table. He said he had $200 in the sergeant major's safe which he could recover tomorrow and asked me to trust him for that amount. I certainly had qualms about accepting bets with no money on the table but, heck, I was playing with the house's money and, more importantly, Stanley was a nice guy and a guy you could trust. We played a little while longer with Stanley making large bets. Suddenly, after a series of losing hands, he said the money with the sergeant major was exhausted and he would pay me tomorrow. And that's what he did. This left me with more than $600, which I sent home via postal money order. Why was this event such a big deal? Because $600 was about a year's pay!

During our entire stay in New Zealand we kept a nightly poker game going in one of the tents. The stakes were pretty high for our level of poverty — ten cent ante, with a pot limit. Even with this modest start pots could get pretty substantial since you could raise up to the amount in the pot on each card. Pots over $100 were not uncommon. Of course gambling was illegal in the Corps but that rule was largely ignored by all hands, including the officers who had their own game.

The Corps dealt harshly with homosexual activity in those days. One day they turned out the entire regiment in a formal dress formation to demonstrate punishment for breaching this regulation. The poor culprit was forced to stand at attention while the charges and results of the General Court Martial were read aloud by the adjutant. The charge was "oral coition" and the sentence was ten years in Naval Prison at Portsmouth, NH, and a dishonorable discharge. After the reading the MPs marched him off to the brig.

7

Tarawa

On October 17, 1943, we broke camp and trucked down to Wellington Harbor to board our assigned ships. Of course they didn't tell us where we were going but we had no illusions that the destination would be peaceful and friendly. I couldn't believe my eyes when I saw the ship our battalion had drawn. It was the USS *Harry Lee*, a converted peacetime freighter drafted into federal service in 1940. In a sense it was the laughingstock of the fleet, for its crew could never get it trim — it always listed to one side or the other. It was known throughout the fleet as "the listing Lee." Moreover, it was a homely bucket with only a single stack perched atop high superstructure. After boarding I discovered it was no worse below decks than other transports I had been subjected to.

We sailed out of the beautiful Wellington Harbor with regret for leaving the friendly people of New Zealand and with the usual pre-combat apprehension. However we soon learned we were not going immediately to a fight but to more maneuvers and practice landings in the Hawkes Bay area. I remember little of these landings but am sure I welcomed the chance to get the platoon ready for the real thing. Most of them had never descended a cargo net into a bobbing landing boat and needed basic instruction on how to secure their weapons and equipment to prevent them from falling and braining someone in the boat below. They had to be drilled to grasp only the vertical strands of the cargo net to keep their hands from being stepped on by the men following them. After a few days of this practice we sailed back to Wellington. We stayed in the harbor for a week and finally sailed north, on November 1, to Efate in the New Hebrides group of islands where we again made a practice landing. I remember this landing because of a most embarrassing occurrence; I got seasick in the landing craft. I don't know why it happened for I had pretty good sea legs, and it was humiliating as hell to throw up in front of the entire platoon; Marine sergeants don't do that!

We left that anchorage on November 12 and sailed for an island the Corps had named Helen, but its real name was Betio, one of the islands of the Tarawa atoll in the Gilberts Group. A coral reef 500 or more yards wide surrounded the entire island. The depth of the water over the reef was crucial for many of the Marines would be coming ashore in LCVPs, landing craft sometimes called "Higgins boats," equipped with a bow ramp and capable of holding a platoon of infantry. However, the first assault wave would be carried in 87 LVTs, amphibious tractors we called "amtracs." Each of the amtracs was armed with two 50-caliber machine guns. It seemed to me that 174 heavy machine guns banging away simultaneously should keep a lot of Jap heads down and permit the first wave to get ashore with minimum casualties. That is assuming there would be any Japs left alive after the island had been subjected to a week of aerial bombing and the "D-Day" Naval bombardment. Some Navy officers opined that any Jap left alive after the bombardment would be too addled to fight. This was truly the heaviest amount of ordnance, 2,700 tons, ever laid on a target of this size.

The original plan of attack was uncomplicated. "D-Day" would be

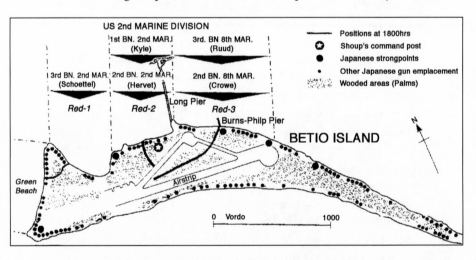

Betio Island, the largest of the Tarawa atoll. The map shows where the assault battalions landed on "D-Day" and the front line at 18:00 that evening.

120

November 20. We would land from within the atoll on the north shore of the widest part of the island. The landing area was divided into three sectors labeled Red Beach 1, 2 and 3. The first wave would be comprised of three battalions: the Third Battalion, 8th Regiment (3–8) on the left on Red Beach 3, the Second Battalion, 2nd Regiment (2–2) in the middle on Red Beach 2, and the Third Battalion, 2nd Regiment (3–2) on the right on Red Beach 1. My battalion, the First Battalion, 2nd Regiment (1–2), would land from LCVPs behind 3–8 on Red Beach 3, but would delay landing until the assault wave had carried its attack clear across the island. We would move in to the conquered area, wheel left and attack east down the long narrow tail of the bird. It would be a two company front with B Company on the left and A Company, with my platoon leading, on the right. This was the narrow two platoon assault we had been trained for in New Zealand. But the battalion was also the division reserve and could be employed at any time and place the situation warranted. As it turned out all our pre-invasion plans were for naught.

On "D-Day" minus 2, I had a confrontation with Vince Paskas, my platoon guide. Vince was a sergeant when he joined us as a replacement on Guadalcanal whereas I didn't make the rank until we were in New Zealand. Hence he was senior and was seriously upset to be serving under me. Vince was an acerbic personality at any time. His previous posting at Marine Corps Headquarters in Washington had given him a sense of superiority that did not go over well in our combat oriented outfit. He had no friends in the company. His resentment came to a head when I ordered him to draw ammunition, grenades and rations for the platoon in response to an announcement over the ship's PA system. Vince stayed in his bunk and told me to do it myself. Past dislike and my pre-combat state of tension caused me to explode and drag Vince from his bunk and onto the deck where, kneeling on him, I explained that drawing supplies was the primary duty of a platoon guide and he had better damned well get to it. This persuasion was successful and Vince drew the supplies.

It's difficult to remember my mental state as we waited to begin the attack. I am sure I had the usual pre-combat jitters but don't recall any morbid fear. Pearl has told me that she could detect some concern from my last letter before the landing. We had been told the pre-invasion bombardment would be the heaviest in history, with two battleships and several cruisers dropping 2,700 tons of high explosives on the island. Army and Navy bombers would hit the target daily for a week before "D-Day." There was speculation that the landing might be a breeze with only a shell-shocked remnant of the original garrison left to welcome us. I had my doubts about that scenario for I had suffered Jap shelling on the Canal and knew it took a direct hit to kill a well dug-in Marine. The maps of Betio we had studied in the days before the landing showed the emplacements constructed by the enemy to be well done and almost too numerous to count. I'm sure I followed the rule of thumb which had served me well throughout my Marine Corps career — always expect the absolute worst and no matter what happens you will be mentally prepared.

"D-Day" breakfast was a pleasant surprise — steak and eggs rather than the beans and cornbread the Navy fed us before the Canal landings. The only people who didn't approve of the menu were the doctors who anticipated being called upon to deal with stomach or abdominal wounds. After chow, contrary to orders, I went topside to look around. It was still dark but I could see some of the other transports nearby. While gazing idly at a ship on our starboard side I saw a geyser of water shoot up between us. It didn't take me more than a second or two to figure out that what I saw was the detonation of a Jap shell. Hey, they are not all dead or shell-shocked. Our Navy took exception to this effrontery and opened up with all its firepower. The display was awesome! The 14-inch shells from the battleships and the smaller shells from the cruisers leave a fiery trail as they arc towards their target. One of the first salvos hit an ammunition dump and caused a tremendous explosion. In a short time the island appeared to be burning from end to end.

After a while I went below to check on the platoon and get a bit of sack time. The only place to wait for the order to disembark was in our bunks and the men were all sacked out waiting the call. I hit the sack and, despite everything, dozed off and dreamed I heard the ship's speaker system announce there were torpedo tracks in the water. This aroused me, for the hold of a ship is not the place to be if torpedoes are swimming. Of course there were no torpedoes. I either dreamed the message or it was a mistake.

7. Tarawa

At dawn, or shortly thereafter, we assembled at our debarkation stations. I took the roll and personally inspected each man to ensure he had all his assigned equipment and had it properly secured. Within a short time we descended the cargo net into a waiting LCVP. A bit tight, but these boats will handle an entire 40-man platoon. We joined the other boats from our ship and circled while waiting for the order to go to the beach. The sea was a bit choppy but calmed a bit as we entered the lagoon and approached the line of departure. I am unsure as to how long we circled in the boat but estimate we arrived at the outer edge of the island's 500-yard reef at about ten o'clock. The assault wave had been ashore for less than one hour. The scene presented to us was discomforting to say the least. Good size-caliber shells were hitting around us, and not all were missing. To our right, close to the reef's edge, I saw a tank lighter turn on end and slide beneath the sea. A second landing craft was on fire upon the reef. All my doubts about the strength of the Jap's resistance were quickly dispelled.

Within minutes of our arrival our battalion CO, Major Wood Kyle, pulled up to our side in the Battalion headquarters boat and directed, "Grab empty amtracs as they return from the beach and go to Red 2, they need help." As luck would have it the first empty amtrac I saw came directly to our boat. In a brief confab we told the crew what the orders were and they responded, "Let's go!" Of course the amtrac won't hold the entire platoon so I directed Sergeant Bob Sewell to put in his squad and I added about two or three men from another squad. I thought the lieutenant would want to go with this first group but he directed me to lead them in. At about this point Lieutenant Ross said the only words he had ever spoken to me which were not in the line of duty. He said, "Bill, I hope I awake tomorrow with the worst headache I've ever had." I don't remember what, if anything, I responded but know I was pleased to see that he was human like the rest of us.*

I jumped into the amtrac and took the forward spot on the star-

---

*Unfortunately, Lt. Ross did not survive the battle and he died an unsung hero. A Private Dale told me he died making a lone frontal attack on a Jap machine gun emplacement. According to Dale, he told Ross you can't successfully knock out a machine gun with a frontal charge but Ross accused him of cowardice and went alone. He was dead before he had gone ten feet.

board side. In very few minutes I heard our tracks hit coral and we were on the reef. Since we were no longer in danger of sinking I ordered the men to uncover their cartridge belts by removing their lifebelts. These hollow rubber belts went around the waist and could be inflated by squeezing an embedded CO_2 cartridge. At this time one of the men, a kid we called "Hollywood" because that was his home town, stood up in the front of the compartment behind the port side 50-caliber machine gun. He wanted to see ahead to our landing beach. It was a fatal mistake. A 37 or 40-millimeter shell hit the ammunition box of the machine gun, exploded and almost decapitated "Hollywood." The force of the explosion threw his body to the rear of the amtrac, showering everyone on the port side with blood and brains. WELCOME TO TARAWA!

The amtrac continued toward the shore and I ordered the men to load and lock their weapons. The Jap gunner ashore punctuated my command with a second projectile, an airburst type which exploded directly over the tractor and punctured all of us with fine shell fragments. Two additional rounds exploded overhead in rapid succession. I felt the fragments hitting me and noticed I had a sizable bloody hole on the inside of my left knee. I wasn't sure what was happening to the other men but I was sure a lad named Dub Taylor sitting opposite me was dead, for I saw a hole appear in the middle of his forehead. Fortunately, my diagnosis of Taylor's wound was incorrect. He survived.

As we got closer to the shore the airbursts were replaced with machine gun fire. The bullets were bouncing off the armored front of the amtrac but a few entered the port side of our compartment and caused an unknown number of casualties. Bob Sewell, sitting opposite me, took one in the leg. One entered the viewing slits on the front and, judging by the screams of agony from the cabin, seriously wounded one of the crew. As we neared the beach the machine gun fire ceased. We had moved to the right and out of its field of fire. When the amtrac stopped I stood up and yelled, "Let's go!" and went over the side. As I was disembarking I looked to my left and could clearly see the long barrel of the gun that clobbered us. The barrel protruded from an emplacement somewhat elevated from those around it. I found out later this was the "strong point" which was not reduced until D plus three.

The beach I had landed on was protected by a coconut log seawall about four feet high. I took inventory and discovered only Bob Sewell and four of his men, Foster Tusing, Duane Terrell, James Allred and Channing Miller, had emerged from the amtrac. They all had small punctures but were capable of fighting. Crouched down behind the wall were a lot of the first wave Marines. This is as far as they had gotten and, from their appearance, it looked as if this was as far as they planned to go. I was instantly obsessed with the thought we had to get all these people dispersed inland before enemy mortars found them. I asked the nearest group if there were any officers among them. Some of them just looked at me, apparently resenting my intrusion on their reverie. My question was soon answered by the appearance of a young officer who crouched near me and peered intently at the "strong point" about 100 yards to our left. I got his attention and reported, "Lieutenant, I have five men, all wounded but able to fight." He didn't say anything but continued to stare toward the "strong point." I then offered this: "Lieutenant, if we can get that tin can out there on the radio I can spot for its gunfire to blast the gun that got my amtrac and is still shooting at incoming vehicles." He turned to me and barked, "Stop calling me lieutenant. I am Major Rice. Colonel Amey has been killed and I am in charge of the battalion. We have no radio, it was lost with the colonel."

I then said, "Major, we have to get these men off this beach before the Japs drop some mortars on it." I believe he detected a tone of criticism in my voice for he snapped, "Every man who tried to go over that seawall got shot between the eyes. You had better find a corpsman and get that shoulder taken care of." With that he duck-walked back to our right from whence he had come. I hadn't realized my shoulder had been hit but I looked and saw my blouse had been shredded and was bloody. A couple of small fragments had entered my shoulder, where they still remain. They didn't bother me but the silver dollar-size hole in my leg was another problem.

As best I can determine I landed pretty close to the boundary between Red Beaches 1 and 2. Instead of going dead ahead toward the "strong point" on Red 2, the tractor had veered westward toward Red 1. If our driver had gone straight in as ordered, we may not have survived. However, at least one amtrac hit the beach east of my position. I didn't see it come in but shortly after landing I saw some Marines about 100 yards to my left, behind the seawall but directly under the strong point's machine guns. As I looked in that direction I saw the most heroic act I witnessed during my combat career. One of the Marines, in obvious distress, staggered out into the water and into the sights of the machine gunners, who instantly splashed bullets all around and into him. Suddenly, a figure ran out from the seawall into that maelstrom of fire and dragged the berserk Marine back to shelter. I subsequently found out the wounded Marine was Corporal Clinton J. Ecker Jr. He was a big kid and we called him "Moose." His rescuer was Sergeant John G. Stanley, one helluva Marine! Unfortunately, Moose Ecker died just after Stanley got him ashore. Stanley's act was never reported to medal giving authorities and his action was never formally recognized.

After the conversation with Major Rice I gathered my flock and went over the seawall. We didn't draw any fire and holed up in a very large shell crater. There was one other occupant, a very dead Jap who appeared to be smoldering. At first we thought we were being fired on by a sniper, for widely spaced shots cracked in our ears. After awhile I discovered the shots were coming from the corpse as the fire exploded cartridges in his ammo belt. We covered him with sand and ended that annoyance. I hadn't a clue as to what was going on with the rest of my company or battalion. We were apparently on the front line for there were no Marines in front or on either side of us. I toyed with the idea of exploring two large structures about 50 yards in front of our position but concluded they were unoccupied storage facilities. Besides, my leg was stiffening up and hurting like hell. I tried to bandage it but the bandage fell down every time I bent my knee. It wasn't necessary anyway, for the wound had stopped bleeding and was full of sand. I chewed the antibiotic pill from my kit and hoped for the best.

In retrospect, our isolation in the big shell hole seems strange. We were apparently east of the bulk of the Third Battalion people and west of the survivors of the Second Battalion. The only activity I saw during the day was the foray of a lone Sherman tank. It was amusing in a way. The Sherman came under fire from a Jap tank almost completely buried in the sand with only its turret protruding. It would bounce its small shells (37mm?) off the Sherman with no effect other than causing the crew to swivel their turret as if searching for the source of the shells hitting them. Finally the Sherman's gunner saw the small target and blew the turret completely off the Jap with one round.

A letter from Bob Sewell in 1984 relates that we moved out of the shell hole later in the day and encountered a surgeon who was tending some badly wounded men. According to Sewell the doctor asked us to protect his rudimentary sick bay and that I and private Tusing, also hit in the legs, acquiesced and stayed behind while he and the other two guys went on. I've got no memory of this at all but it could have happened. As night approached we dug rudimentary foxholes in the slippery sand in anticipation of the night attack I was certain would come. Just at dusk a figure draped with machine gun belts stumbled by and caved in the end of my hole. It pissed me off and I yelled something pungent at the culprit, who turned to me and said, "Rogal, is that you?" There was no mistaking that voice, it was Witzel! I remember well his next comment: "Bill, the good lord had his hand on my shoulder today." I told him I too was blessed that day but had a hole or two that needed patching. I asked him what in the hell he was doing with machine gun ammo. He told me his mortar had been lost in the landing and he had been assisting on a machine gun all day. With that he hurried off to rejoin his group.

The night was almost uneventful. I vaguely recall a bombing by a lone Jap plane but no artillery or mortar fire came our way. Shortly after dawn I witnessed the worst tragedy to befall our division in the war. The First Battalion Eighth Marines (1–8) had been wallowing in LCVPs all night waiting orders to land. They were first given orders to land on the far eastern tip of the island, orders which made good sense, but the orders were changed and the battalion was directed to land on Red Beach 2, directly into the field of fire of the "strong point" which devastated our landing on "D-Day." But these Marines weren't in steel amtracs, they were in LCVP landing boats which drew too much water to get over the reef. The explanation given for this disaster is that the orders to land specified they were to land "close to the pier," a comparatively safe route, but this phrase was lost in transit and the battalion headed into the jaws of death. When their flotilla of landing craft reached the edge of the reef, the Japs' heavy guns cut into them, sinking several before they could disembark their troops. The surviving boats could make it only a few yards shoreward before grounding, where they dropped their troops into waist-deep water. The Jap machine gunners had a field day cutting up the men as they slowly slogged through the water. The guns were firing not only from the Red Beach 2 "strong point" but also from a small merchant ship wrecked on the edge of the reef.

The carnage was terrible! The water to my front was soon dotted with the floating bodies of the dead and wounded. Most of 1–8 had been eliminated — more than 300 casualties. But the remnants that made it ashore received immediate orders to attack inland, but not against the strong point. It wasn't reduced until D plus three. During the landing several Navy airplanes, F6F Hellcats I think, dive-bombed the wrecked merchant ship but made, at most, one direct hit. Most of the bombs missed by many yards. I remember being appalled at their poor marksmanship.

No one who witnessed the Eighth Marines bloodbath will ever forget it. Even experienced war correspondent Robert Sherrod was appalled at the carnage. In his award-winning book *Tarawa: The Story of a Battle*,* he writes:

> One of the fresh battalions is coming in. Its Higgins boats are being hit before they pass the old hulk of a freighter seven hundred yards from shore. One boat blows up, then another. The survivors start swimming for shore, but the machinegun bullets dot the water all around them....
>
> Some of the fresh troops get within two hundred yards of shore, while others from later waves are unloading further out. One man falls, writhing in the water. He is the first man I have seen actually hit, though many thousands of bullets cut into the water....
>
> But the machine guns continue to tear into the oncoming Marines. Within five minutes I see six men killed. But the others keep coming. One rifleman walks slowly ashore, his left arm a bloody mess from the shoulder down. The casualties become heavier. Within a few minutes more I can count at least a hundred Marines lying on the flats.
>
> The Marines continue unloading from the Higgins boats, but fewer of them are making the shore now. Many lie down behind the pyramidal concrete barriers the Japs had erected to stop tanks. Others make it as far as the disabled tanks and amphtracks, [*sic*] then lie down behind them to size up the chances of making the last hundred yards to shore. There are at least two hundred bodies which do not move at all on the dry flats, or in the shallow water partially covering them. This is worse, far worse than it was yesterday.

*New York: Duell, Sloan and Pearce, 1944, p. 89.

Marines at the seawall. It took a lot of willpower to go up and over the seawall into a nightmare of shrieking bullets (U.S. Marine Corps).

Two friends I met after the war played a role in that bloodbath. The first, Bill Crumpacker, told me he got down below water level, made like a skin diver and got safely ashore. The other fellow, Dean Ladd, wasn't so lucky. Here is part of his story, excerpted from his book, *Faithful Warriors*, mentioned previously:

> I jumped out of my LCVP at 0615 hours with others in my landing wave onto the reef about 600 yards out from the beach. Then I began the murderous wade ashore. Red Beach 2 was to the right of a prominent feature the long wooden pier that divided Red Beach 2 from Red 3. We discovered, in a disastrous manner that this area was still an enemy strong point.
>
> There was an inter island freighter hulk rammed on the reef. This provided the enemy with a strategic position to rake us with devastating, flanking machine gun fire in addition to the strong fire coming from the beach....
>
> I turned to look over my right shoulder to see how my thirty-one men were doing. Some were still jumping off the ramp too slowly to suit me. I

urged them on with a shout, "Let's go!" I walked a few more steps and heard cries of wounded men from the adjacent platoons intermixed with ours, yelling for corpsmen. I faced the reality of a desperate situation.

I soon found myself at the mercy of the grim reaper. A sickening splat, like an inner tube snapped across my abdomen, shocking me. I realized a bullet had hit me nearly dead center below the navel. I quickly removed my pack, small radio, carbine, helmet and web belt. I was too weak to maintain my balance, forgetting about everything but trying to keep my head above water.

Dean Ladd was rescued by a brave Marine from his platoon, Pfc. Thomas H. Sullivan. He dragged Dean back out to a landing boat "as the hailstorm of bullets continued." The boat transported Dean to the transport he had arrived on, the USS *Sheridan*, where he was taken immediately to an operating room where his luck began to improve. One of the three doctors who attended him was an abdominal specialist from the Mayo Clinic, Lloyd Sussex, who later told him he could not have survived another two hours without surgery. But Dean did survive, returned to active duty and eventually retired as a lieutenant colonel.

Later on that day, D plus 1, I'm not sure of the time, I decided to take my group to find a Marine unit to join. My leg was now becoming a problem. It didn't hurt a great deal but had stiffened and metal fragments in the knee made themselves known when I walked. Nevertheless we set off to the west, where we had seen Marines moving around. The first group we encountered was from our company. They were led by Platoon Sergeant Paul Boyd, one of my close friends. Their experience was pretty much the same as mine but they suffered fewer casualties while in the LVT. I don't remember what we discussed with regard to what action we should take but I suppose it had to do with finding the rest of A Company. At some point Paul looked at my leg and opined that I should get the hell out of there. He said he had heard they were evacuating wounded from Green Beach at the western end of the island. Paul detailed two of his men to help me get there. We set off walking with my arms over the shoulders of the guys walking on both sides. During the trip we were shot at several times, with bullets kicking up the sand at our feet. Twice we hit the deck but the third time I said, "Screw it, let the son of a bitch hit us," and continued walking erect. We made it to the beach without further incident. I thanked the guys and sent them back to Paul.

The evacuation beach was covered with wounded and dead. I remember lying next to a dead Marine officer. The thing that sticks in my mind was his wristwatch. He was flat on his back with his left arm bent in a vertical position from the elbow. The second hand on the beautiful watch revealed it was running and I was sorely tempted to relieve him of it. This thought was not pure avarice, for watches were much-needed but hard to come by pieces of gear. I had been without one for much of the time on Guadalcanal and had to guess at the time when supervising the nighttime guard force. I was certain that someone would put that watch back in circulation before the officer was buried. But, of course, I resisted that temptation. I wonder who ended up with the watch.

My memory is very hazy as to how I got off the beach and into an LCVP but I have a vivid memory of the casualty sitting opposite me in the boat. He was cradling the torn remains of his scrotum in his left hand. His right hand had no flesh on the finger bones, which seemed almost intact. It was clear that a grenade, probably Japanese, had gone off in his right hand when he tried to throw it back. We didn't talk. I assumed he had been given a heavy dose of morphine by the corpsmen. In fact no one talked during the ride to the ship. We were a subdued bunch. I, for one, had a feeling of shame or remorse that I was leaving the company while it was still engaged in combat. It was a feeling that I was in some manner guilty of deserting my post in time of danger.

The boat ride ended at the side of a Navy transport, the USS *Arthur Middleton*, APA 25, which had been ordered back into the lagoon to receive wounded. Although not a hospital ship, it had been equipped with the gear needed to treat the seriously wounded and had a first rate medical team. I was taken into an operating room where my clothing was cut off and my wounds examined. The doctor told me they could do nothing for me because the wound in my knee was too big to sew shut and would have to be closed by plastic surgery when I reached a Naval hospital. Since they couldn't close the wound they cautioned me to not take a shower for fear of further contaminating the wound. I was then given a bunk in the hold with the other wounded. The first thing

I did was take a shower. My body was encrusted with sweat and muck and I simply could not endure the discomfort and stench for the duration of the voyage to a hospital, which I correctly assumed would be in Hawaii. At any rate, I did not get infected.

A Company suffered severely at Tarawa. We lost 33 killed in action. Eighty-one of the 967 men deployed by my First Battalion died. The company command group led, by Captain Bill Bray, landed about 150 yards west of the pier. Bray found about 15 A Company men and with them and others, including some sailors armed with weapons from fallen Marines, went on the attack, reaching the edge of the airfield's taxiway. There they teamed up with what remained of B and C Companies and some stragglers from F and G Companies. The group, numbering about 150 men, spent the night between the main runway and the taxi strip. The next day they were ordered to attack across the main runway and suffered severe casualties in doing so. They built up a line on the south side of the airfield where they repulsed severe counterattacks and almost ran out of ammunition and grenades. They succeeded in cutting the island in two by the evening of the second day, when they pushed on to the south shore and occupied the enemy's beach defenses.

A Company's Men Killed on Tarawa

Lieutenants
John E. Anderson
Robert J. Harvey
Armstead E. Ross

Gunnery Sergeant
Paul Perkins

Platoon Sergeant
Leonard E. William

Sergeants
William R. Gibbons
James J. Maine
Wesley O. Williams

Corporal
Clinton J. Ecker

Privates First Class
Ray E. Adkins
Theodore J. Alger
Olan Ard
Harold R. Burch
Charles L. Cantrell
Jess R. Harrison Jr.
Henry Lorenz
Marvin Schwartz

Privates
William E. Brandenberg
Faris G. Byrd
Marvin G. Chudej
Harry Cronkhite
Aaron Daniels
Walter E. Harris
Gerald R. Hull
James C. Kneff

132

7. Tarawa

Privates
Roger V. Maidment
Albert L. Parker
Forest R. Sturges
Christofer W. Trotter
Ernest E. Tucker
Charles D. Walker
James A. Whitworth

For his exploits on Betio, Bill Bray was awarded the Navy Cross. The citation reads, in part:

> For extraordinary heroism as Commanding Officer of Company A, First Battalion, Second Marines ... mustering his men and finding that only a small number had reached shore he promptly organized numerous scattered leaderless units in the vicinity and began a determined attack inland, leading his men across the exposed taxi strip in the face of violent machine gun, mortar and rifle fire to reinforce the battered remnants of another company despite the heavy casualties sustained by his own. Later, under his brilliant leadership, his company crossed the bullet-swept area of a fighter strip and although he was seriously wounded during the action, succeeded in capturing an important part of the south beach....

I had entertained a rather dim view of Captain Bray's leadership of the company after my run-in with him over my record book in New Zealand. Maybe he didn't know how to mark a record book but he sure knew how to lead a company in combat. I met him once after the war in 1967, at a friend's house at Camp Lejeune. He died of leukemia that year, which was discovered during his physical exam for promotion to general.

Below is a famous picture taken on "D-Day" plus one from near the base of the pier looking west along Red Beach 2. The amtrac number 44 canted against the seawall was driven there by Platoon Sergeant Fredrick Clemments. Fred told me after the war that the standing order for the amtracs on "D-Day" was to take them as far inland from the beach as possible. Several made it over the seawall but Fred's got hung up, not by enemy action at that juncture but by engine failure. The craft's hull had been pierced by shells on the way in and when it canted up on the wall the water ran to the rear and killed the engine.

One of the combat heroes of Tarawa, who became a close friend

The sad scene on "D-Day" plus one before the dead on the sand and floating in the water could be retrieved (U.S. Marine Corps).

after the war, was William Sanders of Princeton, West Virginia. Bill, or "Sandy" as we used to call him, was then serving as a reconnaissance officer with our First Battalion headquarters group. That he became a hero was a great surprise to me, for he didn't look like a tough Marine — he was just too pretty and boyish looking.

I first saw Sandy in New Zealand as I was walking down a company street in our tent camp and I was instantly struck by his extremely youthful and pretty face. In a smartass tone I said to Bob Boyd, who was accompanying me, "My Gawd, look at what they are sending us as leaders!" It was said loud enough for Sandy to hear but he ignored me.

In the vernacular, "Appearances don't mean nothing." Here, excerpted from Sandy's Navy Cross citation, is what Sandy did at Tarawa:

When intense fire from enemy shore emplacements inflicted heavy casualties on our forces as they waded toward the beach, First Lieutenant Sanders voluntarily prepared to attack the hostile positions with the aid of a Sergeant of his company. Bringing a 75mm pack howitzer into use and neutralizing the devastating fire of the first pillbox, he courageously rushed the position despite heavy fire from another emplacement and destroyed the pillbox with hand grenades ... he then crawled twenty five yards to the first of a group of four connecting emplacements and, completely destroying the position with TNT unhesitatingly advanced on the second emplacement and annihilated the defenders with hand grenades.... By his splendid initiative, First Lieutenant Sanders put out of action three enemy .25 caliber and two 13-mm machine guns and one 20-mm antiboat gun....

Sandy did not escape from that fracas scot-free. A rifle bullet hit him at the left base of his neck and exited through a much larger hole lower down on his back. He spent four months in the hospital recuperating on Oahu and returned to active duty on the "Big Island" about the same time as I did.

The cruise to Hawaii seemed endless, for I had nothing to read. We spent our time discussing the battle, getting each man's story and viewpoint on the conduct of the operation. To a man we thought there had to have been a better way. While under way, we ambulatory cases were repeatedly called topside to witness burials at sea. I thought it was an impressive little ceremony and a fitting ending to a combat Marine's career. The only other thing I remember about the voyage was the music blaring from the ship's loudspeaker system. The knucklehead feeding the machine kept playing a hillbilly tune in which the vocalist warbled something that sounded like "tweedle lo twill." After a few days of that torture we denizens of the holds rebelled and threatened to invade the upper reaches of the ship and do bodily harm to the record player. We eventually got it stopped.

Another friend I met after the war is Norman Hatch, a now retired Marine major. Norm was a motion picture photographer for the Second Division during the Tarawa battle. He did a fantastic job—so good in fact that his film was used to produce an Academy Award–winning documentary about the battle. Norm was commissioned and went on to win further honors, leading a photography group at Iwo Jima. But during the Tarawa battle Norm took the time to aid a scared and needy island resident. Here is a picture of then–Staff Sergeant Norm Hatch sharing his scarce canteen water with a kitten.

Compassion amid chaos! Sergeant Hatch shares his water with a kitten (U.S. Marine Corps).

We arrived at Pearl Harbor on December 7, the second anniversary of the Japanese assault on the island. There was some apprehension that the Japs might try another sneak attack just to show us they were still around. And sure enough, that night, as I was being transferred to the hospital, the air raid sirens started wailing and I was carried into some sort of concrete shelter. I can remember being sorely pissed off that the dammed Japs had followed me all the way to Hawaii and were still trying to get me. But the disturbance was short-lived and in a short while I was carried to a reception room at the old hospital on Hospital Point in the Navy Yard. A jolly, plump middle-aged nurse kidded me and tried to get me to laugh but I remained stone-faced. I wasn't in shock, just didn't feel like smiling. I was put to bed in a large ward and immediately fell into a sound sleep, the best in months.

The following morning I was x-rayed and examined by a team of doctors and was told two things: there were shell fragments in my left shoulder and left knee but they would not operate to remove them because such surgery would cause more injury than was warranted and they would probably not cause any problem in the future. The second thing they told me was the silver dollar-size hole on my knee was too large to be closed by suturing but that given time it would heal "the way a tree heals from an injury to its bark." This would take time and I would stay in the hospital to guard against infection until the healing was complete. They considered plastic surgery but discarded that as too difficult and hard on me. All in all this sounded like a pretty good deal to me — three squares a day and nothing to do but stare at the nurses, some of whom were real lookers.

A day or two later I was sitting up in bed with my knees drawn up and brushed my arm against my left knee. I felt a sharp pain which, upon examination, came from an inch-long scrap of metal resting just under the skin on my shin bone. I called the corpsman to take a look and he quickly said, "I'll take care of that." He took me to the dressing room at the end of the ward and directed me to sit on the operating table. He cleansed the area, injected local anesthesia and started cutting with a scalpel. I was watching him from a sitting position but suddenly began feeling lightheaded. The corpsman noticed this and told me to lie down. This was a bit embarrassing but there were no witnesses. When the procedure was over he offered me the piece of metal but I declined and it was thrown into the trash. This was my first experience with a senior hospital corpsman. I think his rank was first class. The dressing room was his bailiwick and he was in charge. Although the nurses outranked him they did not even enter his territory without his permission.

In a very short time I decided this enforced hospital stay was the ideal time to have my right knee operated on to correct the old football injury which almost laid me low in New Zealand. I raised this question with a doctor who said he'd take it up with the head surgeon but he cautioned that such "non-emergency" surgery for a pre-existing condition was rarely performed in this hospital. Such patients were sent back to the mainland for the surgery or a medical discharge. However, after some delay the operation was scheduled. It seems that I had a scarce military specialty, "Combat-Experienced NCO." An exception must be made for

Cincpac File
Pac-F052- pp
P15/ P
Serial

UNITED STATES PACIFIC FLEET
AND PACIFIC OCEAN AREAS
HEADQUARTERS OF THE COMMANDER IN CHIEF

7 DEC

From: Commander in Chief, United States Pacific Fleet.
To: ROGAL, William W., Sgt., USMC.

Via: CO., U. S. Naval Hospital, Navy Number 128.

Subject: Purple Heart - award of.

Enclosure: (A) Purple Heart Medal.

1.   In the name of the President and by direction of the Secretary of the Navy the Purple Heart is awarded by the Commander in Chief, United States Pacific Fleet to:

SERGEANT WILLIAM W. ROGAL, USMC

for wounds received in action during the Gilbert Islands Occupation, November 1943.

C. W. NIMITZ

Copy to:
    SecNav
    BuPers
    Personnel Jacket
    Comdt., USMC.

My Purple Heart citation, signed by Admiral C.W. Nimitz.

people in this category. Standard operating procedure dictated they must be repaired and sent back into the fray.

I was told I was fortunate, for the surgeon who would operate was a highly respected expert brought into the service from his practice in New York. I was given a spinal anesthesia which turned me into stone from the waist down. Any anxiety I may have felt during the operation was alleviated by the presence of a very beautiful, full-lipped nurse who held my hand and talked to me. All in all, it was a painless and very successful procedure. The knee functioned perfectly thereafter until old age took over and made me a candidate for replacement surgery.

The remainder of my hospital stay was among the most enjoyable period of my time in the Corps. I soon mastered crutches and was able to go to the mess hall, which had excellent food, the best GI food I had savored to date. I played chess with some other patients with reasonable success. Later on, when I was able to drop the crutches, I made friends with several senior NCOs from the Navy Yard's Marine guard detachment. They would pick me up in one of their vehicles and take me to the NCO club for lunch, usually a big steak washed down with copious amounts of draught beer. Sometimes lunch stretched out to late evening. This caused me a good deal of trouble with the nurses running my ward. However, they were good sports and never reported my indiscretions to higher authority.

As the weeks passed I became fully ambulatory and the hole in my left knee gradually closed. A new nurse in the ward, a shapely redhead from Texas, gave me special attention and incurred her supervisor's displeasure for spending too much time at my bedside. Near the end of my stay in the hospital we made arrangements to meet ashore at Waikiki Beach. We met at a hotel on the beach which had been taken over as an officers' R and R facility. I had no problem passing as an officer since I was wearing Navy khakis with no insignia, the only clothing I had. We rented a surfboard, one of those long, hollow plywood contraptions, and paddled out toward the breakers with her on the board and me doing the pushing. Unfortunately the surf was not running and I was forced to push the board back to shallow water. After the swim we had dinner at the Waikiki Tavern and went our separate ways. We exchanged letters for about a year.

On or about April 1 I was discharged from the hospital as "fit for duty." The Corps had a casual center camp called Camp Catlin located on Oahu next to Hickam Field, the island's large military airfield. Our tent camp was situated just off the end of the airfield's main runway. The huge four-engine transports loaded with fuel barely cleared our tent tops when they took off. If one had ever lost power on takeoff a lot of Marines would have died. They made me a bit nervous.

While waiting for transportation back to my Division, which was now quartered on the "Big Island" of Hawaii, one of those really odd wartime events occurred. One morning, while doing my laundry at a wash rack, I encountered Johnny Kobal, a high school classmate. Johnny told me that he had accidentally encountered two other Lehighton High School graduates in the camp, Alan Fritzinger and Bob Clemmons. Within a few hours we all got together and went ashore. Needless to say it was a rather wet outing. The mathematical chances of four guys from the same small town running into each other in that fashion must be astronomical. Here is a photo of Kobal, Fritzinger and me ashore in Waikiki. I'm on the left, Kobal in the middle and Fritzinger is on the right.

While engaged on Tarawa I gave no thought to the many questions and issues created by the battle. But as soon as the lead stopped flying I fell heir to many doubts that the operation was necessary and that the frontal assault was the proper tactic. Over the years much ink has been spent explaining and, in some cases deploring, the campaign. The most

Three high school chums reunited in Hawaii — author (left), Kobal, and Fritzinger.

recent and the best writing to come to my attention is by retired Marine Colonel Joseph H. Alexander, in *Utmost Savagery*, (Annapolis, MD: Naval Institute Press, 1995). In precise and authoritative terms, Col. Alexander does a yeoman's job in answering many of the questions I have entertained over the years.

Many years after the battle I met and became fast friends with Robert Sherrod who, as Time Life's correspondent, went ashore in the first wave at Tarawa and described his experience in his famous book *Tarawa: The Story of a Battle*. Bob and I spent hours arguing the central issue: Should the battle even have taken place? I always took the position that more than 1,000 dead Marines was too steep a price for only 300 acres of sand and coral. Bob defended the strategic decision to invade but had reservations about the tactics. At the end of the 1973 edition of his book, Bob reports the opinions held in 1953, ten years after the battle, of some high-ranking planers and participants. In his corner he had Admiral Nimitz, who opined that Tarawa was needed "...as an unsinkable carrier in our operation against the Marshalls, and to eliminate Tarawa as a threat to our important communications between our west coast and Australia and New Zealand." Then–Major General Merritt A. Edson, my former battalion CO in the Fifth Marines and Chief of Staff of the Second Division during the Tarawa fight, offered the opinion that it was "the one battle of the Pacific campaign that had to be fought." The gist of most of the favorable opinions is that we learned how to assault a defended hostile shore, lessons that made possible all the subsequent landings at Saipan, Iwo Jima and Okinawa.

As for me, I am still not convinced the frontal assault on the machine guns and artillery that lined the Tarawa shore was necessary. The island adjoining Betio in the Tarawa atoll, Bairiki, was relatively undefended and could have provided a platform for our artillery to methodically eliminate all opposition on Betio. According to Col. P.M. Rixey, then CO of the First Battalion, Tenth Marines, there was an "alternative plan" which would have landed his howitzers on "Bairiki to gain the maximum use of these supporting weapons in preparation fires and pre–H-hour concentrations." Sure, the operation would have taken a few more days, but the U.S. casualty toll would have been a fraction of the actual totals of 1,027 killed and 2,292 wounded. The alternative plan was developed by the Second Division CO, Maj. Gen. Julian Smith, his Chief of Staff, Col. Merritt Edson, and the CO of the Second Regiment, Lt. Col. Dave Shoup. The plan they prepared called for a preliminary bombardment several days in length, the advanced taking of the neighboring island Bairiki for an artillery base, and a decoy simulated landing somewhere on the coast of Betio. Since the Marines are part of the Navy and subservient to its top officers, the plan was submitted to Admiral Nimitz, the overall Pacific commander. He destroyed it, limiting the pre-invasion naval bombardment to three hours and rejecting the taking of Bairiki and decoy landing as too time consuming. This left the Second Division with no options other than a frontal attack across the coral reef.

Startling support for my negative view appeared in 1984 with the publication of a book by retired Gen. Holland M. Smith, the general who was the supreme commander of Marine forces in the Pacific during the war. In his memoir titled *Coral And Brass*, which was serialized in the *Saturday Evening Post*, he described the Tarawa battle as "strategically useless" and "a terrible waste of life and effort." I believe General Smith's view is a bit extreme, for we made good use of the captured airfield in subsequent attacks in the Marshall Islands. It's just that we could have accomplished the job without the extreme loss of American lives.

In summary, my view is that Tarawa was a useful, not necessary, operation which should have been accomplished with far fewer casualties. In fairness to the Navy, its insistence on speed to protect its ships is somewhat justified, for the loss of a single ship can produce a staggering number of casualties. The submarine threat around Tarawa was very real. On November 24, the small aircraft carrier *Liscome Bay* was sunk by a Jap sub less than 100 miles away with loss of 644 sailors.

Before leaving this discussion of Tarawa, one more thing must be said and emphasized. The greatest hero of the conflict was its commander, the Second Division CO, Maj. Gen. Julian Smith. I say the greatest hero for several reasons; first, because of his embracement and presentation of the original plan to land first on Bairiki. Secondly, and more significantly insofar as the final outcome is concerned, was his insistence, in the face of Naval opposition, to acquire a sufficient number of the latest model amtracs to get his men over the reef.

7. Tarawa

Before the operation it was not certain that it was absolutely necessary to have tracked vehicles to ferry the attacking troops across the reef. Rear Admiral Harry Hill, the CO of the amphibious force, had consulted with local mariners and reached "the cautious consensus that neap high tide in the lagoon on November 20 will surely be close to five feet deep" (article by Michael Kernan, *Smithsonian Magazine*, September 1939, 118–131). This would have been adequate to float Higgins boats (LCVPs) for they draw only three-and-a-half to four feet of water. But Julian Smith, bless him, didn't buy that and insisted on getting at least 100 more of the latest model amtracs to augment the 75 older models he had on hand in New Zealand. Gen. Smith again ran into a Navy roadblock, this time in the personage of Rear Admiral Richmond Kelly Turner. Gen. Julian Smith conveyed his needs to his superior, Maj. Gen. Holland M. Smith (known to many Marines as "Howlin Mad" Smith), who took up the request with Admiral Turner, who objected, insisting that more amtracs would not be needed. This outraged "Howlin Mad" Smith, who in a manner living up to his nickname, told Turner, "No amtracs, no operation!" Turner relented and Julian Smith got his amtracs and the rest is history. The thought of wading 400 or more yards to shore from a grounded LCVP in the face of the type of fire I experienced while going ashore in my amtrac gives me the shudders to this day. Thank you, thank you, General Smith.

But how did the Marine Corps thank Gen. Julian Smith for masterminding the successful operation? They fired him, that is, took away his division and placed him in a non-combat staff role as second in command to Holland Smith. It wasn't only the firing that was contemptible, the manner in which it was done was low class. Here is a close-to-the-source narration of the affair as related by Julian Smith's widow, Harriotte "Happy" Smith, in her 1992 book *But That's Another Story*.*

> The battle was over, we had taken the island of Tarawa. The 2d Marine Division was encamped at the Parker Ranch on the big island of Hawaii for much needed rest and recreation. Plans were already under way for the next battle in which the division would be engaged, the Battle of Saipan.

*New York: Vantage Press, 1992.

Julian received a call from Archer Vandergrift, [*sic*] the new commandant, ordering him to Honolulu for a conference with Holland M. Smith and Archer. Since conferences are a common part of the military structure, Julian never gave it a second thought. However he was looking forward to seeing his old friend and college Archer Vandergrift again, especially now that he was commandant. At last Julian would have the opportunity to congratulate him in person....

Later, he recalled, as the conference got underway, an air of mystery prevailed, but he could not put his finger on its source. General Vandergrift looked across the table at Julian and asked, "How's the division doing?"

"I'm pleased to report we are in fine shape, Archer, and already itching to get back in the fight," was Julian's reply.

Archer never responded but went on to other topics on the agenda. After the conference, Julian said he thought it strange that Archer never brought up the plans for Saipan and that troubled him. After seeing the commandant off, he went back to Holland's office and casually asked, "Did Archer say anything to you while he was here about Saipan or what he had in mind? I have a feeling something is in the air."

Holland gave him an evasive look, shrugged his shoulders, and said in an offhanded manner, "Nothing that I know of." ...

Julian went back to Camp Tarawa but spent a restless night trying to find a reason for his uneasiness. As dawn broke through he still had no clue about what was troubling him. He put aside his thoughts that something was amiss and went on about his day carrying out routine matters. Later in the day, one of his aides walked in and handed him a telegram that came through on the wire from Marine Corps headquarters in Washington. The message was brief and to the point:

"YOU ARE HEREBY RELIEVED OF COMMAND OF 2D MARINE DIVISION"

...Military protocol had been totally bypassed. According to protocol, those orders should have gone through the chain of command: General Vandergrift would have notified Gen. Holland Smith and Holland, in turn, would have been the one to break the news to Julian.

Anger and frustration filled Julian, and a sick feeling swept over him! He was crushed and understandably so. He could not understand why his friend and longtime associate Archer Vandergrift had not extended him the courtesy of telling him in person. After all, they had been together when the decision to relieve him of his command was made.

Gen. Julian Smith retired in 1945 to his home in Northern Virginia. But he was not completely idle. He founded the Second Marine Division Association, an organization still going strong today with thousands of members. The idea to start the group was generated by the many letters forwarded to him from Marine Corps headquarters that were written by Marine veterans trying to locate buddies who had fought with them in the division. Also, beginning in 1947, on the anniversary of the Tarawa battle, the general had invited Washington-area veterans to his home for a get-together to honor those who did not return. Among those present at the second meeting in 1948 were Dave Shoup and Carl Hoffman, still on active duty in Marine Corps headquarters, and the writer-correspondent Robert Sherrod. This group kicked around the idea of forming an organization which would enable Second Division veterans to find each other and get together. In a few months Julian, Shoup and Hoffman had drafted a charter and bylaws, borrowed $3,000 from the Post Exchange fund and filed a certificate of incorporation in Washington, D.C. The first meeting was held on December 30, 1949, and Gen. Julian Smith was elected president. My former battalion commander, Lt. Col. Wood B. Kyle, still on active duty, was elected Third Vice President. I attended the first annual reunion held August 11, 1950, and have been a member ever since.

After the war I got in touch with Bob Sewell, the sergeant squad leader who accompanied me on the wild ride to the beach. He was able to confirm my recollections of the attack and to supply the names of his squad members who landed on the beach with us. Bob returned to the tiny town of Claude, Texas, and went back to herding cattle on the range. He supplied me with a copy of a letter he had written to a mutual friend in which he records that A Company had some post-battle excitement on the trip from Tarawa to our new home in Hawaii. Here is what he wrote:

> It was about sundown on the fourth day when the island was called secure, still several hidden in those pill boxes. We made contact with what was left of the battalion, not many.
>
> The next morning we went aboard the USS Doyen. A Jap submarine had surfaced among our transports and a destroyer had rammed him when they tried to crash dive. The destroyer was crippled. We left [in] five transports heavily loaded with casualties and the crippled destroyer, but it turned out we weren't through yet. I believe it was the second night out, just at midnight the Doyen just died in the water. A real large transport, I think it was the Harrison, was right behind us. I'll never know how it missed us. With

both ships loaded with casualties it would have been terrible. We were just off some Jap held islands that had been bypassed. The next morning the navy said we were drifting toward shore, that walking wounded might have to knock out another beachhead to have a place to unload the hard hit boys

Bob Sewell and friend on the range after the war.

146

until help could arrive. It was just at noon that they suddenly got the Doyen cranked up. It sure was a good moment. We went on to Pearl Harbor.

Bob Sewell did not return to A Company after Tarawa and I regret I did not get to meet with Bob after the war. He was one of my favorite guys in A Company but I never went ashore with him and really didn't know much about his background. Before he died, in 1992, he sent me a picture of him in his working clothes.

8

Saipan and Tinian

After a few days in that transit camp on Oahu I boarded a small ship and sailed to Hilo on the "Big Island" of Hawaii. From there a truck carried me to Camp Tarawa, the camp established by my Second Division while I was in the hospital. I rejoined A Company and was instantly assigned as platoon sergeant of the First Platoon. Almost all of the men were new to me, including the platoon leader and the platoon guide. I instantly liked the new platoon leader, 2nd Lt. Bill Herber. He was a real comedian with a clever quip or story always at the ready. More importantly, he knew that he was an amateur among veterans. During one of our first conversations he told me the most important advice he got while in officer training was from an old gunnery sergeant who told him to always seek and follow the advice of his platoon sergeant. For the most part he followed that advice, but we had several disagreements during combat.

Our tent camp was located on the Parker Ranch near the town of Kamuela. The location was ideal, with cool nights and warm, sunny days. We kept to a rather rigorous training schedule. Some features of the schedule should have alerted me to anticipate the nature of our next operation. The company marched down to a small beach where we spent a few days practicing with rubber boats. That should have raised a red flag that we were slated to do something other than going ashore in LCVPs or LVTs but I didn't think much about it for I had trained with rubber boats several times at Quantico and in New Zealand. We also maneuvered in the jungle at night, making assaults on dug-in "enemy" from another battalion. This too should have warned me that we would be doing something a bit unusual in our next combat mission. The most unusual part of our training was practicing being supplied with ammo, rations and water by air drop. The practice was a disaster, for the containers were not dropped by parachute but merely dropped from low-flying Navy dive or torpedo bombers. The falling containers were a menace. It was hairy looking up and trying to decide which way to run to escape the falling packages. We were told they could not use parachutes in a combat situation for fear they would drift off target and into enemy hands.

By this time I should have realized that we were slated to make a rubber boat landing at night, attack the enemy and hold a restricted piece of ground necessitating resupply by air. Perhaps more ominously, our company was reorganized. The weapons platoon was split off, leaving the three infantry platoons and company headquarters, a total of about 129 men, down from about 200. Obviously a hairy operation was coming up.

The mystery was solved in June, when the stripped down 120-man company marched down off the mountain and boarded our ship. And what a ship, the World War I destroyer USS *Noa*, APD 24, a sister ship of the APD *Little* I had sailed around the Atlantic in during my tenure in the Fifth Marines. Part of the reason for paring the company down was to accommodate it on this small ship. The other companies in the battalion had been similarly reduced in size to fit on five similar ships. The six APDs were all equipped with depth charges and 40-millimeter antiaircraft guns. When, in a few days, we joined a convoy of large transports and warships, our APDs took up positions on the flanks of the convoy as anti-submarine protection. One day we had a bit of excitement when we went on a high-speed run and dropped several depth charges. There was no evidence that our attack was successful or that the alert that caused it was real or a false alarm.

Because of the need to accommodate passengers the Navy crew on APDs was somewhat truncated, making it necessary to employ Marines for some shipboard duties such as lookouts and ammunition handlers for the guns. On this trip I was put in charge of the forward damage control party consisting of three sailors and two Marines. The ship's first lieutenant mustered us on the well deck and showed us the small locker containing the damage control equipment. The array was amusing; it consisted of sledges, axes and an assortment of wooden plugs of varying

149

diameter from one to about six inches. In response to my query as to what we should do in case of a major hit he said, "Jump through it." During this meeting one of the sailors, an assistant cook, was whining and bitching to the officer in a manner and in such terms that amazed me. We wouldn't let a Marine private talk to his corporal like that. The state of discipline on the ship worried me if lowly swab jockeys could talk to the ship's first lieutenant like that.

On or about June 9 we sailed into the immense lagoon of Eniwetok, one of the Marshall Islands captured by the Marines four months earlier. We were absolutely awestruck by the number of ships anchored in the lagoon. There were dozens of LSTs and large troop transports. Every type of warship, from battle wagons and aircraft carriers to tiny rocket bearing LCIs, was present. We knew then we were going into a sizable operation and we were soon given the word — we were going to attack and take Saipan, one of the Marianas Islands, the group that includes Guam, captured from us in December 1941. As explained to us, this would be a three-division operation with the Second and Fourth Marine Divisions landing abreast on the island's west coast and the Army's 27th Division in reserve.

Saipan is a large island, about 72 square miles, located about 1,500 miles southeast of Tokyo. The terrain is dominated by a 1,500-foot peak called Mt. Tapotchau. The island was garrisoned by an estimated 24,000 Japanese soldiers who had a long time to dig in. Japan had taken over the island during World War I and had extensively colonized it. The native population, Chamorro, had been completely subjugated and used as laborers in the sugar cane fields which covered much of the arable land of the island and the neighboring island, Tinian. The west coast of Saipan had a small city, Garapan, with an estimated population of about 20,000 Japanese civilians.

On June 10 or 11 we sailed from Eniwetok and were told our destination and mission. The mystery of our battalion's mission we had trained for was disclosed simultaneously with the news that it had been cancelled. We had been scheduled to land the night before "D-Day" in rubber boats on the east side of the island at a place called Magicienne Bay. We were to move rapidly inland to the top of Mt. Topotchau before daylight, set up a perimeter defense around the peak and hold it until

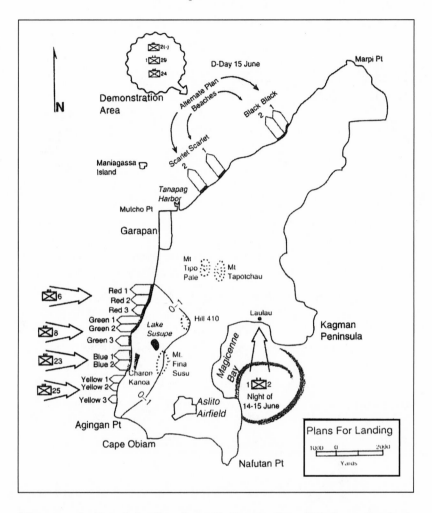

Saipan map showing the landing plan, including the aborted Magicenne Bay landing.

relieved. The planners had envisioned that from that lofty site we would have been able to observe enemy positions and actions on the whole island and at the same time deny that observation point to the enemy. The plan had been concocted at V Amphibious Corps Headquarters. The Second Division staff had opposed it from the start arguing strongly that the mission could not possibly succeed and would produce nothing but dead Marines. They finally prevailed and corps commander, Lt. Gen. Holland M. Smith, cancelled it. It's a darned good thing he did for had it gone ahead I would not be alive and writing this memoir. It was later learned that the Magicienne Bay beaches were heavily defended with emplaced machine guns and underwater mines. Moreover, had we gotten ashore the terrain to the top of the mountain was so formidable we could not have gotten to the top before daylight. In fact, it was later concluded that the torturous route from the beach to the peak could not have been covered in time in broad daylight with no enemy present.

Our changed mission was to act as division reserve but be prepared to land anywhere on orders. Thus, on June 15, we were positioned a mile or so off the beachhead and in a great position to observe the action. It was quite a show, with battleships and cruisers pummeling the shore with their big guns and carrier aircraft strafing and dropping bombs. One sad event took place. One of our aircraft, clearly visible as a Grumman, flew directly over the armada participating in the landing and was shot down. I was disturbed because the plane was so clearly visible as one of ours but the navy gunners kept firing until they shot it down. Our ship's loudspeakers were tuned to the frequency of the TBS (talk between ships) radio being used as the operation's communication link. Thus we could follow a bit of the action. The only message I remember was the admiral giving a cruiser's captain hell for sinking Japanese ships tied up or anchored in Tanapag harbor. He told the miscreant, "We are going to use that harbor!" We were not on the frequency used by Marine units and had no news as to how the landing was going. We were too far at sea to see what was going on.

Our respite ended the next morning when we got orders to go ashore and join the rest of our division. We embarked in LCVPs and headed for the beach but again, as at Tarawa, we had to abandon those boats and change to LVTs, amtracs. Saipan had a reef 1,000 yards offshore which could not be crossed by boats so it was back to the tractors. Again it was a piecemeal operation in which we sort of thumbed rides with ingoing amtracs. I got one to stop and jumped in with about half the platoon. Too late, I observed he was loaded with five-gallon cans of fuel for the vehicles ashore. There would be no survivors if we took a hit from the artillery fire which was exploding around us as we approached the reef. That fire peed me off—this wasn't "D-Day," this was D plus one, those guns should have been silenced yesterday.

We landed at a place called Charon Kanoa, on the extreme south border of the Second Division's assigned beachhead. A badly shell-damaged factory with the remainder of what had been a tall chimney dominated the beach. It had been a refinery producing sugar from the sugar cane grown everywhere on Saipan and its close neighbor Tinian. I had no time to enjoy the scenery for this was a "hot beach" constantly under fire from artillery and mortars. Fortunately the beach was in defilade and the small arms fire from the front line somewhere beyond the beach passed harmlessly overhead. The surprising thing about this beach was the group of Marines assigned to unload ammo and other supplies from the constant chain of amtracs—THEY WERE BLACK! This was an entirely new thing to me, for the Marine Corps I knew had no blacks.

The first wave at Saipan keeping their heads down waiting to continue the assault (U.S. Marine Corps).

I learned later these men were part of an all-black company trained at Montford Point, Camp Lejeune, North Carolina. Whatever their origin, they were doing a hellova dangerous job. Two of them were wounded by shell fragments while we were mixed in with them.

In short order the rest of the battalion came ashore and we moved out to the north. We had just started when I experienced a close encounter with the angel of death. An artillery shell impacted the sand a yard or two in front of me and skipped harmlessly out to sea like the flat stones we used to throw across the pond when we were kids. The caliber of the round and the type of weapon which fired it on such a flat trajectory are unknown. What is certain is that had it detonated I would not be writing this recollection.

We had quite a distance to go for we were assigned to backup the Sixth Marines, who held the extreme north end of the beachhead. We reached the area and dug in 20 or 30 yards from the beach behind the front line, ate chow and settled in for the night. It was absurdly quiet with almost no firing from our side or theirs. Except for Lt. Herber, who dug in alone, the rest of the platoon dug in two to a hole. Sgt. Daniel Sprague,* my platoon guide, and I dug in together Although we were nestled in behind the Sixth Marines we set a 50 percent watch, with one man awake in each hole at all times.

It was a night to remember! At some time after midnight we were hit with one of the most intense artillery barrages I experienced in the war. It was big stuff too, probably about 150-millimeter. Most of the platoon had never experienced a shelling of any kind and began whimpering and crying out. It was new to the lieutenant also and he called to me, "Rogal, tell the CP I am going to take the platoon out of here." Of course that was ridiculous and I ignored it. Sprague and I yelled at the troops to knock off the chatter and stay low in their holes. One kid yelled to me his rifle had been cut in half so I ordered all of them to put their weapons in their foxholes.

The artillery fire slackened after a while but it was soon replaced

---

*Dan Sprague had been assigned to my platoon from the weapons platoon when the company was pared down to 120 for the special Magicienne Bay mission. The regularly assigned platoon guide was a Sergeant Clymer. He rejoined us later and Sprague went back to the weapons platoon.

by a hellish curtain of machine gun fire, the cracking of some sort of flat trajectory shell fire and the rumble of heavy weapons. At the time it was not apparent to us what in the hell was going on except there was no question that the Sixth Marines in front of us were in a heck of a fight. Indeed they were — a thousand or so Japs accompanying and mounted on more than 24 medium tanks had attacked with their usual ferocity and disregard for casualties. Our bivouac area was almost in the middle of the fight but we could not fire a shot. At any rate our help wasn't needed. The Sixth Marines knocked out almost all the tanks and killed 700 or more enemy troops. The tanks were no match for our bazookas and 37mm antitank guns.

At 07:30 on D plus two, the Sixth went on the attack and we were assigned the task of "cleaning up the battlefield." This meant we were to mount a sweep across the area and determine if all the dead enemy were really dead. The aftermath of a battle is not a pretty sight. The first gruesome sight to greet us was the remains of the Marines who manned the line at the corner where the north-south line joined the east-west line from the beach. A heavy water-cooled machine gun had been emplaced here to cover both the north and east fronts. Its jacket had been holed by enemy fire but the gray condition of the metal evidenced it had continued to fire until it overheated and froze. Its crew lay dead from many wounds, with the gunner draped over his frozen gun. What a fight those guys put up! I don't know how many casualties the 1-6 had that night but there were dead Marines all over the place. We did not disturb them. The "graves registration" people would follow us and take care of the bodies, properly identifying them and removing them for burial in a trench being dug closer to the beach.

More than 20 Jap tanks littered the area, some of them draped with Jap bodies. Dozens and dozens of Jap soldiers covered the field as far as I could see. I had the feeling the Japs had thrown their "Sunday punch" to no avail. I relieved one corpse of his sword and Nambu pistol. I later rigged a shoulder holster for the pistol and wore it that way for the rest of the campaign. It was a sweet shooting piece. I put a Jap mess kit on one of the tanks as a target and was amazed at how well I could shoot the thing.

As we proceeded across the battlefield we came upon a number of

Japanese light tank. Jap tanks were poorly armored and no match for our anti-tank weapons, including the infantry's hand-held bazooka (U.S. Marine Corps).

deep, partially covered emplacements dug to serve as bomb shelters. The first one we hit contained what appeared to be a dead Jap soldier. One of our men from the Third Platoon jumped into the hole to investigate and was shot dead by the Jap, who had been playing possum. After that we threw grenades in the holes to make sure they contained no live Japs. But that procedure resulted in tragedy. The Second Platoon, operating to my left, heard a noise of some sort in a large, almost completely covered emplacement and dropped in a grenade. To our horror the explosion produced screams and crying of children. Six or seven little Chamorro girls in school uniforms had taken shelter in the hole. Our corpsmen did what they could for their wounds but some of them looked pretty far gone. This was the only time I saw combat Marines with tears in their eyes.

The next day produced excitement of a unique kind. We, and every-

Fortunately, casualties among the native Chamorro population were light. They had hidden in prepared bomb shelters during the pre–invasion bombardment. Here, a Marine rescues a Chamorro women and her children (U.S. Marine Corps).

one around us, became mightily concerned when an ominous green cloud appeared a mile or so to our south in the Fourth Division area. Someone whispered, "Gas," and a near panic began with everyone, including this writer, regretting having followed the usual practice of discarding their gas masks shortly after hitting the beach. I wasted no time and returned to the area where the Sixth Marines had received heavy casualties. I quickly found four or five gas masks and carried them back to the platoon and passed them out to the guys I first encountered. The alert was over in a few minutes when the word was passed that the green cloud was composed of some harmless chemical exploded by our artillery.

I received a nasty blow while in this area. One of the batteries of the Tenth Marines was situated nearby and I paid it a visit, looking for a friend who had been a fellow patient in the hospital at Pearl Harbor. I asked around and eventually located a first sergeant who informed me that my friend was dead, killed the day before by an accidental discharge of his own weapon. He had stood the carbine against a bush. When he retrieved it he leaned over the bush and pulled the weapon toward him. The trigger caught on a twig and the weapon discharged into his face killing him instantly. I was really disturbed by this for I had grown really fond of this guy during our hospital stay. We would spend hours talking about our pre–Marine Corps lives and our plans for life after the war. He had been wounded in the buttocks at Tarawa while wading ashore. Apparently the bullet which struck him was tumbling, for it cut an awful deep groove across his left cheek which could not be sewn shut but had to grow shut like the wound in my knee. His death, and particularly the way it happened, saddened me for I had formed few close friendships in the Corps.

On D plus three we were assigned an area on the left of the line of attack and moved off to the north. We met very light resistance and suffered no casualties in the company. A defensive line was set up south of the coastal city of Garapan and there we stayed for about a week. Our section of the line had easy going over small hills and agricultural land in contrast to the troops on our right who had the heavily wooded Mount Topatchau to contend with. Small groups and single Japs probed our line at night and inflicted some casualties. One man died from a bayonet wound. He was sound asleep when the Jap pinned him to the ground with the bayonet on the end of his rifle. His buddy, also asleep in the same hole, awakened and shot the Jap. Another fellow was nicked by a sword. This sword incident was amusing in a macabre sort of way. It happened on a black rainy night. I was on watch when I heard a loud CLANG, a scream, some cursing and a single shot. I investigated and found that a single Jap had infiltrated and gotten to the rear of our line. He approached one of our men, sitting erect on watch in his foxhole and, of course, looking the other way. The Jap had raised his sword and brought it down with full force squarely on the helmet of the sitting Marine. The noise awakened the sitter's foxhole mate, who shot the Jap. The intended victim got off with only a fright, a creased helmet and a severe headache.

I played a part in another amusing incident on this line. I was sharing a foxhole with my lieutenant, Bill Herber, who had just relieved me and was standing one of his first watches in a combat situation. I had curled up in my poncho to keep off the rain and was trying to sleep. Herber nudged me and whispered, "There's a Jap out here." Thinking he was experiencing a typical "new man" syndrome I said something to calm him and pulled the poncho back over my head. This didn't work and he gave me a violent shake and whispered more loudly, "Goddammit, there's a Jap out here!" This aroused me and I sat up, looked around and there, clearly outlined against the night sky and less than ten yards away, was a Jap soldier holding a rifle! I hurriedly grabbed my carbine and banged two shots at the guy. I may have hit him but probably missed, for we found no body the next morning. Herber never let me forget the incident.

During our stay on this line we had some fun shooting a small Jap artillery piece we had captured. The only problem was we had no fuses for the shells and thus were shooting duds. The only Jap activity was to drop a few mortar rounds on us from time to time. I have always feared mortars for, unlike artillery shells, you can't hear incoming mortar rounds until it's too late. Thus it would piss me off when Captain Brooks would force me and the other senior NCOs and platoon leaders to leave the protection of our holes and report to his CP only to get the word that he had heard from the battalion CP and they had nothing to tell us. We would look at each other in disbelief and sprint back to our foxholes. But Lou Brooks was a good guy who had been an enlisted man before the war. He was a weightlifter with an amazing muscular physique. He was courageous and took care of his men. You can't ask more from a Marine officer.

Robert Sherrod's second book covering his adventures as Time-Life's war correspondent in the war against Japan, *On to Westward*,* describes an occurrence during the Saipan battle which produced one of the biggest brouhahas of World War II. Bob's reporting of the incident gave ammunition to the Hearst press to use in its campaign for the aggrandizement of General Douglas MacArthur and its criticism of Marine Corps tactics.

*New York: Duell, Sloan & Pearce, 1945.

During the first couple of weeks of the Saipan battle we made slow progress. Our movement north stopped for days at a time. The problem with such slow progress, as the Marines see it, is that static units, just sitting around, continue to take casualties and lose strength from sickness and other causes while gaining no ground and inflicting no harm on the enemy. It's a zero sum game and combat effectiveness suffers. I well remember these delays, for the Jap mortars had our range and made it risky to get out of your foxhole. The cause of our inertia was the failure of the Army 27th Division, on our right flank, to move aggressively. The Marine lines on the left could not move forward, for it would leave a dangerous, in fact untenable, hole in the front line. The 27th Army Division was a National Guard outfit commanded by Major Gen. Ralph Smith, a leader much loved by his men. Faced with this situation, Lt. Gen. Holland M. "Howlin' Mad" Smith, the overall commander of the operation, did the unthinkable, on June 24 he relieved the Army general. Here is Bob Sherrod's account of what happened:

> The Army division had only a 2000 yard front with six battalions to cover it, but its progress was too slow for the Marine Tactics. (We've got to win this battle quickly, so these ships can get out of the harbor and get on with the next operation.) Last night, I was told at corps headquarters, one Marine outfit had taken a hill in front of the lagging Army troops, "rather than risk losing it back to the Japs." The third Army regiment, the 105th was still stalled in the coral-packed southeast corner of the island, Nafutan point. Holland Smith had ordered two of the regiment's battalions out of this area, on the theory that one battalion should be able to clean out the Japs down there, where three had not yet succeeded.
>
> "We cannot attack mount Tapotchau until the Twenty-seventh division moves up," said a staff officer at corps headquarters, "and we've got to have that high ground so we can look down the Jap's throats instead of letting them look down ours. Besides, if we don't keep pressing 'em they'll reorganize and dig in deeper, and casualties will shoot up higher. We can't sit back and expect artillery and naval gunfire to blast 'em out of those caves.
>
> I saw General "Howlin' Mad" at his headquarters; he was nervous and remorseful. "Ralph Smith is my friend," he said, "but good God, I've got a duty to my country. I've lost 7000 Marines. Can I afford to lose back what they have gained? To let my marines die in vain? I know I'm sticking my neck out — the National Guard will try to chop it off — but my conscience is clear. I did my duty. When Ralph Smith issued an order to hold after I had told him to attack, I had no other choice but to relieve him."

8. Saipan and Tinian

Bob points out that the war correspondents on Saipan didn't even think about writing a story on the incident for, in the first place, the Navy censors would never have let it go by. But someone leaked the story and, ironically, Ralph Smith's relief was first publicized by the source who sought to defend him. Hearst's *San Francisco Examiner*, on July 8, carried a front page story which, among other bad things, stated, "Allegedly excessive loss of life attributed to Marine Corps impetuosity of attack has brought a breach between Marine and Army commanders in the Pacific.... The controversy hangs upon Marine tactics versus Army tactics, the Marines seeking a swift decision at high cost, while the Army moved more deliberately — at lesser cost." The Marines were outraged. They had to take the beachheads with high losses while the Army, coming in later, had to merely walk ashore. Moreover, the Marines had done almost all of the fighting to that date. Hearst continued the attack on July 18, but this time in the *New York Journal-American*:

> The American people were shocked by the staggering casualties on Saipan, even before the fall of the island. The Army's advocate of more cautious tactics has been relieved of his command.... The supreme command in the Pacific should, of course, be logically and efficiently entrusted to General Douglas MacArthur.... The important and significant thing the American people DO know is that equally difficult and hazardous military operations conducted in the Pacific War under General Douglas MacArthur have been successfully completed with little loss of life in most cases and with an obvious MINIMUM loss of life in all cases."

This made many Navy and Marine commanders see red. They considered they had done a pretty good job in moving the Central Pacific front line from Hawaii to Saipan, 3,700 miles, with a loss of only 4,277 lives. General Alexander Vadegrift's memoir, *Once a Marine*,* states the former Marine Corps commandant's view that Navy Admiral Ernest King and he stood completely behind General Smith:

> Any commander traditionally and by law holds the right to relieve any subordinate right or wrong in peace or war.... Under the same conditions Holland would have relieved a Marine officer and so would I.... Furious at this obviously unfair [newspaper] attack, I told the Secretary of the Navy and

*New York: Ballantine, 1966.

Admiral King that I stood completely behind Holland. King did too but thought that in the best interests of fighting the war we should adopt a "no comment" policy. Logic forced me to agree.

The last week in June we launched an attack to the north. The principal opposition was artillery and mortar fire. We had the help of our own artillery and aircraft. Late in the day we moved up on a stone mountain and ran into heavy opposition. Within a few minutes we had two guys killed and another wounded. At this point Herber ordered me to go around the east side of the vertical stone promontory and "consolidate the line." I hadn't the least idea what he was talking about but "good soldier Rogal" ran north along the rock wall until it gave way to a canyon There weren't any troops out there, only empty foxholes and some discarded equipment. By this time I was all alone, about 100 yards in front of our company line. My presence did not go unnoticed and some Jap machine gunners opened up on me. They were located in caves on the rear, northeast face of the rock prominence I had passed. I hit the deck and tried to find cover in a shell hole, but this was rocky ground and the shell hole was too shallow. I tried but couldn't deepen it with my entrenching tool. The machine guns kept firing but the rounds passed over my head. Their firing positions were slightly lower than my ridge line. They couldn't hit me if I stayed in my shallow hole, but I couldn't get away — if I stood up to run they would have me cold. I didn't relish the idea of staying out there until dark, 100 yards in Jap territory, but it was the only option I had. After what seemed like an hour but might have been less, the fire suddenly stopped. I glanced to the rear and saw the source of my salvation — one of our Sherman tanks was approaching along the ridge line and began firing into the caves that harbored my tormentors. A Marine was walking behind the tank and directing it using its external telephone. I wasted no time, grabbed my pack and weapons and ran for the tank. The walking Marine raised his weapon but fortunately held fire. When I got closer I saw that the Marine directing the tank was my close friend Bob Boyd. I got back to the platoon and declared to Herber that I didn't appreciate weird orders that can get people killed. I thanked Bob but he told me he had almost shot me for he didn't think there were any Marines out there. He had brought the tank to get the machine guns. Saving me was serendipitous.

On the following day, June 22, we moved left and took up a position on an east-west running ridge on the south side of Garapan, the island's largest town. We had an excellent view of the ruins left by our naval gunfire and bombing. Since our automatic weapons had not been fired for a few days and may have gotten wet during the landing, I requested and received permission to test fire our BARs into the town. We got them all going and laid down a pretty good curtain of fire into a sort of octagon-shaped large stone building in our immediate front which had withstood the bombardments and still had its roof. Its open windows provided good targets for our guns and the troops were enjoying the firing opportunity. While we were not firing tracers, in time our rounds ignited something inside the building and black smoke billowed from the windows. And then, surprise, surprise, about ten uniformed Jap troops burst from the building running north, away from us. By the time we brought fire to bear on them they disappeared into the rubble of the town. What a missed opportunity!

Something far more significant occurred while we occupied that ridge line. Since it was the front line and provided an excellent view of the enemy's positions in the ruined town, the ridge was populated with observation posts for naval guns, our artillery and mortars, and air support. The air observer was just a few yards from my position and I could clearly hear his directions to supporting aircraft. The aircraft he was working with were Grumman torpedo bombers, TBFs, equipped with air-to-ground missiles. They would start their approach to our south and fly directly over our heads to impact their missiles in the town. This meant the missiles would be released while the plane was well behind us. When aimed and dropped correctly the missiles would pass safely overhead and hit in the town. The observer would talk to the pilots while they were making their runs. As a plane approached and the pilot was on the correct glide path he would say something like, "OK, good, good." I was having my morning coffee when suddenly the observer's voice went up in volume and he was screaming to the incoming pilot, "NO, NO, NO!" I spun around and saw the incoming plane just as it released its missiles directly at us. I dived backward into a large Jap-built emplacement a split second before the missiles hit the ridge. I didn't get a scratch but many Marines on the ridge were killed, including the executive officer of the Tenth Marines, who was acting as forward observer for his artillery.

On the next day we launched an attack. The opposition in my immediate area was light. I could see that B Company on our right was meeting serious machine gun fire but quickly overcame it with the aid of a couple of Sherman tanks. We reached our objective, an east-west street we christened "Radio Road," well before dark. While I was trying to determine where to have the platoon dig in, a kid named Lucas from Paul Boyd's platoon approached and struck up a conversation. We were standing on a street corner next to a brick column which formed part of a gate to a destroyed mansion. Suddenly a bullet struck the pillar. I hit the deck and immediately discovered the bullet had gone through Lucas' chest before it hit the column. This created a classic combat problem — how to get help for Lucas without getting hit by the same sniper. Lucas was moaning and asking me if he was going to die. I tried to reassure him, told him he had a "dream wound," and in a few minutes was able to persuade a passing tank to park in a position to screen him from the sniper. With that protection we were able to get a corpsman to treat Lucas and help get him out of there. I wonder if he did survive.

This episode teed me off. The Jap could have shot me instead of Lucas, for we were standing only a couple of feet apart. I determined to try to find the guy before he got any more Marines. The general direction of the shot was revealed by the crater where it had hit the pillar after hitting Lucas. I started off in a general northeast direction and soon hit pay dirt. A crew trying to set up their 37mm antitank gun had come under fire from a sniper and one of them told me he believed the guy was in a spider hole partially covered with a sheet of corrugated metal roofing. A depression on the south side of the hole enabled the occupant to fire his weapon and then sink back into obscurity. These metal sheets from knocked-down houses made perfect camouflage, for the ground was covered with them. I circled north of the spider hole he pointed out and dropped an incendiary grenade into the opening the occupant had used to aim and fire his rifle. (A fragmentation grenade was out of the question for its explosion, if rejected by the hole's occupant, would injure me and the gun crew.) There was no doubt I had the right hole for the grenade came right back out and began burning harmlessly on the ground. It was the only one I had so I asked the 37mm crew if they had one. They passed me a strange-looking grenade they told me was a new type of incendiary. I pulled the pin, dropped it down the hole and ran back a few steps, for I didn't know what to expect from this new weapon. It was well I moved back, for the Jap also threw this one out. It exploded in a ball of fire and lumps of white phosphorous flew everywhere. Fortunately, none hit me but one of the 37mm crew was slightly burned. A few seconds later an explosion inside the spider hole revealed the Jap had taken his own life with a fragmentation grenade. I got a lot of satisfaction out of killing that guy; it was kinda personal.

That night we dug in along the south side of a street which ran from the city up into the hills. It was a quiet night with very little firing from either side. On the following morning I had another hair-raising escape from a premature demise. As I walked the line, one of the men fired a shot into the rubble across the street. I got angry when troops fired their weapons needlessly. It puts everyone on edge and on the deck for fear of incoming fire. When I asked this kid what he had fired at he pointed to a Jap body lying face down on the rubble across the street. I ordered him to knock off the firing at a clearly dead body. He remonstrated, insisting he saw the Jap move. To prove him wrong I walked over to the body for a closer look. When I got about ten feet from the corpse it rolled on its right side and fired at me with a small automatic pistol. The round missed me by inches and I quickly ended the threat with two rounds from my carbine. Why he missed me became apparent when I turned the body over. He was blind! His face had been severely burned by some source, probably napalm. I marveled then, and still do, at the fighting resolution of that soldier. Instead of seeking aid for his terrible injury he determined to go out fighting, killing one last enemy.

My memory is hazy about activities for the next few days but I think we stayed in place for a while and then resumed the attack northward through the eastern suburb of Garapan. This area was semirural with fallow fields and an occasional knocked-down farm house. By July 4 the town was behind us but there was still a lot of fighting going on in the central part of the town to our left rear. We were advancing in a skirmish line against little or no opposition. About midday we arrived at the south edge of a large flat field which was completely devoid of vegetation. A brush-filled depression running along the east boundary provided cover for an advance. I was concerned that the trees and shrubbery which bordered the north side of the 500-yard field could conceal an army of Japs with their weapons. I told Lt. Herber we should take the platoon in column via the depression and reform into a skirmish line after we got past this wide-open field. He asked our company commander, Captain Louis Brooks, for permission and, I was told, Brooks asked the battalion CP, which denied permission saying, "The orders are to advance in a skirmish line." This idiocy teed me off for I was certain there were Japs in the tree line on the other side of the field.

And I was right. We got about 100 yards into the field when a Jap tank pulled out of the brush and laid into us with machine gun fire. In seconds I had three men down seriously wounded. I had found protection from the fire in a deep pit which had apparently been dug to house some sort of heavy weapon. But how do we get the wounded out of the bare field without losing the rescuers? A partial answer arrived in a few minutes in the form of one of our halftracks, which blew the turret off the Jap tank with one 75mm round. With that problem out of the way I stood erect to begin getting the downed men to medical assistance. Suddenly someone hit me on the back of my head with a baseball bat, or that's what the blow to my head felt like. I slumped down to the ground in a sitting position and looked rather stupidly at my helmet lying on the ground by my left side. The helmet revealed what had felled me; it had a sizeable hole in back and the left side of the inner liner was slashed from rear to front. In a daze I knew I had been hit by a bullet and I suspected it was in my head, nestled behind my forehead. That fear was quickly dispelled when I felt a burning at my beltline, reached down and recovered a red-hot jacketed bullet which had apparently lost momentum after circling inside the helmet and fell inside my blouse. I dropped it, which was a mistake, for it would have solved a question which has nagged me ever since. Was it a Jap bullet or American from the fight going on in downtown Garapan? I'll never know but suspect it might have been the latter, for I was facing northeast when hit.

Head wounds bleed a lot and the bullet had cut a three or four-inch groove where it grazed the back of my head, so I headed back to the rear to get sewed up. I was ambulatory so I hitched a ride in a passing jeep which dropped me at a forward aid station where they put me on a stretcher. The doctor there tried to talk me out of the Jap pistol I wore in an improvised shoulder holster, saying, "You won't be needing it where you are going." I knew I'd be back with the company in a few days and told him to get lost. After a short ride in an ambulance I arrived at a field hospital housed in several large tents. The staff took care of my wound and assigned me a cot in a large tent made into a ward. The division CO, Major General Thomas E. Watson, visited the tent one day and asked me what had happened to me. Stupidly, all I said was, "I got shot." He looked as if he expected more of an answer but left without further comment.

A day or two after I entered the hospital they brought in my company commander, Lou Brooks. As soon as I could, I went to see him. He was quite a sight. Hit by dozens of fragments from a Jap grenade, or other explosive, he was spotted with small bandages from head to foot. He asked me to tell the gunny, Bob Boyd, to save his Jap oil can. I laughed and told him he was not coming back to the company in his condition but he insisted he would make it. Of course it never happened and, when I got back to the company the next day, Bill Sanders, the executive officer, was company commander. That was OK with the men; we liked him.

While I was in the hospital on the early morning of July 7, the Japs launched their final, all-out desperate banzai attack against two battalions of the Army 105th Regiment. The suicide attack by about 2,000 army and navy troops demolished the 105th's line and was finally stopped by Marine artillerymen of the 10th Marines. The Second Marines were not involved with that fracas but A Company had repelled a smaller banzai attack the following night, which earned Bill Sanders a bronze star and Bob Boyd a Silver Star. I returned to the company the next day and missed all the fun. In a weird sort of way banzai attacks were almost pleasurable for defending Marines. Here at last were the elusive enemy soldiers you had been fighting against for weeks, fully exposed to your counter fire and dying like flies. It sure beat digging them out one by one from strong defensive positions and taking a lot of casualties in the process. Our defensive preparations, with interlocking machine gun and BAR fire behind barbed wire and Marines throwing lots of grenades, were usually sufficient to repel attacks with minimum defensive casualties. Of course, it is doubtful that any defensive line could have resisted the 2,000-man attack which hit the Army on July 7. That one would not have been fun!

The island was declared secured on about July 9. In Marine Corps usage the term "secured" meant the end of organized resistance but ignored the hundreds of enemy soldiers hiding out in the jungle or hills. A Company had a few casualties cleaning out these remnants long after I had left the island for the States. One of the guys killed was Channing Miller, a friend and a heck of a Marine. For about ten days we rested, cleaned weapons and fought flies. The flies of Saipan were somewhat larger than the common housefly and were somewhat greenish in hue. And they were present in the trillions. Simply eating became a chore for you could not bring spoon from can to mouth without a load of flies piggybacking on the spoon. We guessed the presence of thousands of dead bodies provided them with places to lay their eggs. Our standing joke at mealtimes was to direct one of the group to "take a crap and bunch these goddamn flies!"

During the ten-day rest, the cruiser which had supported our regiment with naval gunfire sent us a few cases of beer, about one beer per man, or maybe a few less. That served as a catalyst and all kinds of Japanese potables emerged from the men's packs. The large two-liter bottles contained sake and the smaller 750ml brown bottles contained a potent Jap whiskey. In our dehydrated, half-starved condition, this booze had a smashing effect and, in a short time, half the company was soused to the gills and raucously enjoying life. We made so much noise the battalion CP sent word to tone it down or knock it off. The drinks had a strange effect on me — my head and speech were clear but my legs would not work. Herber had to half carry me back to our foxhole.

During the party I did something I am ashamed of. At the beginning of the rest period we received a replacement lieutenant who instantly made himself obnoxious by trying to reform the way we were running the company. We operated on a "rank has its privileges" basis and officers and senior sergeants never stood in line for chow or anything else. Also, Bob Boyd had liberated a room-size mosquito net which we erected and used as a mess hall for the officers and sergeants. These actions upset our new lieutenant and he made his feelings known in the hearing of the entire company. This open criticism infuriated Sanders and annoyed the rest of us in the leadership group. Moreover, his egalitarianism did not go over well with his platoon — they wanted a leader, not a friend. For some unknown reason the lieutenant selected me as a confidant and, near the end of our drunken frolic, he asked me, "Bill, I am not getting along in this company, can you tell me why?" In sotto voice I told him, "Lieutenant, there's a clique in this company which feels you can't run a platoon worth a damn." I waited a second and then added, "And I'm one of them." He said nothing and spun away. Shortly thereafter he was transferred and I never saw him again. In recent years I have read at least two articles by the lieutenant relating his combat experiences on Tarawa and Saipan.

One other thing of note occurred while we were in this bivouac. The battalion was informed the division had authority to commission five second lieutenants. For unknown reasons the officers in A Company felt I should be a candidate and sent my name to battalion for consideration. In response I was summoned to be interviewed by the battalion CO, Lt. Col. Wood B. Kyle. The interview was a disaster, for Col. Kyle's only question was, "Why do you want to become a second lieutenant?" This caught me unawares and I blurted out this asinine answer: "Well, I've led a platoon in three campaigns and feel I might as well get paid for it." I am sure this answer went over like a lead balloon but it probably didn't matter, for we learned later that all five commissions had been awarded to men working in division headquarters.

About July 20 we were informed our job wasn't finished — we were slated to attack and conquer the neighboring island of Tinian. My reaction to this news was one of anger but reluctant acceptance. I had survived the war so far against heavy odds and wondered if I would make it through another campaign. I was no longer an eager warrior, but a tired and resigned one, hoping to survive one more foray "into the cannon's mouth." My mood was lightened somewhat by the scuttlebutt that the men who had made the original landing on Guadalcanal, i.e., those with more than 24 months abroad, would be sent to the States after this next action. Also, we got the welcome word that the Fourth Division would make the initial landing on "D-Day" and we would land later. Here is a map showing the landing plan, including site of the fake landing diversion.

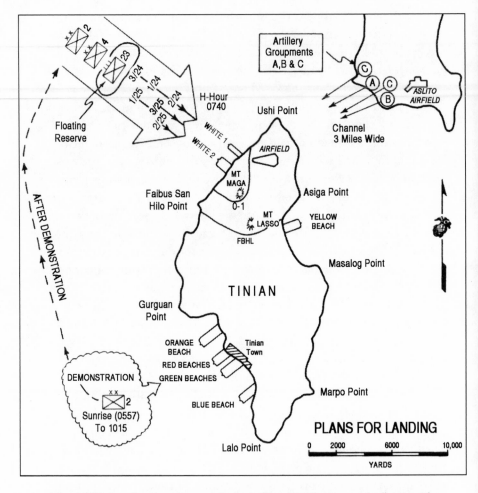

Map of Tinian showing the assault, including the "demonstration" area, where the battleship *Colorado* and destroyer *Norman Scott* suffered many casualties.

Tinian was three miles south of Saipan. Artillery based on Saipan was able to support the initial landing and subsequent attacks east and south on Tinian. Thirteen battalions participated in the bombardment. Tinian is slightly smaller than Saipan, about 11 miles long by five miles wide. A large airfield, named Ushi by the Japs, covered the north end. Under our management and with some improvements, it became the launching pad for the *Enola Gay*.

170

8. Saipan and Tinian

On July 24 we boarded a transport and were given the heavenly opportunity to take a hot shower and wash our filthy clothes. The ship sailed a few miles south and, together with other transports and numerous fighting ships, battleships, cruisers and destroyers, simulated making a landing on the southwest coast of Tinian, off Tinian Town. This feint produced a lethal and unexpected response from the Jap defenders. A previously undiscovered battery of big guns scored hits on the battleship *Colorado* and the destroyer *Norman Scott*. Both ships suffered severe casualties. Thank heaven they ignored my transport. But apparently the feint worked, for the Fourth Division landing on the northwest beach went smoothly. The enemy didn't attack the beachhead until late that night, after the Fourth Marines had installed a perimeter defense and were well dug in behind barbed wire. The attackers were decimated, losing 1,500 soldiers. All in all the assault on Tinian was a "text book" operation.

On July 25 we embarked in LCVPs and headed for the beach. As at Saipan, I was a bit surprised and irritated when we came under artillery or mortar fire as we neared the beach: "Why hadn't those Fourth Division clowns gotten rid of these irritants?" One of the shells made a near miss on Paul Boyd's boat, making a hole in the port quarter which was quickly closed with a kapok life preserver. Nevertheless, we got ashore without casualties and attacked eastward across the immense Ushi airfield. Aided by artillery fire from our batteries sited on the south coast of Saipan, we took the field in a few hours. The trek across the airfield was interesting for the revetments held the remains of Jap planes and, if memory serves, a fighter or small bomber with black cross German markings. The attack was also noteworthy as it was almost unopposed and we took no casualties.

When we reached the east coast we turned south along the shore. We maintained that left flank position for the rest of the campaign. And, fortunately for us, that eastern shoreline was lightly defended. But it wasn't deserted. On the second day of the southward advance I had an amusing encounter with the enemy. Two Jap soldiers, wearing knee pants, leather puttees and white shirts, emerged from some trees and waved a white flag almost in my face. They were unarmed and obviously not a threat so I beckoned them to approach. The older man spoke a little

English and I learned he was a colonel who acted as paymaster for all Jap troops in the islands. He told me he resided in Tokyo with a wife and two kids whose photos he proudly displayed. I asked him if he knew who we were. He responded, "U.S. soldiers." "No, no," I said. "We are Marines, U.S. Marines." He smiled and repeated, "U.S. soldiers." In desperation I pointed to the Marine Corps emblem and the letters USMC printed on my uniform blouse but he never got it. So much for the Marines' belief that the Japs knew about us and were deathly scared of tangling with "U.S. Marines."

During the march south we encountered something new to us, Japanese civilians. Almost all were women, many with small children. They were weak and sorely in need of water. I offered my canteen to one mother who took it, unscrewed the cap and gave water to her two small kids by pouring a few drops into the canteen's cap and serving it that way to the kids. She drank a little the same way from the cap.

As we neared the southern tip of the island the Japs counterattacked several times but mostly at the Eighth Marines area to our right. These attacks were repulsed with light Marine casualties but the CO of the Third Battalion of the Sixth Regiment, Lt. Col. John Easley, lost his life during an attack on his CP.

During our attack on the high rocky ridges near the island's end we were supported by a new weapon, improvised napalm bombs dropped from aircraft. The results were spectacular but of uncertain effectiveness. Other weapons new to me were the rockets launched from racks fixed atop trucks. A dozen or more of these large rockets could be fired in rapid sequence so that all were in the air before the first one struck. The impact area virtually exploded, with trees, rocks and bodies erupting in a fountain of yellow flame. It was awesome and I thanked my lucky stars the enemy didn't have a similar weapon. However, one of those rockets almost did me in. When a rocket truck situated about 50 yards behind me let go its barrage, the propellant of one of the rockets failed and the rocket, spinning laterally, headed right for me! Like a darn fool I tried to run away but stumbled and sprawled flat on my face as the rocket landed beside me. Needless to say, the rocket didn't explode. We got a few nervous laughs out of that incident.

As we continued the advance we began taking more and more Jap civilians prisoner; almost all were women and children. There were exceptions. Among one group I spotted a nervous male in army pants with a civilian shirt. He was, like many of the refugees, carrying a woven straw bag which contained personal effects. We always searched these bags but this guy at first refused to hand it to me. The reason soon became obvious. Beneath his clothing in the bag were four grenades! I resisted the urge to kill him; butt stroked him with my rifle and sent him to the rear.

Not all the Japs were surrendering. Some were doing as their countrymen had done on Saipan — leaping from the cliffs into the sea. The soldiers were killing themselves in caves and on the rocks before us. One brave soul decided to have us send him to his maker. He laid down on his back on a rock at the foot of the cliff about 200 yards from us. We decided to help him and detailed one of our best shots to try to put him away. Our man took three shots at him and missed each time. After this

Time-out for a little kindness. Staff Sergeant Federico Claveria offers a candy tidbit to a little Chamorro in the internment camp on Tinian (U.S. Marine Corps).

display of marksmanship the Jap got up slowly and disappeared into a cave under the cliff. I assume he took care of the job himself.

One day at dusk I was standing on a coral rock watching one of our Landing Craft Infantry (LCI) cruising along and broadcasting messages in Japanese urging the holdouts to surrender. Suddenly the gunner on the ship cut loose with his 20-millimeter and I saw balls of orange flame coming right at me! I dove off the rock and cut my left elbow and hand on the sharp coral. The corpsman bound up the arm but it rapidly became infected. In a few days the arm began to swell and exude a sticky liquid. I probably should have gone to the rear to have one of the doctors look at it but I was concerned they might slap me into sick bay and make me miss my scheduled evacuation back to the USA. So I stuck it out and stayed with the company.

Within a day or two of this event we were informed the island was secured and our battalion was taken off the line and moved to the rear. This provided an opportunity to clean our weapons and get all our gear and clothing back into shape so that we would resemble a Marine platoon and not a bunch of itinerant bums. I passed the word and set all hands to cleaning weapons for inspection. They went busily to work and later in the day Herber and I went through the ritual of inspection, found everything in reasonable order and dismissed the platoon. Within a few moments a weapon discharged almost in my ear and the dreaded cry of "Corpsman!" rang out. What a mess! One of the men didn't want to go to the trouble of stripping down and cleaning his BAR so he hid it in a bush and fell in at inspection with a rifle. When he retrieved the BAR he grabbed it by the muzzle and pulled it from the bush. The trigger caught in the bush and the weapon went off when the muzzle was only a few inches from his upper arm. The bullet and muzzle blast almost amputated the arm. It was hanging by a piece of flesh and skin. We had trouble getting the bleeding stopped but quickly got him to the battalion aid station where a doctor took over. I hope he survived.

I remember that accidental discharge vividly for it was the last casualty I saw in World War II. And it was such a senseless event, with a young man losing his arm, if not his life, after the combat was over.

On August 4 the orders came; men with more than 24 months in the Pacific were detached and directed to proceed to the western shore for evacuation. I would be lying if I said I had mixed feelings about leaving A Company, for I was combat weary and had the thought that I was living on borrowed time. One cannot indefinitely travel in harm's way without paying the ultimate price. Sooner or later some Jap was going to get lucky and end my tenure on this globe. Moreover, I was not leaving any old friends behind; all the guys who were with me the whole way from Guadalcanal on were going with me, including the Boyd brothers and Ralph Wycoff. I think there were eight of us who had made it all the way. When I said goodbye to Herber he asked me to leave my issue wristwatch for, as usual, working watches were scarce and needed to set the nighttime sentries. He assured me he would send my samurai sword I had left in safe keeping with a guy in regimental headquarters on Saipan. After I had arrived stateside he wrote saying he had boxed and mailed the sword, but it never arrived. I did carry some souvenirs off the island, my Nambu pistol and some stuff from a Jap officer's trunk I found in a cave, including a flag, a "belt of a thousand stitches" and several personal photographs.

At the beach we boarded LCVPs and motored out to a transport anchored offshore. Here I ran into a problem. I couldn't climb the cargo net hanging over the side of the ship. My arm had swelled to double its regular size and was oozing a clear serum its entire length. But worse yet, it had lost all strength and would not permit me to go up the net. The problem was solved when some sailors rigged a line with a loop and hoisted me up the net. Whew, what a relief! It looked for a while I might be sent back ashore to a hospital.

When I got aboard I was given a bunk in the sick bay, which was merely a number of bunks arranged around an open cargo hatch. I had no sooner laid down when my space was invaded by a Jap antitank gun, which was swinging wildly as it was being lowered to a deck below. I escaped unscathed but angry as hell. I was told the gun was being shipped to the states for evaluation. The reason it was swinging wildly during its descent to the hold was the winches were being operated by the ship's inexperienced Navy gun crew. The ship's civilian crew refused to work unless paid overtime wages, which the captain refused to do. I was appalled, but had a more serious personal matter to think about — my injured arm.

175

This is the Japanese flag found in the cave on Tinian and the samurai sword from Tsingtao.

The next morning, after a sleepless night, I was visited by two Navy doctors who got into an argument over what to do about my arm. One suggested they "use the new stuff." The other demurred, saying, "We are only supposed to use it on serious cases." The first doc said, "What do you think this is? He may lose that arm." Fortunately, the first doc won the argument and I was given successive shots of the "new stuff," which turned out to be penicillin. In four days my arm had dried up and returned to normal. What would have happened without that brand new wonder drug?

We had a bit of excitement after a few days of sailing. One of our cargo holds contained a hundred or more Jap prisoners. They became restive and mutinous for some reason, probably the food. After a few anxious hours we discovered the problem was stimulated by our failure to separate officers from enlisted. After the few officers were segregated in separate quarters the near riot was over. In a few days we arrived at Maui, where the prisoners were disembarked for retention in a large prisoner camp.

The ship dropped us off on Oahu and we were assigned tents in the large tent camp near Pearl Harbor, the same camp I bunked in after my discharge from the hospital. The only noteworthy thing which occurred during our three or four-day stay in this camp was the theft of my Nambu pistol. Like an idiot, I hid it under the pillow on my cot while I went to a movie. It was gone when I returned. I still had my other souvenirs, the rifle, flag and photos, but I valued the pistol most, it was a sweet shooting weapon.

On August 26 we boarded the USS *Sea Scamp* and sailed for the States, arriving at San Francisco on September 4, about 27 months after leaving from San Diego. We were billeted in a barracks on Treasure Island and were immediately given shore leave. The problem was we were broke, except for one guy who had a half dollar. Also, the only clothing we had was the camouflaged utilities we had worn in combat. Nevertheless, we jumped on a bus and went ashore. We thought that a grateful civilian populace would buy us drinks if we acted thirsty enough. Our group of six or seven men went into a bar or club, commandeered a large round table and ordered one beer with the 50 cents we had and passed the beer around the table giving each of us a sip. Almost instantly drinks began to arrive and never stopped coming for the entire evening. Things got hazy after awhile but I vaguely recall the scenario was repeated at other nightspots until we were all drunk as hell. Somehow we got back to the base without casualties.

9

Camp Pendleton

In a day or two I departed from Frisco and reported to the Recruit Depot at San Diego. I have forgotten what method of transportation got me there, probably a train. After being completely outfitted with new uniforms, shoes and underclothes, I received the disappointing word that I would be stationed on the West Coast at Camp Joseph Pendleton for an indeterminate time up to a year. I had hoped to get an assignment on the East Coast near my home and Pearl. But the Corps needed combat-experienced NCOS as instructors at Pendleton and that's where I was going to spend the next 12 months.

In a few days I was given a thirty-day leave and, on September 12, I departed by train for home. Of course, I had to pay for my ticket and spend six or more days of my precious leave in round-trip transit. When I arrived at Lehighton I immediately went down to Washington to get Pearl. We had a little talk and I popped the question. She accepted and I bought a tiny diamond ring with all the money, about $125, that was left from the hundreds I had sent home for safekeeping.

While in Lehighton I was given a hero's welcome by everyone I encountered in town. The most noteworthy event was a huge party thrown by Eddie Mandour, a family friend and owner of a hotel and bar. It was a grand affair but none of my high school buddies were there; they were all away in military service. I was invited to a Rotary Club luncheon and gave a brief speech telling them we were winning.

In a few days we ran out of things to do and friends to see and took off by train for Pearl's home in Melmore, Ohio. Meeting her parents was quite an adventure but it went smoothly and we learned to like each other. Pearl's only sibling, her brother Gerald, was away in the Marine Corps. He later participated in the battle for Iwo Jima. I stayed in Melmore a couple of days and then entrained back to California and reported to Camp Pendleton on October 20, 1944.

My first assignment was as a student in classes preparing us to become instructors to recruits preparing for assignment to combat units. For weeks I attended needless boring lectures presented by unqualified teachers. Sure it was boring, but hey, it beat the hell out of being in combat. My first assigned homework assignment was to prepare a lesson plan for instructors to use in teaching the nomenclature, assembly, maintenance and tactical employment of the Browning Automatic Rifle, the BAR. The lesson plan was an outline of the teaching course showing the amount of time to be allotted to each segment of the program and included the text of each lecture to be used verbatim by the instructor. For reasons not explained to me, the presiding officers liked my plan so well they assigned me the job of preparing lesson plans for all of the subjects taught at the school, including small weapon tactics and weapons unfamiliar to me, such as the flame thrower. This was an office job without end, for the infantry school taught the maintenance, use and employment of all infantry weapons and the tactics employed by small units. I worked at this task for the remainder of my stay at Pendleton and produced a two-inch thick volume of text which is still in my possession. Of course, much of it was excerpted and paraphrased (plagiarized?) from the basic Field Manuals which covered each subject.

My office was at Tent Camp 2, located near the "back," north entrance to Camp Pendleton, not far from the pretty little town of San Clemente. We bunked in Quonset huts — not regal quarters but a far cry from the poncho covered foxholes I endured in the Pacific. After a few months in a foxhole you will never complain about an indoor, dry sack again.

In early December I made one of the dumbest mistakes of my life. The Marine Corps had been urging me to ship over (reenlist) after my four-year enlistment expired in early September. I was scornful of these efforts and determined to become a civilian as soon as the war was over. I was happy with my "COG" status, which meant I was retained in the service at the "convenience of the government." But then, in December, events in the European theatre changed my thinking. I read in a newspaper that the German army was putting up stiff resistance and would not be defeated within the next 12 months. The same article predicted the war against Japan might take another two years after the German defeat. At this time the Marines were offering men on COG status a bonus of about $250 to extend their enlistments for two years. I reasoned, incorrectly, that I should take the offer, for I was going to be in service for at least that time until the Japs surrendered. On December 5, like a dammed fool, I took the money and signed on for another two years. In less than nine months the war was over and I was stuck in the Corps until December 1946. But wait, there is more to this horror story. I got the money in cash, put it in my wallet and headed for San Diego in a friend's car. We stopped on the way at a tavern in Oceanside for a quick beer. When we arrived in the city my friend dropped me off near the Marine base and drove off. I intended to hail a cab and felt for my wallet. It was gone! I had no idea where my "friend" was headed. Since I didn't have a nickel and had no pass or identification, I checked in to the Marine base, told my story to the OD (officer of the day) and was put in the brig overnight. They put me on a bus back to Pendleton the next morning. The wallet and money never turned up. I believe it fell out of my pocket in the car and was retrieved by my "friend," the driver.

In January of 1945 Pearl arrived from Washington. Initially she stayed on Coronado Island in the home of a Navy captain's widow, Mrs. Ghent, who was the mother of a lawyer Pearl worked with at the National Labor Relations Board. It was a lovely home but its owner was a bit hard to take. She was horrified by the fact that Pearl was engaged to, egad, an enlisted man. In a short time Pearl found a room in a nice boardinghouse on 5th Avenue and a job in the offices of the Consolidated Vultee bomber plant, which was then building B24s, "Consolidated Liberators."

Back at Pendleton I kept scribbling away on my lesson plans but had trouble seeing much of Pearl, for I had no place to spend the night in San Diego when I got a day off. Bob Boyd's wife, Janie, and Ralph Wycoff's wife, Babe, had found and rented a house in San Diego but they had no room for an extra body, although I recall that Paul Boyd and I occasionally bunked on the living room floor. I think I also slept on a cot at the YMCA now and then.

After several months of this we decided that waiting to see if I survived the war made no sense and decided that we needed to start a home together right away — let the war bring what it may. On June 18 we tied the knot in the Methodist Church of Santa Anna. The preacher was a nice guy who questioned us at length before the ceremony. He told us he was concerned about the viability of wartime weddings and strove to officiate at only those he was sure had a chance to be successful. My old buddy from the Fifth Marines, Mike Adamoyurka, and his wife Jane, also a Marine, were stationed at nearby El Toro Naval Air Station. They were best man and maid of honor. Our honeymoon was short, for I had only a 72-hour leave. We strolled around "The Pike" at Long Beach, had a carnival-type picture taken and spent a night in a nice hotel.

Finding a place to live in wartime California was challenging, but we found a pretty good spot, one half of a two-car garage. There was a partition down the middle to separate us from the family next door, a sailor with wife and baby. We shared the kitchen and toilet located in the rear of the garage. Pearl protected me from the spiders and scorpions which shared our bedroom. The garage was situated at the juncture of Route 1, El Camino Real, and the road into Tent Camp Two, my workplace, so I had no difficulty in getting rides to and from work.

Fortunately we soon found far better quarters. One of the officers in my office who had received orders suggested we should try to get the apartment he and his wife had been renting in San Clemente. The apartment was situated on the second floor of a two-story stucco house occupied by the Jones family: husband, wife and two young kids, a girl and a boy. Dr. Jones was a dentist with an office in Capistrano. They were a typical

The way we were — our June 1945, wedding picture.

181

Californian family. Mrs. Jones' only costume was shorts and a halter. In addition to the goat in the backyard they had a cocker named Veronica and a cat I labeled Saipan. Our apartment was perfect for our needs: living room, bedroom and kitchen, and a view of the ocean.

Pearl soon found a job in a small defense plant, Reeves Rubber. She worked in the office and enjoyed the place. We made some friends, some with automobiles, and saw a bit of Southern California, including Lake Elsinore. We ate pretty well, for Pearl turned out to be an excellent cook. Although we had ration books, red meat was scarce so we ate a lot of unrationed fresh rabbit, which Pearl turned into a gourmet dish.

About this time some of the officers in my office encouraged me to apply for a commission. This sounded good to me and I went to see our sergeant major. He was cooperative and started to get an application form. But he stopped short when I told him that I had turned 23 on my birthday the week before. "Sorry," he said, "this program is for applicants who are no more than 22 years old." But then he said, "Wait a minute, there is another program which will accept you at your advanced age." But after looking at some papers he said, "Wait another minute, didn't you get married last week?" This program is only available for unmarried men." And so went my second shot at a commission. It was probably a good thing, for with a commission I would probably have stayed in the Corps and gotten killed in Korea.

We settled in at the Jones manse and enjoyed married life to the fullest. In fact, these were the happiest years of our lives. The war was a remote event of which we heard little, for we had no daily newspapers nor broadcast media to keep us up to date. We simply ignored it and were completely unaware that it was rapidly coming to a close. We were brought back to earth on August 15 while shopping in Oceanside. Suddenly the Navy ships in the harbor started blowing their horns and shooting volleys of tracers into the sky. The clerk in the drugstore told us the Japs had signed the surrender papers and the war was over. What now we wondered? We rather quickly found out.

In a few days the entire enlisted staff of the school was assembled in an auditorium at the main base. We were directed to "listen up as your name is called." And listen we did, for as a name was called the number of "discharge points" the man had accumulated was read and his future announced. The point system allotted one point for each month of service, two points for each month overseas, five for participating in a campaign and five for each medal or decoration. You needed 85 points for discharge. I had accumulated almost twice the required number, but discharge was not for me. When Bob and Paul Boyd's names were read their point totals were announced followed by the word they wanted to hear: "DISCHARGED." Like most of the men in the room, Bob and Paul were Marine Corps Reserves called in for the duration of the war. But, alas, that was not my situation; I was a "regular" Marine who had signed an enlistment contract to serve for a fixed time without regard to the existence of the war. And, due to my stupidity the preceding December, I still had about 15 months to serve. Thus I was assigned to a group preparing for shipment to China.

10

China

September 11, 1945, found me aboard the USS *General William Weigel* bound for Pearl Harbor, where we arrived and disembarked on September 16. Prior to embarking I had been placed in charge of about 80 boots headed for their first overseas assignment. All I had to do was take charge of their papers and take a roll call daily. Upon arrival at Pearl we were placed in the tent camp I had visited twice in 1944, after my hospital stay and on the way home after Tinian. It was the transit center of the Pacific.

During our brief stay I had to keep my charges busy doing something so I had them field stripping and cleaning their weapons and doing close-order drill. After a couple of weeks of this routine they began to resemble a real Marine outfit. This came to a welcome end on October 9, when we boarded the USS *Menkar*, a rather small Coast Guard manned transport. While aboard we took a sort of "Cook's Tour" of the South Pacific, stopping, but not disembarking, at Makin Island in the Gilbert Islands, at Majuro and at Kwajalein in the Marshall Islands. The tour ended at Guam, where we disembarked on October 26.

The stay in a makeshift tent camp on Guam was short. I remember only two things about it. First, I hitched a ride to one of the immense airfields our B29s had used while bombing Japan. The bombers were still there, lined up in rows with tropical vegetation breaking through the tarmac and beginning to engulf them. I heard a rumor a Japanese salvage company had gotten a contract to disassemble the planes for scrap. So soon, I thought, commercial relations so soon? The other unforgettable memory of Guam was the infestation of monstrous-size rats. I don't know what these ten-pound monsters had been feeding on (some said Japanese corpses) but they were truly outsized.

10. China

On October 29 I sailed from Guam aboard the USS *LST 588*. Because I was the senior Marine passenger, I was given a bunk in the chief's quarters, well forward on the port side. At some point I was informed we were headed for Tsingtao, China, a city occupied by the Sixth Marine Division, recently arrived from its first and last battle on Okinawa. The boredom of the trip was alleviated two or three times by the appearance of lethal floating mines. These were apparently antiship mines sowed by our aircraft which had now broken their tethers and were floating on the surface. They were clearly a terrible hazard for all shipping. The standing orders for all U.S. ships mandated they could not proceed on their trips without destroying any encountered mine. We sank the ones we discovered by gunfire from the ship's antiaircraft machine guns and by fire from the Marines' rifles. Two of the mines merely sank when their shells were pierced by bullets but one exploded with a huge roar and waterspout. For the remainder of the voyage I slept rather nervously thinking of what would happen to my flimsy LST if we hit a mine during the night, when they could not be seen.

We arrived at Tsingtao on November 7, where I located and reported in to Sixth Division headquarters. The adjutant's staff had discovered that my office duty at Camp Pendleton had given me a secondary military specialty classification as a writer. Their first plan was to make me an office worker but when they discovered I could not type they assigned me as a reporter on the division's "house organ" publication, whose name I have forgotten. The editor, Ed Maloof, had been a reporter on the New Orleans *Times-Picayune*. This job gave me a jeep and freedom to explore the city. What more could you ask for?

Tsingtao was a truly cosmopolitan city. During the early 20th century, when China was partitioned and controlled by the European colonialist powers, the city had been occupied and controlled by Germany. The Germans left their mark by erecting large stone buildings of unmistakable Teutonic design. These large office and school buildings and a magnificent Catholic cathedral dominated the cityscape. But there was also a healthy sprinkling of modern buildings erected by the Japanese who attacked and drove out the Germans in 1917. The Japs were our allies in the First World War. They occupied the city and surrounding countryside until 1922, when it was returned to Chinese control. However, that sovereignty only lasted until 1937, when the Japs attacked and took over. Thus, they had an excellent port to facilitate their invasion and conquest of almost the entire country in the 1930s. Of course there was also some Chinese architecture, a pagoda or temple here and there.

We evicted the Japanese occupants of all suitable large buildings and used them for offices and to billet troops. My first billet was in a three-story stone building which had housed a high school. The chemistry lab on the top floor burst into flames during my tenure. The pitifully under-equipped Chinese fire department was unable to quell the flames but our fire trucks from the airfield did the job in good order. Our tank battalion was billeted in a sizeable collection of buildings which had been the campus of Shantung University. During the final months of our occupation of these school buildings, young Chinese launched "Back to School" protest demonstrations. As the division was pared down in size we "liberated" school buildings as soon as possible.

The principal mission of the Sixth Division was to accept the surrender of the Jap troops who occupied the city and province, some 60,000 of them. On October 25, a couple of weeks before I arrived, almost the entire division, about 12,000 men, were mustered at the race track for a ceremony to accept the surrender of about 10,000 Jap soldiers. A Jap major general, Eiji Nagano, signed the surrender document and, together with his staff officers, took off their swords and presented them to our division commander, Major General Lemuel C. Shepherd Jr., and a nationalist Chinese, Lieutenant General Chen-Pao-tsang. Interestingly, the surrender document states the Japanese Commanders "...hereby surrender unconditionally all of the forces under our command to the Generalissimo Chiang Kai-Shek." Protocol had to be served.

When we arrived, the population contained a large number of Japanese civilians, some 30,000 in the city and another 40,000 in the province. Many had been born there during the 30-year occupation. Of course, they had many businesses and controlled the commercial heart of the city. But it was all over for them when we took over. Without regard for any property rights, or rights of any kind, we put all Jap civilians on LSTs and other transports and shipped them to Japan. For many of them it was a strange country. Their property was turned over to the local Chinese, who were ruled by a warlord named Li.

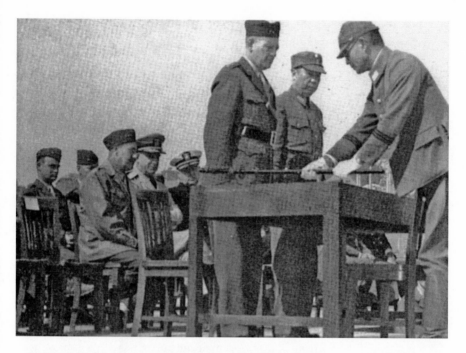

Major General Eiji Nagano, commander of all Japanese Forces in the Tsingtao area, lays down his sword as a token of unconditional surrender before Sixth Division commander Major General Lemuel C. Shepherd.

I had only one direct contact with the Jap troops. In the interval before I became a reporter, the division executive officer gave me an order to go to the Jap headquarters and get some office chairs. Our clerks and typists were without chairs and could not function standing up. The Japs had been made aware of our need and had agreed to supply the chairs. All I had to do was direct them to where the chairs were needed. When I arrived at Jap army headquarters, I was escorted into the office of their commanding general. He was seated at a large desk in a very large room, at least 40 feet long by 20 feet wide. Of course, he was surrounded by flunkies of various ranks. When I told his interpreter my mission he told me I was expected and escorted me to a parking space near their building where I met a junior officer who led me to a truck manned by about four enlisted men. No one in this group spoke English so I had no idea where this working party was going to get chairs. I was soon informed. We drove off with me in the cab with the driver and headed into the city office buildings section.

The procedure for getting the chairs was brutally efficient. We would enter a large office full of civilians typing and working away at their desks. When we entered all would rise and my crew would simply yank away their chairs and carry them out to the truck. This scenario was repeated a dozen or more times until the truck was fully loaded. I directed the party back to Sixth Division HQ, where a Marine work party took over. During this affair I was uneasy. During the preceding three years I had never seen a Jap soldier I hadn't tried to kill or who hadn't tried to kill me. And here I was hobnobbing with uniformed enemy troops who could have put an end to me with ease.

There was a small German population in Tsingtao but it was of recent vintage and not the remnants of the pre–World War I settlers. These were also shipped back to their homeland as soon as arrangements could be made. The city also had a sizeable Russian group. These were the so-called "White Russians" and their descendents who had fled east through Siberia when the Communists took over Russia in 1918. They had a rough life during the Jap occupation but it was better than life would have been back in Russia, for many of them were of royal blood. One of the group, a "Princess" Tamara, opened an excellent restaurant where I was introduced to and fell in love with beef stroganoff. Some of the Russian girls were quite pretty and had no shortage of Marine suitors. I attended a fancy dress-up wedding of one of these girls to a Marine friend.

My stay as a reporter on the paper was short-lived, for it was shut down a few weeks after I came aboard. The assignment I remember was to locate memorable or interesting sights in and around the city and write an article describing them. The most interesting place I discovered was a Chinese temple called the "Temple of Five Religions." The story, as I got it, was that a group of Chinese had become convinced that the various faiths being presented to them had two things in common, a single supreme being or some sort of heaven and an earthly disciple. Thus they built a temple to honor five of the most prominent faiths or disciplines: Christianity, Buddhism, Islam, Confucianism and Taoism. Thus, they built a beautiful temple honoring all five equally. The altar, or perhaps I should say altars, were located in an open-sided, roofed structure at the rear of an open courtyard. Arrayed in line across this building were statues of Christ, Buddha, Mohammad, Tao and Confucius. It was a beautiful and solemn place.

My next assignment was Headquarters Battalion police sergeant. Mostly my duty involved supervising a small number of Marines and a sizeable group of Chinese coolies who kept shipshape the various buildings and their grounds occupied by the battalion. I had a number of corporals who did the actual supervision of work parties assigned to the various buildings so I had a lot of free time, which I occupied studying the math and English literature correspondence courses I had subscribed to.

My blissful tenure in this sinecure was disturbed by a most unusual event. I was handed the task of making good Marines out of a group of about 20 men who had, in effect, mutinied and refused to do their assigned duties. The problem was heightened by the fact that these guys were black. They were Marine stewards assigned to the division officer's billet, which was located in a modern hotel named, I believe, the Edgewater. They rebelled because the hotel was fully manned by Chinese, and these fellows refused to take orders from Chinese chefs and supervisory staff. As they told me, "We ain't taking no orders from no goddamned gooks!"

I assigned the group to one of my corporals and told him to keep them busy policing up around the battalion barracks. The first morning of this arrangement did not go well. At mid-morning the corporal reported to me the blacks refused to come out of their bunk room and go to work. I went to the room and found them sitting and lying around listening to a record player. I couldn't believe what I was seeing and let out a bellow of outrage. In seconds I was flat on my back with two large men holding me down. One of them informed me, "No white son of a bitch is going to yell at us like you done!" I told them to get off me or I would see they went to the brig for a year. This threat didn't have any effect, but help came from the unofficial leader of their group, a very large man named Washington. He ordered them to desist and apologized to me for the attack. I got the names of the two culprits and escaped with what little dignity I still had. I put them on report and testified against them at "office hours," or a deck court marshal conducted by the battalion executive officer. He gave them five days in the brig on bread and water, sometimes irreverently called "piss and punk."

I solved the problem of what to do with the rebellious group by placing Washington in charge and agreeing that all orders for them would go to and through him. It worked, and I had no further difficulty. The group was sent back to the States within a short time as part of the general dissolution of the division. At the time I had little sympathy for this detachment of negroes. As I viewed it then, these people had volunteered to serve as stewards and, like all of us, were supposed to do their jobs. My view has now changed and I can sympathize with that group of segregated men, assigned to only menial duties and denied full membership in the Marines. Thank goodness that has changed and negroes now form a significant of part of, and perform essential duties in, today's Marine Corps.

On January 9, 1946, my long-delayed promotion to platoon sergeant came through. According to my Record Book I was "examined and found qualified for promotion to Platoon Sergeant" on 1 Aug 44. At that time we were in combat on Saipan and something got screwed up and the promotion was never effected. I didn't know that entry was in my Record Book until a long time after I was discharged. Had I known, I would have agitated for the promotion when I got to Camp Pendleton.

At any rate, the promotion enabled my move to staff NCO quarters, which was located in a large vine-covered mansion which had been built and owned by a British shipping firm. It was quite regal, with a three-story atrium surrounded by balconies which fronted the bedrooms. The ground floor had a huge stone fireplace and a bar attended by a native Chinese bartender. I shared a large room with an interesting Marine who had been an Olympic wrestler. He was a middleweight, about 150 pounds, but would take on allcomers. He participated in a competition in Peiping while we roomed together and "threw out his back" wrestling a 225-pounder. He was in real pain for most of the time we roomed together but the Navy medics had no answer. We kept an ample supply of local "Huba" vodka and American beer in the room for medicinal purposes.

By June the Sixth Division had been substantially dissolved and I

The Sixth Division Headquarters Battalion's staff NCO billet and club.

was transferred to the First Battalion of the Fourth Marine Regiment and given command of a platoon in C Company. It was good to be back in an infantry outfit but it was not the same as it had been during the war. This outfit was a bunch of crybabies who had not actively participated in the war but were now forced to serve far from home. Their morale was low and their job performance abysmal. We went through the motions of training and began studying the makeup and procedures of our next enemy, the Soviet Union.

I had to move out of the Headquarters Battalion NCO club and move closer to the Fourth Marine area. However, my living quarters actually improved for I was given a suite of rooms in a walled compound near the First Battalion barracks. Four other staff NCOs occupied similar suites in the compound. We set up a mess and hired an excellent Chinese cook. He did all the shopping for groceries and produced outstanding dinners. My favorite dish was fried breaded eggplant. Also, I acquired a personal servant, a "room boy" who kept my quarters, my gear and clothing in top shape. I called him "Hayseed," an approximation of his Chinese name. I have forgotten what I paid him but am sure it was very little. He was about 30 years old and quite homely with buck teeth. I also acquired some pets, a monkey, a dog and numerous parakeets. The monkey was a character. During our frequent beer parties I would give him a small amount of beer in a saucer. The results were spectacular: He became amorous, sat on my shoulder and rubbed his face on my chin. He was friendly with all Marines but seemed to hate all Chinese.

My tenure in the Fourth Marines was more of a vacation than an occupation. I went through the motions of instructing my platoon in the mornings and spent the rest of the day in recreational pursuits. A fellow Marine was a tournament-class tennis player. He taught me the game and I became almost good enough to beat him. We would play for a couple of hours and take jeep rides to the beach for a swim and sun bath. After a shower we had dinner in our private dining room and then walked a few blocks to the Fourth Marines staff NCO club, where beer was a dime and mixed drinks a quarter. This was the first time in my experience that enlisted men were authorized to have hard liquor. Heretofore only officers had access to whiskey and the enlisted of all ranks had only beer. This was a great club — so great, in fact, that one of our regular patrons was Brigadier General William Clement. He told me he patronized our club because he was more comfortable with senior NCOs he had served with as a junior officer than with the inexperienced youngsters at the officers club. We were overstocked with old senior NCOs, six-stripers, who had headed back to China as soon as the war was over. Some of them had temporary commissions during the war but had now reverted back to their old ranks. But with the dissolution of the Sixth Division there were no billets for this influx of talent. They spent most of their time in the club.

The club was also a financial success. When we had to close it up upon leaving Tsingtao we had a sizeable sum in the treasury. After some discussion we eschewed the option of giving the sum to Naval Relief and sent the club secretary to Shanghai to purchase mementos for each of the remaining club members. He came back with solid silver engraved club membership cards and good-quality leather wallets for each of us. I still have my membership card.

During our stay in Tsingtao the Chinese communists had been content to leave us unmolested in the city. They controlled the countryside and dealt harshly with intruders. Late in the fall of 1945 they wreaked havoc upon a battalion-sized force of Chinese Nationalist troops which debarked from transports and marched through the city and into the countryside. I was impressed with their appearance as they marched by in perfect drill order. They were armed with 30-caliber Springfields, the same rifle we used on Guadalcanal. They had machine guns, jeeps and artillery. All in all they appeared to be a formidable force capable of handling the commie peasants who surrounded us. Alas, it was not to be — within days a tattered remnant of the unit straggled back into town sans weapons and vehicles.

Things began to change for us in the summer of 1946. The "Chicoms," as we learned to call them, sent infiltrators into town and things got a bit dicey. Two Marines on liberty were murdered and the sentry on the gate of my battalion's compound was killed by a sniper one night. I tried to be careful where I walked alone but one evening, on the way to the club, two military-age men stepped out of a doorway and positioned themselves across my path. The street in this residential area was otherwise deserted. I did not think turning around and running away was an acceptable procedure for an American Marine so I held my swagger stick in my right hand, positioned it across my body and, without changing pace, moved right at them. Fortunately, the bluff worked and they moved aside and my sphincter relaxed. During this dangerous period we were ordered to carry swagger sticks and Marines below staff NCO ranks were not permitted to go ashore alone — they had to go in pairs or larger groups.

Sometime in early August (I do not have the exact date) we, i.e. the battalion, boarded a huge transport and sailed for the States. I have completely forgotten the name of the ship. This was the finest ride of my career. I had a large bunk with inner-spring mattress in a cabin I shared with three other guys. The cabin had its own toilet and a large round table for eating or card playing. As for the latter, a poker game was played almost endlessly for the entire trip. Since the cabin had no porthole we soon lost track of time and were unsure whether it was night or day outside. There was an open galley on our deck so we could eat whenever we felt the urge.

One of my roommates who worked in the battalion office aboard ship asked me if I would like to have a duplicate of my Service Record Book, the book that sets out every significant event of my service career. I accepted the offer and, in about a week, he delivered the finished duplicate record to me. What a boon it has been while writing this memoir. It gives me the dates of all moves and the names of all ships and even included copies of citations and Purple Heart awards.

The monotony of sailing was relieved by passage through the Panama Canal and a liberty in Colon where, as the photo below reveals, we spent a few hours in a nightclub called Claridge.

In a few more days we disembarked at Norfolk and I caught a train for Quantico. I was stationed at the base for a couple of weeks while my

Staff NCOs and a couple of lieutenants living it up in a Panama nightclub. My last foreign liberty as an active duty Marine. Author is sixth from the right.

discharge was processed. As I recall, the discharge procedure took about a day to complete. I believe they kept guys there for a few days until they had accumulated a sufficient number to justify setting up the medical and administrative personnel to screen the dischargees. They had rigged up a series of offices with prominent signs directing us where to go. I clearly remember one sign which directed you to an indicated office if you had suffered named diseases, including malaria and filariasis. I followed the direction arrow on that sign and was interviewed about my experience with malaria. I told them it had not recurred during the past year. I was told to seek medical help from the Veterans Administration if it did. Another sign directed those who had been wounded to an office manned by several doctors who asked a lot of questions and conducted a perfunctory physical examination, which I apparently passed. I was unaware that these doctors were from the Veterans Administration. Still another sign directed the wounded to a panel of representatives from the various veterans associations, including the American Legion and the Veterans of Foreign Wars. At first I thought they were recruiting and sort of resented it, but I was quickly disabused and told they were there to represent us in filing disability claims with the VA. I opted to let the VFW process my claim but I assured them I was not disabled and quickly dropped the subject from my mind. But I was dead wrong, for in December I received a letter from the VA telling me I had been awarded a 30 percent disability pension. Later, while in college, the VA called me in for a more extensive medical examination which took almost a full day. When I got home that night I told Pearl to kiss goodbye to the pension, but in a few days I received a letter telling me the pension would continue for life. It wasn't much money but at that time every cent counted.

My only assigned duties at Quantico were standing 24-hour "officer of the guard" watches, one day on and one day off. During my off hours I was free to go to Washington to see Pearl, which I did whenever I could find transportation. Also during this time I successfully resisted repeated efforts to get me to join the Marine Corps Reserve. When I asked these recruiters why I should sign up for the Reserve their laughable answer was to preserve my rank.

My extended enlistment was up on December 10 and I was content to continue serving the rest of my time at Quantico. It was too late to

Enlisted at Philadelphia, Pennsylvania *on the* 6th *day of* September *, 19* 40 *to serve* Four *years*

Born 21 June, 1922 *(Date)* *at* Wilkes-Barre, Pennsylvania

When enlisted was 70 *inches high, with* Blue *eyes,* Brown *hair,* *complexion:* Ruddy *citizenship:* U.S.

Previous service: None

Rank and type of warrant at time of discharge: Platoon Sergeant (TWL) 25Jan46

Weapons qualification: 8Sep45-Rifle Marksman
15Oct40-Pistol Sharpshooter

Special military qualifications: Infantry Chief

Service (sea and foreign): 18Dec40-8Apr41
American Theater of Operations
9Jun42-4Sep44 & 11Sep45-10Oct46
Pacific Theater of Operations

Wounds received in service: Wounded in action on: Gilbert Islands, Nov43. Saipan Island, 8Jul44.

Battles, engagements, skirmishes, expeditions: Participated in action against the enemy at: Guadacanal, BSI, 7Aug42-9Aug42; South Solomons, 10Aug42-31Jan43; Tarawa Atoll, GI, 20Nov43-21Nov43; Saipan & Tinian, MI, 16Jun44-1Aug44.

Remarks Awarded Navy & Marine Corps Medal of Honor for Heroism in action. Issued Honorable Service Lapel Button and Marine Corps Discharge Button. No time lost. Awarded Good Conduct Medal 6Sep43. Awarded Good Conduct Bar 7Sep46. Second Good Conduct Bar period commenced 8Sep46, no offenses since that date. Extended enlistment for (2) years from 4Dec44.
Character of service excellent.

Serial number 293903 Captain, , U. S. M. C.

Is *physically qualified for discharge.* Requires neither treatment nor hospitalization.
I *certify that this is the actual print of the right index finger of the man herein mentioned.*
, U. S. N.
and Medical Officer.

Monthly rate of pay when discharged One Hundred-twenty-six and 50/100 dollars
I *hereby certify that the within named man has been furnished travel allowance at the rate of* five *cents per mile from* Quantico, Virginia *to* Lehighton, Pennsylvania *and paid $* 265.45 *in full to date of discharge.* Paid $100.MOP"Z".

Captain, , U. S. M. C.
(Signature of man.) *Commanding Officer.*

My honorable discharge papers.

enroll in the fall semester at any college and I had no civilian job in sight. It was a short jaunt to Washington and Pearl and, besides, when I did get out I would receive two months pay for unused furlough time. But it was not to be. The Corps decided that I would now take the unused

196

leave whether I wanted to or not. I objected to no avail and, in effect, the Corps kicked me out on "Terminal Leave" on October 8, but the order cautioned I was still subject to military law until December 10. This was the final insult. All the government saved was $253, two months pay. In those days that was a lot of money.

11

Rejoining the World

Pearl still lived in the Marleeta, a boardinghouse on 16th Street just above Scott Circle, but that was not available for us so we found another boardinghouse across the street. It was a rather small room on the top floor, which meant climbing four flights of stairs. We didn't mind that so much for we were young and strong. The only qualms we had about the place was how to exit in case of fire, the narrow stairway was the only way out. If fire made it unusable we were trapped. But we had no choice, for living space of any kind was scarce. The post-war building spree had not yet started.

My first duty was to find a job. My "Special Military Qualification" in the Corps, "Infantry Chief," was not saleable in the civilian economy. Of greater importance than a job was taking steps to get into college for the spring semester starting in February. I concentrated my efforts on schools in the Washington area, for Pearl had a good government job with enough income to support us while I was matriculating. I applied to only two, American University and George Washington University. I was accepted by both schools but the acceptance by George Washington was conditional. Because of my dismal high school record I was admitted to the "Division of Special Students," a category which required the maintenance of a "C" average to remain in school. I felt I could manage that and opted to enter GW.

As for the job, I paid a visit, still in uniform, to Sidney West, one of Washington's elite men's clothing stores, located at 14th and G streets. They asked if I had any experience and I fibbed a bit, telling them I had worked in a department store in Lehighton, Pennsylvania, before the War. I really had a tiny part-time job but I had never been on the sales force. They asked if I would like to sell "furnishings," and I said sure, although I was not sure what the word meant. Nevertheless, they hired me to sell furnishings (shirts, ties, underwear, belts and socks) as a temporary employee for the pre–Christmas shopping season. I was to be paid 7 percent of my sales but was guaranteed $40 a week. Of course I had to show up for work in suitable civilian attire so I hurried and bought an ill-fitting double-breasted grey suit, which I had to replace with a more acceptable garment at the first opportunity. I was a really bad salesman who rarely sold enough to "make my draw," that is actually earn my $40 stipend, but Sidney West kept me on for the holiday season and rehired me for the season in succeeding years.

During the holidays, and afterward, we spent a lot of time looking for a place to live. It was tough going, but then, in early February, as I was entering GW, we had fantastic luck and landed a place — not just an ordinary apartment but a two-story garden type in a South Arlington development called "Arlington Village." It was ideally located, on a bus line and within walking distance of grocery stores. We liked it so well we stayed there for nine years. We got the place because a friend had a sister who was married to a war buddy of the builder and owner, Gus Ring.

In college I had no difficulty in maintaining the requisite C average and, in fact, did a lot better than that. I was majoring in psychology because my cousin, Dr. Howard Goheen, then employed at the Pentagon and who had gotten his Ph.D. at George Washington, persuaded me to follow in his steps. While some of my classmates were youngsters fresh out of high school, most of them were returned veterans like me. I met and became lifelong friends with two of these fellows, Rupert (Rip) Mulhearn, a former army lieutenant, and Leroy (Lucky) Yarnoff, a Navy pilot.

During my junior year the school announced a program which greatly appealed to veterans like me who had lost a good deal of time during the War. The program provided that undergraduates with only three years (six semesters) of successful study could apply and be admitted to law school. I toyed with the idea of med school but quickly decided I wanted to be a lawyer, applied and was accepted for admission to law school. By the calendar I had been in college for only two years but I had garnered three years of credits by attending summer school, a procedure I repeated in law school.

Law school was a breeze and I got good grades but could have done better. In early June, 1950, while starting my fifth semester, I learned that Virginia would permit law students who had completed only four semesters, i.e. two years of law school and, of course, lacked an LLB law degree, to take the Virginia bar exam and, if they passed, be admitted to practice. Still obsessed with the need to make up lost time, I determined to give it a try. But, of course, the bar exam would deal with the entire field of law, including subjects I had not yet been exposed to in school. Thus I felt I had to take a "cram course" teaching all the questions which might come up in the exam. Fortunately, such a one-week course, taught by Dean Woodbridge of the William and Mary Law School, was scheduled to be held at Washington and Lee University in Lexington, Virginia, a week before the exam. I decided to take the course and the exam as a sort of "dry run" to prepare me for the real thing, i.e. taking the exam after I got my law degree. The course was really excellent, for I took and passed the bar exam and was admitted to practice in Virginia in August 1950.

I completed law school and received my LLB (later changed to a JD, Juris Doctor) in February 1951. After passing the bar I spent my spare time as an associate attorney with the firm of Crouch and Crouch in Arlington. This experience convinced me that finding a legal job was certain to produce a livable income quicker than opening a practice. So in early 1951, I went looking for a job with the biggest employer of lawyers to be found, the U.S. Government. I first tried the Department of Justice but was told there that I needed a recommendation from "The Hill," i.e. from a member of Congress. But the clerk in the personnel office told me the Federal Trade Commission was hiring and may not require congressional endorsement. I had no knowledge as to what the FTC actually did but I walked down Pennsylvania Avenue to its building at 7th Street and was hired that afternoon after appearing before a committee composed of the agency's top officers. I worked for the FTC for 19 years, until July 1970. I started as an investigator working out of the agency's Chicago field office. After a transfer back to Washington, I traveled for a few years as an investigator and then spent a few more years as a trial attorney. After that I was assigned to a group writing the Commission's opinions and eventually became the officer in charge of that group. From there I was promoted to become Attorney in Charge of the

Washington Field Office. After a couple of years in that slot I was raised to the position of Assistant Director of the Bureau of Deceptive Practices. By this time I had achieved "Super Grade" status and was making a comfortable living wage, but for reasons still not very clear to me, I became increasingly restive and determined to leave government service and enter the private practice of law. So, in June 1970, I submitted my resignation to the Commission chairman, Casper Weinberger. He left that position shortly thereafter to become Secretary of Defense, but before leaving, on July 8, 1970, he awarded me the Federal Trade Commission's highest honor, the "Award for Distinguished Service."

In private practice, I first became a partner in Dow, Lohnes and Albertson, a firm primarily engaged in communications law before the Federal Communications Commission. After a few years I formed a partnership with Edward Sloan, a law school friend and a member of my Lutheran Church. This ended when Ed became disabled with a brain tumor. From then until I hung up my shingle, I shared office expenses with other attorneys but was essentially a lone practitioner. During this period I served a number of business clients who produced and sold promotional games of chance to supermarkets. A principal client in this field was Telecom Productions, a leader in the field. Also, I spent many years as general counsel of the American Advertising Federation, the home body of regional advertising groups around the country.

By far the best client I had as a private practitioner was the Direct Selling Association, the association of about 200 "door-to-door" selling companies such as Amway, Avon, Kirby and Mary Kay. I spent 18 years as the administrator of the Association's Code of Ethics, a tough set of regulations which cleaned up the practices which had raised the ire of consumer protection groups and government agencies, including the Federal Trade Commission. I resigned that position and effectively left law practice in May of 1997.

In retirement, Pearl and I still reside in the home we bought in 1967 in Annandale, Virginia. We love to travel abroad and cruise the high seas. We have a second home, an apartment on the beach in Rehoboth Beach, Delaware, which we enjoy. Shortly after arriving in Annandale in 1967, we founded and became charter members of Hope Lutheran Church, where we still worship.

Bibliography

Alexander, Joseph H. *Utmost Savagery: The Three Days of Tarawa.* Annapolis, MD: Naval Institute Press, 1995.

Bartsch, William H. "Operation Dovetail: Bungled Guadalcanal Rehearsal, July 1942." *The Journal of Military History* 66 (2), April 2002, pp. 443–476.

Cass, Bevan G. *History of the Sixth Marine Division.* Washington, D.C.: Infantry Journal, Inc., 1948.

Clemens, Martin. *Alone on Guadalcanal—A Coastwatcher's Story.* Annapolis, MD: Annapolis Naval Institute Press, 1998.

Dickey, John L. *A Family Saga—Flush Deck Destroyers 1917–1955.* Waldoboro, ME: Prints Charming Printers, 1999.

Frank, Richard B. *Guadalcanal.* New York: Random House, 1990.

Hoffman, John T. *Once a Legend.* Novato, CA: Presidio, 1994.

Johnston, Richard W. *Follow Me: The Story of the Second Marine Division in World War II.* New York: Random House, 1948.

Ladd, Dean. *Faithful Warriors: A Combat Marine Remembers the Pacific War.* Annapolis, MD: Naval Institute Press, 2009.

Lundstrom, John. *The First Team and the Guadalcanal Campaign: Naval Fighter Combat from August to November 1942.* Annapolis, MD: Naval Institute Press, 1994.

Miller, John. *Guadalcanal: The First Offensive.* Washington, D.C.: Center of Military History, U.S. Army, 1949.

Sherrod, Robert. *History of Marine Corps Aviation in World War II.* San Rafael, CA: Presidio Press, 1952.

_____. *On to Westward.* New York: Duell, Sloan and Pearce, 1945.

Smith, Harriotte Byrd. *But, That's Another Story.* New York: Vantage, 1992.

_____. *Tarawa: The Story of a Battle.* New York: Duell, Sloan Pearce, 1944, 1954; Fredericksburg, TX: Admiral Nimitz Foundation, 1973.

Smith, Holland M., and Percy Finch. *Coral and Brass.* New York: C. Scribner's Sons, 1948.

Vandegrift, Alexander. *Once a Marine: The Memoirs of General A.A. Vandegrift, United States Marine Corps.* New York: Ballantine, 1966.

Index

Adamoyurka, Michael 22, 181
Alexander, Col. Joseph H. 141
Allen, Patrick (Pat) 1
USS *Alhena* 43
American Legion 195
USS *American Legion* 117
Amey, Col. Herbert R. 125
amtrac (amphibious tractor) 120, 123, 124, 125, 127, 133, 142, 143, 152, 153
Aola 61, 62, 64, 65, 73
APDs (transport high speed) 26, 27, 28, 29, 31, 35, 36, 60, 149
Armstrong, Dooney 80
Arthur, Col. John 83, 105, 106
USS *Arthur Middleton* 131
Atabrine 98

Baker, Harold 80
BAR *see* Browning Automatic Rifle
Bartsch, William 2, 49, 67, 91, 92
Bauer, Maj. Harold 71
Bayonets 11, 13, 51, 52, 82, 84, 88, 158
Betio 120, 122, 133, 141, 142
Blanco 31
USS *Bountiful* 16
Boyd, Bob 40, 96, 134, 162, 167, 168, 180
Boyd, Paul 40, 60, 74, 88, 130, 164, 171, 180, 183
Boyd brothers 40, 67, 96, 175
Bray, Capt. William T. 92, 113, 114, 117, 132, 133
Brooklyn Navy Yard 36
Brooks, Capt. Louis 159, 166, 167
Browning Automatic Rifle 21, 31, 40, 41, 47, 48, 51, 65, 81, 86, 87, 96, 163, 167, 174, 179
Browning machine gun 19
Burgess, Wilbur 42, 64, 66, 67, 86, 88, 89, 92, 114

Camp Catlin 139
Camp Elliot 37, 42
Camp Pendleton 14, 178–180, 185, 190
Campbell, Eugene 86
Carlson, Lt. Col. Evans F. 37, 38, 39, 40, 48
Carpenter, Pl. Sgt. Howard 92
Chamorro 150, 156, 157, 173
Charleston, SC 17, 29, 30
Charon Kanoa 153
Chicoms (Chinese Communists) 193
Clark, Corp. Ed 111
Claveria, SSgt. Federico 173
Clemens, Martin 62, 63
Clement, Brig. Gen. William 192
Clemments, Pl. Sgt. Fredrick 133
Clemmons, Bob 140
Clifton, Pvt. Charles 91
Coast Watchers 50, 62
USS *Colhoun* 27
USS *Colorado* 170–171
Contos, Col. Harry 2
Cooper, Sgt. 114
Coote, Sgt. Bruce 42, 61
Corey, Pvt. Alton 90
Crabs 46
USS *Crescent City* 43
Culebra 22
Culp, Corp. Bill 24, 57
Cummings, Sgt. Daniel 8, 12, 13, 14

Denley, Sgt. Ernest 64, 74, 86
USS *Doyen* 145–146
Dumbo 43
Dunkle, Gy. Sgt. Everette B. 77, 78, 90

Easley, Lt. Col. John 172
Ecker, Corp. Clinton J., Jr. 126, 132
Edson, Lt. Col. Merritt A. "Red Mike" 28, 30, 39, 57, 141, 142

Index

Eniwetok 150
Enola Gay 170

Fiji Group 49
First Raider Battalion 35, 39, 60, 72
Florida Island 2, 50, 57, 103
Freeman, Frank 86
Fritzinger, Alan 140
Fuhrhop, Capt. Paul W. 41, 56, 59, 74, 83, 90, 113
Funk, Sgt. Maj. Charles 115

Gage, James 86
Garapan 150, 158, 163, 165, 166
Gardner, George 77, 91
Gavutu 49, 51, 54
USS *General William Weigel* 184
George Washington University 198
Gilbert Islands 120, 184
Gill, Richard 86
Gitmo *see* Guantanamo Bay
Goetz, Elmer 86
Gohenn, Dr. Howard 199
Gray, Amos 86
Green, Walter 91
Green Beach 130
USS *Gregory* 27, 60
Grumman F4F 66, 71
Grumman Torpedo Bomber (TBF) 163
Guam 150, 184, 185
Guantanamo 17, 18, 21, 25, 57
Guantanamo Bay 21, 23
Gunter, Lt. Howard G. 83, 84

Halavo Peninsula 50
Hale, Henry 86, 89
Hammel, Eric 106
Haruna 70
Hatch, SSgt. Norman 135, 136
Hayseed 192
Hearst 159, 161
USS *Henderson* 16, 17, 22, 28, 45
Henderson Field 60, 61, 65, 66, 69, 80, 91–95, 97, 100, 105
Herber, Lt. Bill 148, 154, 159, 162, 166, 168, 174, 175
Higgins boat 22, 26, 42, 43, 49, 61, 69, 120, 128, 143
Hill, Lt. Col. Robert E. 83, 84, 107
Howe, Charles 91
Howitzer 82, 91, 107, 135, 141
Hyde, Blaine 80

Johnson, Lt. Russell 41, 64

Kennedy, Pres. John F. 67
King, Adm. Ernest J. 161, 162
King Neptune 47
Knee mortar 52, 89, 102
Kobal, Johnny 140
Kongo 70
Koro 49
Kyle, Lt. Col. Wood B. 84, 106, 114, 116, 123, 145, 169

Landing Craft Vehicle, Personnel *see* LCVP
LCVP (Landing Craft Vehicle, Personnel) 21, 43, 109, 120, 121, 123, 127, 129, 131, 143, 148, 152, 171, 175
Lehighton 4, 5, 6, 25, 26, 34, 40, 140, 178, 198
Leineweber, Thomas M. 65
USS *Little* 27, 28, 30, 37, 60
LST 150, 185, 186
Lucas 164
Ludlum, Edward 91
LVT *see* Amtrac

M1 Garand 111
MacArthur, Gen. Douglas 159, 161
Magicienne Bay 150, 152, 154
Majercak, James 86
Malaria 61, 97, 98, 109, 195
USS *Manley* 27
Mann, Lt. Joe A. 91
Marianas Islands 150
Marleeta 198
Marshall Islands 141, 142, 150
Matanikau River 73, 90–92, 95, 100, 106, 107
USS *McCawley* 21, 22, 25
McCullough, Russell 91
USS *McFarland* 71
McKay's Crossing 109, 114
USS *Mckean* 27
Medal of Honor 71, 104
Melanesians 50, 63, 100
Melmore, Ohio 178
USS *Menkar* 184
Miami 28, 29
Miller, Channing 104, 125, 168
Miller, Doyle 80
Miller, Capt. Jack 41, 74, 75, 90
Mitsubishi bombers 71, 93

Mosier 89, 91
Mulhearn, Rupert (Rip) 199

Nagano, Maj. Gen. Eiji (Japanese Army) 186–187
Nambu 51, 96, 155, 175, 177
Napier 111, 114
Narr, Lt. Joseph L. 67
Naval Hospital at Silver Stream 110
Navy and Marine Corps Medal 67, 68, 114
Navy Cross 133, 134
New Zealand 49, 57, 58, 97–100, 103, 108–113, 116, 118–119, 121, 133–134, 137, 141, 143, 148
Nimitz, Vice Adm. Chester W. 138, 141, 142
USS *Noa* 149
Noble, Sgt. Emery "Stud" 83
USS *Norman Scott* 170–171
Noval, Pl. Sgt. Julius 40, 61, 91

Olson 95
Onslow Beach, N.C. 27

Paekakariki 109
Parachute Battalion 49
Parks, Lt. Floyd 62
PBY (Patrol Boat Y; U.S. Navy designation for Consolidated Aircraft, Inc.) 42, 60
Pearl Harbor 34, 40, 136, 146, 158, 177, 184
Petty, Paul 91
Pistol Pete 69, 91, 107
Point Cruz 73, 106, 107
Poppelwell, Beth 112, 114
Portuguese man-of-war 28
USS *President Adams* 43
USS *President Hayes* 43
USS *President Jackson* 43–46, 108
Price, Ben 114
Price, Pearl 2, 32, 33, 34, 44, 121, 178, 180–182, 195, 198, 201
Price, Corp. Thurman 41, 77, 79, 80
Pule, Daniel 62, 65
Purple Heart 19, 58, 67, 138, 194

Quantico 25, 26, 30–32, 34, 37, 116, 148, 194–195
Quinine 97

Raider Battalion 38, 54, 57
Record book 30, 113, 114, 133, 190, 194
Reising gun 56

Rice, Maj. Howard J. 125–126
Rixey, Col. P.M. 141
Roosevelt, Pres. Franklin Delano 34
Roosevelt, Maj. James 38
Ross, Lt. Armstead E. 115–116, 123, 132
Rupertus, Brig. Gen. William B. 56

Sadler, 1st Sgt. Raymond J. 74, 90
San Clemente 179, 181
San Diego 42, 44, 177, 178, 180
San Juan 22
USS *San Juan* 43–54
Sanders, Raymond 80
Sanders, William 134–135, 167, 169
Santa Anna 181
Savo Island 60, 103
Schreiner, William 86
Schuler, Alfred 86
USS *Sea Scamp* 177
Second Marine Division Association (SMDA) 149
Second Marines 39, 43, 57, 61, 93, 112, 133, 167
Shepherd, Maj. Gen. Lemuel C., Jr. 186–187
Sherrod, Robert 67, 128, 141, 145, 159–161
Shotgun 104
Sixth Division 185–188, 190–192
Slusser, 1st Sgt. "Slug" 20, 30
Smith, Lt. Gen. Holland M. 142–144, 152, 160–162
Smith, Maj. John L. 94–95
Smith, Maj. Gen. Julian 142–145
Smith, Oliver 86
Smith, Maj. Gen. Ralph 160–161
Solomon Islands 47, 49–51, 56–58, 62, 67
Sorensen, James 41, 49, 58, 77–78, 86–87, 89
Sparks, Pvt. Joseph "Little Joe" 64
Sprague, Sgt. Daniel 154
Springfield Rifle 13, 40, 51, 193
Stafford, Capt. Richard 65
Stanley, Sgt. John G. 117–118, 126
Stevens, Orville 91
USS *Stringham* 27
Sulfanilamide 111

Tanaka, Capt. Jinzou 92
Tani, Akio 92
Tapotchau 150, 160
Taylor, Pvt. James "Dub" 86, 124
Taylor, John 46, 82, 84

Index

Thompson, Sgt. Otis 86
Thompson submarine gun 64–65
Tinian 148, 150, 153, 169–171, 173, 176, 184
Tongatabu 48
Tsingtao 176, 185, 187–188, 192–193
Tulagi 2, 41, 49–51, 53–55, 57–61, 65, 71, 72, 103

Ushi Airfield 170–171

Vandegrift, Lt. Gen. Alexander Archer 69, 106, 143–144
Veterans Administration (VA) 195
Veterans of Foreign Wars (VFW) 195

Vicky, Zackman 32, 34
Von der Heyde, Pfc. H.A.F., Jr. 8, 14

Washing Machine Charlie 70, 94, 98
Watson, Maj. Gen. Thomas E. 167
Wellington 108–1089, 111–112, 119
Whittington, Dalton 80
Willard, Lt. Chap. W. Wyeth 57
Witzel, Corp. Luther 5, 10–11, 14–15, 19, 40, 127
Wolf, Don 28, 33–34, 37, 57, 72–73
Wycoff, Ralph 175, 180

Yarnoff, Leroy "Lucky" 199
YPs 59, 61–62, 72